DEATH DIARY

DEATH
DIARY

A YEAR OF LONDON MURDER, EXECUTION, TERRORISM AND TREASON

GARY POWELL

AMBERLEY

To my wife Karen.
The bravest woman I know xx

And to Gooner – RIP mate.

Murder is unique in that it abolishes the party it injures,
So that society must take the place of the victim,
And on his behalf demand atonement or grant forgiveness;
It is the one crime in which society has a direct interest

W. H. Auden
(The Dyer's Hand and Other Essays, 1962)

First published 2017

Amberley Publishing
The Hill, Stroud
Gloucestershire, GL5 4EP

www.amberley-books.com

Copyright © Gary Powell, 2017

The right of Gary Powell to be identified as
the Author of this work has been asserted in
accordance with the Copyrights, Designs and
Patents Act 1988.

ISBN 978 1 4456 6502 3 (paperback)
ISBN 978 1 4456 6503 0 (ebook)

British Library Cataloguing in Publication Data.
A catalogue record for this book is available
from the British Library.

Origination by Amberley Publishing.
Printed in the UK.

CONTENTS

INTRODUCTION

Statistically, the number of murders in London is at its lowest since the 1960s. Even though London's population has significantly increased and become more diverse, the capital is the safest it has been for thirty years. However, *one* murder is *one* murder too many; the regularity of youth homicide permeating our news bulletins and newspapers on a seemingly daily basis is extremely disturbing. In actual fact public perception of crime is far greater than the crime rate itself; with London's population standing at around eight million, the likelihood of becoming a victim of homicide in the capital is approximately 1:80,000. The police service and local authorities are pro-active in areas of crime prevention and crime reduction – the use of closed-circuit television (CCTV), the architectural design of buildings, housing estates and transport infrastructure with crime prevention at its core is strategic in efforts to lessen the perception of crime that we all fear.

Of course, murder *is* committed in our homes, on our streets and public transport services, having a devastating effect on the friends and family of both the victim and the offender. Murder has many mainsprings, the motive commonly greed, revenge, jealousy or a feeling of power over another human being. Murder destroys the heart of any family and rips the soul out of a community.

This book endeavours to examine – in short, sharp, daily bursts – the circumstances of murder and execution in London over the past four centuries, drawing on some well documented criminal cases but more so on cases that have rarely been examined, including those of police officers murdered in the execution of their duty. It highlights the levels of depravity and plain evil that we humans are capable of inflicting on each other. Unlike other volumes on murder, this account diversifies to include terrorism, where innocent citizens become the victims of a sometimes-obscure political cause or ideology that they may never have heard of – nor had any opinion on.

In our society, an offender's human rights are arguably paramount, the victim's often forgotten. An offender has a right to a fair trial, a cornerstone of the British judicial system long before the introduction of the Human Rights Act 1998 (Article 6). This book will raise questions about how we, as a society, respect the memory of murder victims and acknowledge the awful suffering of the victim's family. Murder is corrosive, it wears people down, a fact often overlooked or indeed ignored by judiciary, government and media. It is very hard to explain to a grieving relative why the killer of their loved one has received life imprisonment with a minimum term less than that of an offender who robs a bank.

Different methods of execution have been employed by the state: the butchery of being hung, drawn and quartered or burnt at the stake, facing the firing squad for treachery and the hangman's noose for murder. But is there a place for capital punishment in our society today for the most serious of crimes? Some make the case for the return of the death penalty for the murder of children, police officers in the execution of their duty, or the killing of innocent civilians in the name of a political or religious cause. A recent example is the atrocious murder of Fusilier Lee Rigby in May 2013 where live television broadcasts portrayed, repeatedly, the aftermath of the attack; a blood-soaked terrorist proudly spouting his justification for taking the life of a defenceless young man. I would not dare to second-guess the Rigby family's views on capital punishment, but in a case with such irrefutable evidence of murder, personally, I believe the return of such a punishment is warranted. Many will claim that capital punishment is not a deterrent and that we must uphold the human rights of a killer – the same killer who failed to show any such compassion for his victim. It does, however, ensure that a convicted, executed murderer will *never* murder again. Politicians have got their heads buried in the sand when it comes to this issue, frequently failing to consult, listen to and act upon the will of the British people before and during recent parliamentary debates and votes on the subject. We as a nation have taken a major constitutional step by voting to extricate ourselves from the rule of the European Union and hopefully, in turn (in my opinion) abolishing the constraints of the Human Rights Act that seriously restricts the power of our courts to deal with terrorists and murderers in particular.

While reading the harrowing stories featured in these pages, remember the victims of these crimes, those of future crimes and their families and friends who will bear a sentence far greater than that of the killer.

G. Powell

Gary Powell retired from the police force after thirty-three years'
service (thirty spent as a detective) in London. He worked as
a detective on New Scotland Yard's Anti-Terrorist Branch and
played a part in a number of murder and terrorist investigations.

I

JANUARY

1st – *Stumpy's Revenge*

New Year's Day 1926 was barely eight hours old when Polly Edith Walker's life was snuffed out by an act of terrible violence. The Walker family, Polly, her mother and brother, lived at No. 58 Arlington Road, Camden Town. Polly was a pretty sixteen-year-old; she befriended a lonely local disabled tailor named Eugene de Vere, who had suffered the loss of his left leg above the knee. Eugene was a regular visitor to the Walker family address drawn by the mischievous, flirtatious Polly, who would lead him on with sexual taunts and innuendo. Things came to a head during the Christmas and New Year period, 1925. Polly had attracted the attention of a young, good-looking chauffeur named Leonard Miall. Eugene de Vere, increasingly frustrated by his 'girlfriend's' behaviour, commented to Miall – as a warning – that Polly had been 'playing him up' and that she would 'not get the chance to do it again'.

On the morning of 1 January 1926, Polly's mother and brother left the house early as Polly slept in. They returned at 1 p.m. to discover Polly missing. They searched the house and discovered her body under her bed – she had been murdered, strangled by a stocking tied tightly around her neck and beaten around the head. An array of weapons, including a pair of bloodied brass tongs and a poker, lay nearby. Items of jewellery and clothes had been stolen from a locked bedroom cupboard. Detectives quickly learned of the potentially dangerous relationship between Polly and de Vere; they called on Eugene's address in nearby Delaney Street, but he had disappeared. The jewellery was pawned in a local pawnbroker by a man with a limp matching the description of de Vere. His photograph was circulated to all police forces and he was tracked down and arrested on 3 January 1926 in Hitchin, Herts.

His trial took place at the Central Criminal Court, Old Bailey. He offered provocation as a defence, claiming Walker had bitten him and called him a beast resulting in him losing his temper and attacking her. The jury dismissed the defence argument – de Vere was found guilty of murder and hanged at Pentonville Prison on 24 March 1926.

2nd – Business Fallout

Marylebone High Street, London W1, is an area of high-priced residential properties bordering a relaxed but busy shopping street. On Saturday 2 January 1993, successful local businessman Donald Urquhart and his girlfriend left the Queens Head pub, intending to catch a taxi home. As they approached the junction of the High Street with Vincent Street, a motorbike roared up, its rider dismounted and shot Urquhart in the head at point blank range. As Urquhart fell to the ground, the assassin fired two more shots into his victim before remounting the bike and making good his escape.

The killer was eventually identified as unemployed roofer Graeme Nigel West. Detectives, through interviews with West, established the murder had been a contract killing, the most likely motive being the business interests of the victim. West was paid £20,000 for the hit. He appeared at the Old Bailey and was convicted of the murder in November 1994. He never disclosed the originator of the contract.

* * *

A similar 'execution' took place sixty years earlier in 1933. The victim was thirty-five-year-old Cypriot Dr Angelo Zemenides. Witnesses heard two shots being fired from an address in Upper Park Road, Hampstead, and the doctor was found slumped in his doorway – shot in the back. Detectives focused on associates of the victim within the Cypriot community, quickly identifying a suspect who had purchased a gun beforehand. His name was Theodosius Petrou, a fellow countryman of the deceased. Dr Zemenides was an influential community leader who had accepted £10 from Petrou to find him a wife. The deceased failed to keep his side of the deal; Petrou asked for his money back and was refused. It was alleged that Petrou returned to the address and shot Zemenides. Petrou stood trial for murder but, despite the abundance of circumstantial evidence, including the purchase of the weapon, he had a strong alibi (from members of his close-knit community) and the jury found him not guilty.

3rd – *Your Teeth Never Lie*
London's fire brigade received an emergency call to a shed ablaze in the back garden of No. 30 Hawley Crescent, Camden Town NW1, on the evening of 3 January 1933. After extinguishing the blaze, firemen discovered a badly burnt corpse. A suicide note, purportedly signed by the forty-two-year-old occupant Samuel James Furnace, was found in the house, avowing financial difficulties for his self-demise. As with all suspicious deaths, a post-mortem examination was performed during which two bullet holes were discovered in the deceased's back. Doubt as to the identity of the deceased arose when the examination concluded the teeth of the corpse appeared to be of a much younger man. Enquiries identified the dead man as rent collector and long-time acquaintance of Samuel Furnace – Walter Spatchett. A countrywide hunt was initiated and Furnace was arrested on 14 January 1933 at No. 11 Whitegate Road, Southend, Essex, after breaking cover and contacting his brother-in-law for help. Furnace was returned to London and held at Kentish Town Police Station. Overnight, after complaining of being cold, he was given his coat to keep him warm. Unbeknown to the gaoler, he had secreted a phial of hydrochloric acid in the lining which he drank; he died in hospital the following day.

* * *

William Joyce, American-born British fascist and Nazi wartime propaganda broadcaster infamously known as Lord Haw Haw, was executed for treason at London's Wandsworth Prison on this day in 1946. Joyce fled from England to Germany at the start of the Second World War and was recruited by German intelligence as a broadcaster of propaganda on German radio's English service. The broadcasts would chillingly commence with the words 'Germany Calling Germany Calling Germany Calling' and would urge the British people to surrender. He was captured in May 1945 on the German/Danish border, returned to England, tried on three counts of treason and executed.

4th – A Traitor's Death
4 January 1946 witnessed the last person to be executed for an offence, other than that of murder, in England. Private Theodore William Schurch was London born of Swiss parents; in his formative years, he became a member of the British Union of Fascists. Schurch was conscripted into the Royal Army Service Corps during the Second World War. While stationed in North Africa, he became an agent for German and Italian intelligence services. The basis of the charge, which led to a traitor's death, was that he obtained military information from British prisoners, which he passed to the enemy. He was tried in England and convicted by a general court martial of nine charges of treachery and one of desertion with intent to join the enemy. He was hanged at Pentonville Prison.

5th – Poor Child
Is there a more sickening crime than child abuse and murder? Justice finally caught up with one such offender on this day in 1880. Charles Shurety, an unemployed bricklayer, was executed at Newgate Prison for the murder of two-year-old Louisa Piper. Shurety lived with Mary Ann Piper, the child's mother, at No. 2 Payne's Place, Kentish Town. Mary Ann and her two older children worked all day to support themselves and the idle Shurety, whose only responsibility was to childmind the infant Louisa. Shurety subjected little Louisa to long-term abuse over several months culminating on 1 November 1879 with Louisa's appalling violent death. She was found by a neighbour lying on her bed covered by a thin blanket. She had visible bruising and cuts to her thin frame. During the trial at the Old Bailey, Shurety stood

in the dock with Mary Ann, both charged with Louisa's murder. One witness gave a chilling account of a conversation she had had with the defendant in which he stated he would 'like to lay the naked child on the floor, thrash her until she could not move and then starve her to death'. He was found guilty of wilful murder and sentenced to death. Mary Ann Piper was discharged on the direction of the judge.

A mysterious twist occurred on the morning of Shurety's execution; a letter arrived at the gaol marked 'On her Majesty's Service – Immediate'. The missive's author purported to be the home secretary instructing the execution to be postponed. The prison governor was suspicious, questioning its authenticity (he was astute as the letter was a forgery) due to the handwriting, punctuation and grammar. Ignoring the letter, he ordered the sentence to be carried out.

6th – An Unauthorised Loan

Foreign bankers Cartmell and Schlitte occupied business premises at No. 84 Shaftesbury Avenue, London W1. On 7 November 1908, a young, out-of-work, engineer called John Esmond Murphy entered the premises with the intention of acquiring an unauthorised loan. He approached one of the partners, Frederick Julius Schlitte, and threatened him with a Webley–Fosbery service revolver he had purchased the day before at a firing range in nearby Oxenden Street W1 and a knife. He demanded money but was refused, shot Schlitte in the shoulder and then stabbed him six times. He ran out of the bank empty-handed but was immediately tackled by a public-spirited member of the public named George Carter and Police Constable (PC) Albert Howe, who heard the gunfire. Both men were stabbed during the struggle but managed to detain the offender. Schlitte was taken to hospital but died of his injuries two days later.

At his Old Bailey trial, Murphy offered a defence of insanity due to suffering from typhoid fever and sunstroke in India where he was born. His defence team produced several witnesses to give examples of his erratic behaviour in the weeks leading up to the attempted robbery. The jury were not persuaded and took only twenty-five minutes to find him guilty as charged.

Murphy was executed at Pentonville Prison on 6 January 1909. Both Carter and Howe were commended by the judge in recognition of their bravery.

7th – Jack Tarr

Execution Dock, on the River Thames' northern shoreline, was the execution site for pirates, smugglers and mutineers for over 400 years. The last hangings were in 1830. Any person who committed a crime at sea against British interests, anywhere in the world, were brought back to London in chains and tried by the High Court of the Admiralty. Those found guilty would be conveyed to Execution Dock in an open cart, enduring abuse and violence from crowds who lined the route from Newgate or Marshalsea prisons. The condemned would suffer a cruel, inhumane death as the shortened noose, from which they hung, would drop to just below the tide line; the short drop would rarely break the condemned man's neck, therefore it took him many minutes to die. The corpse would be cut down after it had been submerged fully by three tides. Following execution, the most notorious pirates, as an example to those tempted to follow in their footsteps, would be tarred, hung in chains and left to rot.

On 7 January 1817, the dock claimed four more lives. John Pierie, a Lieutenant with twenty-eight years in the King's service, and Swede Jonas Norburgh were executed for 'feloniously conspiring to carry off the *Mary Ann* on her voyage from India'. Daniel Bruce and William Hastings faced a similar fate for 'feloniously and piratically carrying off the ship *Roebuck* on the coast of Africa'. A noose can still be seen today, suspended at the back of the Prospect of Whitby pub in Wapping, as a grisly reminder of the area's past.

8th – A Piece of Cake

The crumpled body of a young boy, aged six years, was discovered on this day in 1914, concealed under a carriage seat of a North London Railway train. The youngster had been strangled with, the pathologist believed, a piece of cord. The victim was William Starchfield, son of Agnes Starchfield and her estranged husband John. Following extensive police enquiries and appeals for witnesses, several members of the public came forward with information. At certain points of the journey, William had been seen in the company of a man who had been bending over him in an aggressive manner. One such witness, Clara Wood, described William eating a piece of currant cake; a subsequent post-mortem revealed a cake substance mixed with currants in the deceased's stomach. Clara Wood identified William's father John as the man she saw. John Starchfield was arrested and charged with the murder of his young son, a charge he strenuously denied telling detectives that he was in his lodging house at the time of the murder and produced alibi witnesses to prove it.

John Starchfield stood trial for the murder of his son at the Old Bailey. The prosecution's case collapsed when one witness attempted suicide and star witness Clara Wood's evidence was discredited by the defence counsel, who proved she had seen a picture of John Starchfield in the papers before she identified him, resulting in the trial judge ordering the jury to return a verdict of not guilty. The case remains officially unsolved; John Starchfield maintained his innocence until he died of natural causes in 1916.

9th – All For Love

We return to the North London Railway for another child murder resulting in the execution of Louise Josephine Masset on this day in 1900. Louise, a piano teacher, had an illegitimate four-year-old son, Manfred Louis, following an affair with a Frenchman who had returned home. From the age of three weeks, Manfred was cared for on a full-time basis by nursemaid Helen Gentle. Louise would visit her son once a week at No. 210 Clyde Road, Tottenham. Louise was living with her sister at No. 29 Bethune Road, Stoke Newington, and had begun a relationship with French student Eudore Lucas. During the early weeks of October 1899, Helen Gentle was informed by Masset that Manfred's father, who had been paying for his care, wanted to take him to France to continue his early education and that she would pick up her son and take him via London Bridge Station, onto a ferry and across to France. Gentle arranged to hand over Manfred on the morning of 27 October outside the Birdcage Pub on Stamford Hill, together with a change of clothes for the journey. Later that day the battered, naked, body of Manfred was discovered in the ladies toilet at Dalston Junction railway station; he had been beaten around the head with such force that his face was hardly recognisable and then strangled, a bloodied stone lay near to the body. Miss Gentle read about the murder, of a yet unidentified child, in a newspaper. Recognising the partial description, she went to the police and informed them of the circumstances under which she had last seen Manfred.

Louise Masset was questioned. She stated that she handed her son over to two women at London Bridge Station, hired by the boy's father to take him to France. Detectives proved this account to be a callous lie; Masset had in fact killed her own son before taking a train to the south coast where she spent a few days with lover Eudore Lucas. Her fate was sealed when good detective work uncovered Manfred's bloodied clothes in a waiting room at Brighton Station. The rock found at the crime scene, used to kill her son, fitted perfectly into a hole in the garden at Bethune Road. The shawl the body had been wrapped in belonged to the murderess. The motive for the killing of her illegitimate son was to save her new boyfriend any future embarrassment. She was hanged at Newgate.

10th – A Jealous Squaddie

Jealousy is a destructive, raw emotion and often features as a motive for murder. George Henry Perry, a former soldier of the Royal Garrison Artillery, was discharged in 1907 having served in India and Aden. George found difficulty settling back into civilian life; with few prospects of employment and little money he went to live with his girlfriend Annie Covell and her parents at No. 1 Florence Terrace, Uxbridge Road, Ealing. Annie's father, a former police officer, realised that Perry had no interest in finding employment and was quite prepared to live off his family's generosity, which created a hostile atmosphere. The situation deteriorated when Annie was invited to be a bridesmaid at a friend's wedding in Hanwell to which Perry, who had become very possessive, wasn't invited. On the morning of 10 January 1910, a scream was heard from the breakfast room. Annie was found by her mother on the floor with Perry bending over her.

He had savagely cut Annie's throat before stabbing her twice and throwing the bloodstained bread knife under a nearby table. Perry left by the front door, later giving himself up to PC Robert Drew on Ealing Broadway. Perry's defence team tried to prove a case of 'Impulsive Insanity' where a destructive impulse, like a delusion, cannot be controlled by the patient; the respected *Taylor's Medical Jurisprudence* was used as a reference source. However, it was successfully argued by the prosecution that a rage that had lasted for three days (since the wedding) could hardly be described as a sudden impulse. Perry, to his credit, always professed his guilt and that he deserved to die. The hangman duly obliged on the morning of 1 March at Pentonville Prison.

11th – You Sold What!

Brick Lane, London, E1 is a racially diverse and vibrant area of the capital. Two characters who were an embodiment of that racial fusion were Frances Tucker, a low-level drug dealer of West Indian and Scottish heritage, and her West Indian boyfriend, unemployed painter Cleveland Reid, who had a more serious criminal record and been recently released from a custodial sentence. On his return to Brick Lane, following his incarceration, Reid discovered Frances had sold many of his personal belongings to fund the purchase of drugs, which resulted in a violent quarrel. On the evening of 11 January 1960, a fire broke out at No. 106 Brick Lane, on the junction of Princelet Street, a building in which Frances Tucker had a small bedsit. The building was burnt down with many occupants just escaping with their lives. Further investigation by the London Fire Brigade led to the discovery of the body of Frances. A post-mortem concluded that she had been strangled, soaked with paraffin and set alight.

Detectives identified boyfriend Reid as the main suspect, witnesses informing them of his recent release and the couple's volatile relationship. Reid was tracked down to his sister's address in Cricklewood, north-west London. Reid at first denied any involvement in the murder and subsequent arson, but his clothes reeked of paraffin. So he was arrested and charged. Reid tried to justify his actions by telling the police, and later the judge and jury at his subsequent trial, that Tucker had been blackmailing him with compromising pictures, threatening to show these to his sister, so strangled her with her own scarf and set fire to the flat to destroy the evidence. At a time when the death penalty was under parliamentary scrutiny, Reid escaped the hangman's noose and was sentenced to life imprisonment on 17 March 1960.

12th – A Smiling Geordie

When a man of previous good character cuts his girlfriend's throat, admits culpability and 'only wants to die', refuses legal representation and stands in the dock at the Old Bailey smiling as he pleads guilty – insanity must be considered highly likely. James Robert Vent, an unemployed miner from Newcastle, had been courting forty-nine-year-old Clemintina Balchin of Church Street, Camberwell. On the evening of 12 January 1935, Vent returned to the address drunk. Balchin, angry about his inebriated state, allegedly started to tease Vent over a man she had met, a chef who lived in Hastings. Balchin seriously underestimated Vent's tolerance threshold; overcome with jealousy he took a knife and cut her throat.

During his trial, the judge rightly questioned Vent's fitness to enter a plea of guilty; the prison doctor from Brixton gave evidence that in his professional opinion the defendant seemed to be of sound mind. Judge and prosecution discussed whether a jury should be empanelled to decide on Vent's mental state, but the judge decided this was not needed and sentenced Vent to death. The execution date was set for 6 March 1935 until a reprieve arrived from the home secretary; Vent was incarcerated in Broadmoor Criminal Lunatic Asylum until his death.

13th – Husband and Pimp

Prostitutes often take measures to safeguard their security: carrying a weapon or being physically able to defend oneself should the need arise. Having your husband as your pimp and your driver who escorts you and your client to your own flat, waits until the business end has been completed before repeating the scenario – is another. That is how husband and wife Ruby and Ernest Bolton operated. On the night of 13 January 1956, Ernest had already made several trips between their home, No. 32 Westbourne

Terrace, W2, and Mayfair where Ruby plied her trade. The last client Ruby was entertaining was a regular punter. Ernest relaxed his guard and fell asleep in his car. When he woke in the early hours of the morning, he rang Ruby a couple of times from a nearby telephone kiosk but got no answer. Thinking she was probably putting in a little extra effort for a little extra profit, he didn't disturb her and went back to sleep. By 7.30 a.m., Ernest – now worried – entered the flat to find his wife had been murdered; brutally beaten, suffering repeated blows to her head with a heavy axe. Detectives made significant strides with the investigation, receiving information from normally tight-lipped sources in the world of vice keen to see the murderer of one of their own brought to justice. A prime suspect was identified – Leonard Atter. Atter was arrested and when questioned admitted that he was at the flat and had paid for sex with Ruby but left in the early hours as, he claimed, Ruby had another customer turning up at 3 a.m. This admission would rebut any initial forensic evidence the police discovered such as fingerprints, fibres and bodily fluids belonging to Atter, as he admitted he *had* been in the flat. However, more significant forensic evidence was forthcoming: Ruby's blood in Atter's hair and on his clothing. Couple this with him shaving his beard off the next day to alter his appearance and the discovery of a detective magazine at his flat featuring an axe murder, police believed they had a *prima facie* case and Atter was charged with Ruby's murder and sent for trial.

At his trial, the forensic evidence, on which the prosecution were so reliant, was severely undermined by the defence to the extent that the judge decided it too circumstantial and ordered the jury to return a verdict of not guilty. Atter walked from court a free man and the murder remains unsolved.

14th – A Stroll along the River Lea

Margaret Evans, aged twenty-four, was deeply in love with Edward Hugh Tunbridge, a warehouse clerk and the father of Margaret's two-year-old child. Domestic servant Margaret fell pregnant for a second time and arranged to meet Tunbridge at Clapton railway station on the evening of 14 January 1922 to decide how they were going to cope with another mouth to feed. Tunbridge made it clear to Margaret that he had serious doubts as to whether he was the father of this second child. There can be little doubt of Tunbridge's intention that night; his purchase of potassium cyanide earlier in the day would convince a later jury of an evident level of premeditation. They met as arranged and walked along the towpath of the River Lea near Spring Hill, Clapton. Margaret proposed they get married; this suggestion didn't seem to fit in with Tunbridge's plans for the future – or at least *his* future. As they walked past a bridge, they crossed paths with a police officer on patrol. A few minutes later, the officer heard a splash of something in the water and saw Tunbridge walking hurriedly back along the towpath towards him – alone. The officer stopped Tunbridge and asked him where the girl was. Tunbridge, surprised to see the officer still in the vicinity, was escorted back in the direction from which the officer heard the splash and found Margaret Evans floating face down in the water. At his trial, Tunbridge gave evidence claiming he was having a cigarette when Evans took the bottle from his pocket and drank the contents before fainting and falling into the river and drowning.

The post-mortem revealed a large quantity of cyanide in Margaret's blood-system and injuries to her face consistent with several punches from a clenched fist. The judge summed-up to the jury that if Evans had taken the poison willingly, as claimed by Tunbridge, of which there was significant doubt, she may have thought it some sort of abortive. The jury did not believe Tunbridge's story, found him guilty of murder and he was sentenced to death. Tunbridge's legal team submitted an appeal to the home secretary, which was dismissed. Tunbridge was executed at Pentonville Prison on 18 April 1922.

* * *

Also on this day in 1997, compulsive gambler Brandon Hale was found beaten and shot through the eye in Queens Woods, Highgate N10. Detectives suspected the murder to be one of a growing number of contract killings in the capital. The motive for this unsolved homicide was believed to be connected to the disappearance of a large amount of money.

15th – Baby Killer

Frances Lydia Alice Knorr, born Minnie Thwaites in London in 1868, emigrated to Sydney, Australia in 1887. Frances married Randolph Knorr, a German immigrant, but life in Australia was tough due to a financial recession and Randolph received a prison sentence for selling furniture that he had obtained on hire purchase. This left Frances alone, penniless and starving. She moved to Brunswick, Melbourne and advertised her services as a child minder. She took on the care of mainly illegitimate babies, a practice referred to in London as baby farming (baby farming was a widely followed practice in London at the time she emigrated and will be discussed later) and on occasions passed children on to other women, but paying them a lower rate. When she couldn't come to such an arrangement, she would either return the child to its mother or simply murder the infant. She returned to Sydney on her husband's release from prison. A grisly discovery was unearthed by the new tenants in Frances' former Brunswick home. While preparing a flowerbed, they discovered the remains of three small children.

Police traced Frances back to Sydney and she was arrested for murder, found guilty and sentenced to death. The authorities ignored vociferous objections and appeals from women's groups in Australia and executed Knorr on this day in 1894; Knorr was one of only five women ever to be executed in the state of Victoria.

16th – Killer Husband

George Albert Crossman was a murderer and serial bigamist who, by 1898, had already married three women, been convicted of bigamy and sentenced to five years hard labour. But hard labour had not dampened his 'ardour'; on his release, he married wife number four, a Miss Thompson, on 10 January 1903. They moved into No. 46 Ladysmith Road, Kensal Rise, Queen's Park (now Wrentham Avenue). On 15 January, he sent his new wife off to a relative's house, telling her he had to travel to Manchester on business. The very same day of wife number four's departure, Crossman married a young nurse called Ellen Sampson and took her back to Ladysmith Road. Crossman murdered Sampson, his wife of one day, on 16 January 1903.

Just over a year later in 1904, having married two more women, Crossman rented out a room at Ladysmith Road to a man called William Dell. His new tenant complained to Crossman about an awful smell emanating from a cupboard under the stairs. Crossman explained away the smell as residue from plaster that he had used for decoration and promised to remove it. The smell was in fact coming from a metal trunk – containing the body of Ellen Sampson – Crossman had encased in concrete, which had cracked, emitting the awful aroma. Dell was mistrustful of such a bizarre story and decided to report his suspicions to the police. A few days later, while Crossman was having the trunk removed, a PC Rees arrived to follow up the report. As Rees walked up the path towards Crossman, the murdering bigamist panicked and made a run for it, chased by Rees. When captured, he shouted, 'Oh God!' and slid a razor from a coat pocket and slit his own throat, dying in a gush of blood and escaping justice. A subsequent coroner's inquest took place into the deaths of Crossman and Ellen Sampson. The hearing was attended by a number of Crossman's wives (including his current legitimate wife, formerly Miss Thompson). Verdicts of murder (Sampson) and suicide (Crossman) were recorded.

17th – Brothers in Arms

Brothers Daniel and Robert Perreau were executed for forgery at Tyburn on this day in 1776, both having been charged with attempting to defraud Drummond's Bank in London. The trial at the Old Bailey created great public interest as both defendants held high social positions in London society and were described by *The Newgate Calendar* as 'One an apothecary of great practice and the other living in the style of a gentleman'. A portrait of the two brothers, standing in the dock during their trial, can be seen at the National Portrait Gallery in London.

18th – A Hated Wife

The bodies of a mother and her young baby daughter were plucked from the Grand Union Canal near Paddington in December 1802. The grisly discovery was made by boatman John Atkins. The last sighting of mum and daughter alive was on Sunday 5th in the company of estranged husband and father George Foster in the Mitre Tavern on the canal. A somewhat speculative case against George Foster, based purely on circumstantial evidence, was placed before a jury at the Old Bailey on 14 January 1803; the jury, convinced of his guilt, convicted him. He was dispatched with haste on this day, 18 January 1803, hanged by the neck until dead outside Newgate Prison. The jury's decision was vindicated when Foster admitted to the killings just prior to his death, confessing that he hated his wife and that the death of the baby had been unfortunate but necessary. His body was delivered, on the order of the court, to the Royal College of Surgeons to be publicly dissected and anatomised in accordance with the Murder Act passed by Parliament in 1751; an act devised 'for better preventing the horrid crime of murder' and 'that some further terror and peculiar mark of infamy be added to the punishment' and further, 'that in no case whatsoever shall the body of any murderer be suffered to be buried by mandating either public dissection or hanging in chains'. The act also legislated the murderer be executed within two days of conviction, unless the third day be a Sunday, then the execution would be postponed until the Monday.

19th – Let's Go Play Son

George William Austin idolised his young five-year-old son George Gerard. During the latter part of 1898, the boy fell 18 feet from a window of their family home at No. 26 Goswell Terrace, Clerkenwell. George senior anticipated what was about to happen and tried to prevent the fall but failed; fortunately the young George received no permanent injury. George Austin never really got over the shock of seeing his son disappear out of the window and frequently suffered bouts of depression.

During the evening of 19 January 1899, George senior took his young son out of the house on the pretext of playing with his toy locomotive. They went to nearby Lloyd Square where he inexplicably struck George Gerard on the head with a hatchet several times and walked away. George approached a local beat officer PC Denby and calmly informed him that he had chopped his son's head off, pointing back into Lloyd Square. PC Denby escorted Austin back to the scene; the boy was still alive but died at Kings Cross Road police station a short time after.

George was charged with his son's wilful murder. His wife testified at the coroner's inquest into the death of her son that her husband had been suffering severe headaches and never recovered from the shock of George Gerard's fall, which he held himself responsible for. She also described her husband's fear of abject poverty, often threatening to kill them all rather than suffer such deprivation.

The case was sent to the Old Bailey. The court heard from Dr James Scott of Holloway Prison where George had been held on remand. Dr Scott gave evidence of his observations of the prisoner while in custody. In his opinion, George was in no fit mental state to make a plea or stand trial. This tragic case ended with George being detained at HM's pleasure in a mental institution for the rest of his life.

20th – Bite Marks but No Charge

A police patrol attended an emergency call to Royal College Street, Camden Town on 20 January 2002 in response to a man causing criminal damage to a neighbour's property. The offender was Anthony John Hardy, who the police interviewed and arrested in his own the flat. The officers checked the flat for evidence of other offences and found the flat's bedroom door locked. Hardy claimed he let the room out to a lodger, who had the only key. During a search of the prisoner, the key was found in Hardy's trouser pocket; officers opened the door and were shocked to discover the body of a young woman later identified as local prostitute Sally Rose. She had suffered cuts to the head and her torso was covered in human bite marks. The result of the post-mortem examination revealed that although she had been badly abused Sally had in fact died of a heart attack; therefore, Hardy was only charged with the original criminal damage offence and served a couple of weeks in prison.

Nearly a year later, on 30 December 2002, a vagrant was searching rubbish bags for food in an alleyway behind the College Arms pub on Royal College Street when he made a grisly discovery; one of the bags contained human remains. A more thorough search by police found the further remains of two women – minus their heads and hands, which were never recovered. A bloody trail led back to Anthony Hardy's flat where police discovered, amid a scene akin to a slaughterhouse, an electric saw, a hacksaw and a woman's torso. The media labelled the missing Hardy as *The Camden Ripper*. The two women were identified as local prostitutes Elizabeth Valad (identified through serial numbers on her breast implants) and Brigitte MacClennan.

Hardy was arrested at Great Ormond Street Hospital just a couple of miles from the scene of his gruesome crimes. He appeared at the Old Bailey in November 2003 charged with three murders, pleaded guilty and received three life sentences.

21st – Pepys' Day Out
Samuel Pepys, the celebrated seventeenth-century diarist, refers to the brutal public execution of Colonel James Turner for burglary on this day in 1663:

> Up, and after sending my wife to my aunt Wight's to get a place to see Turner hanged, I to the office, where we sat all the morning, and at noon going to the 'Change' and seeing people flock in the City, I enquired, and found that Turner was not yet hanged. And so I went among them to Leadenhall Street, at the end of Lyme Street, near where the robbery was done; and to St. Mary Axe, where he lived. And there I got for a shilling to stand upon the wheel of a cart, in great pain, above an hour before the execution was done; he delaying the time by long discourses and prayers one after another, in hopes of a reprieve; but none came, and at last was flung off the ladder in his cloak. A comely-looked man he was, and kept his countenance to the end: I was sorry to see him. It was believed there were at least 12 or 14,000 people in the street.

22nd – A Family Affair
Bartle Road, East Ham was a peaceful residential street adjacent to the busier Barking Road. Local resident Mary May Palfrey was in a relationship with blacksmith George William Barton, her fifty-one-year-old brother-in-law who lived in Troy Town, Peckham Rye. Barton's wife (Palfrey's sister) had died several years before and they planned to marry. Following an argument on 22 January 1925, in which Barton accused Palfrey (a widow herself) of seeing other men, in particular a sailor, he savagely slashed her throat

with a razor. Barton gave himself up at Vine Street police station; he was arrested, tried for murder and executed at Pentonville Prison on 2 April 1925.

23rd – Theatreland Murder

PC William Fitzgerald died while on duty on this day in 1866. PC Fitzgerald was patrolling London's Drury Lane when he had occasion to arrest a male behaving in a drunken and disorderly manner. The offender was John Daly, a labourer. PC Fitzgerald struggled to direct the belligerent Daly towards Bow Street police station, the shortest route being along the dimly lit Broad Court. Out of the darkness appeared Daly's two friends, John Cahill and Daniel Curtis who intervened, helping to free Daly from the officer's grip. Daly, now at liberty, commenced a vicious attack against the outnumbered PC Fitzgerald, kicking and punching him to the floor. Cahill and Curtis lent a boot or a fist before running off like the cowards they were. PC Fitzgerald, who was in a bad way with a shattered arm and in a great deal of pain, was assisted by colleagues. Close to death, Fitzgerald managed to tell them that 'Long Bob', a name Daly was known to the police by, was responsible for the attack before dying of his injuries. John Daly, Cahill and Curtis were arrested and tried; the charge of murder was reduced to manslaughter. Daly was sentenced to five years penal servitude, Cahill and Curtis for twelve months hard labour. The ferocity of the attack leaves little doubt that these offenders were reckless as to the injuries inflicted and had left Fitzgerald to die, but the court decided this was insufficient evidence to support the more serious charge of murder and the three men escaped the rope.

24th – Look What She Gave Me!

Provocation as a defence to murder is defined in law as '*a concession to human frailty*'. Such a defence was offered to a jury by Canadian infantryman Private George Harman at his trial for the murder of young barmaid Phyllis Earle, a married woman whose soldier husband was fighting for his country in the First World War. A lamplighter found Phyllis Earle's body under a railway arch in Amhurst Passage, Hackney Downs. She had been murdered in the late hours of 24 January 1918; her throat cut after suffering severe blows to her head. The young Canadian soldier proved to be the last person seen in her company. He was traced and arrested on suspicion of murder; when searched, he was found in possession of a bloodstained knife and dried blood splashes were present on his greatcoat. He admitted that he had murdered Phyllis but claimed provocation as Phyllis had passed on a sexually transmitted disease to him. Harman explained to detectives that he had talked to her about the infection that night, but she just mocked him, which led to him losing his temper.

At his trial, the jury rejected provocation as a defence to murder; the fact he had succumbed to such a disease was knowledge he had held for some time and therefore his actions on the night were not instantaneous, even when accompanied by the derisive words uttered by the victim. Harman was convicted of murder but the jury recommended mercy. The judge, by law, sentenced Harman to death. Following a petition signed by residents of London Fields (reading between the lines the victim didn't seem to be the most popular of characters), appealing for mercy to be shown to Harman, and an appeal to the home secretary, the death sentence was commuted to life imprisonment.

25th – Newgate's Last

Charlotte Cheeseman's boyfriend returned from the Boer War in 1902 and discovered she had been seeing another man called George Woolf, a labourer aged twenty-seven of Eagle Wharf Road, Hoxton. A hostile confrontation took place between Charlotte's two lovers, resulting in each (who presumably didn't know about the other) ending the relationship with her even though she was now carrying Woolf's baby. Some attempt at reconciliation took place when Charlotte and George met at a pub on Southgate Road, Hoxton on 25 January 1902, witnesses recalled seeing the pair drinking together. The following morning, Charlotte's body was found in a ditch on Tottenham Marshes between Scotland Green and Park railway stations. She had suffered terrible injuries; her neck and face were badly mutilated. George, the main suspect, attempted to escape arrest by enlisting with the East Surrey Regiment at their Kingston Barracks. His efforts were in vain, as he was detained and charged with the murder of Charlotte Cheeseman. George was tried at the Old Bailey, found guilty and hanged on 6 May 1902. George Woolf was the last person to be executed at Newgate before its closure later that year and its demolition in 1904.

***

British biographer and travel writer James Pope-Hennessy lived with his male partner Leslie Walker-Smith at their flat at No. 9 Ladbroke Grove, North Kensington. Both men had befriended another younger man called Sean O'Brien. O'Brien had encouraged the friendship as he had formed a plan to relieve his new pals of a substantial amount of cash. He and two accomplices, Terence Noonan and Edward Wilkinson, intended to steal an editorial advance, due to Pope-Hennessy, of £150,000, for a book on the life of Noel Coward. On 25 January 1974, Noonan and Wilkinson waited in the Mitre pub 50 metres away on the corner of Ladbroke Grove and Holland Park Avenue for a signal from O'Brien that Walker-Smith had gone out and their victim was alone. Noonan and Wilkinson, having received the signal, went to the house to join O'Brien, but the thieves discovered they had jumped the gun as the advance hadn't actually been paid to the author yet. They were furious and were not going to leave empty-handed. Pope-Hennessy was tied up, a hairnet forced down his throat, stabbed, and beaten severely around the head. In the meantime, Walker-Smith returned in possession of a carving knife he had innocently left the flat to purchase. A fight took place resulting in the serious wounding of Walker-Smith. Police were called to the house and both victims were rushed to hospital; Walker-Smith underwent emergency surgery and survived, and Pope-Hennessy died of his injuries. O'Brien, Noonan and Wilkinson were eventually arrested and appeared at the Old Baily in July 1974; all three pleaded guilty to the manslaughter of Pope-Hennessy and the wounding of Walker-Smith. O'Brien received seventeen years imprisonment with Noonan and Wilkinson receiving fifteen years each.

26th – Bad Cop
Former police officer turned gambler Maurice Freedman was a married man who purported to have a new career as a travelling salesman. He started an affair with thirty-year-old typist Annette Friedson.

Freedman was one of life's losers, selling his clothes and borrowing money to fund his gambling. When Annette's parents found out about Freedman's lifestyle and that he was already married, they implored their daughter to end the relationship. Annette stuck with Freedman on the promise he would divorce his wife and deal with his gambling addiction. Eventually her patience ran out and she followed her family's advice to end the relationship. The desperate Freedman continued to harass the young typist to the point where she became genuinely afraid for her own safety and had her brother escort her to her place of work, H. R. Munns & Co., No. 103 Fore Street in the City of London. On the morning of 26 January 1932, Freedman waited in the vicinity of Fore Street until Annette was alone and about to enter her offices, he approached her and begged her to come back to him, which she refused to do. He claimed in his defence that he took out a razor to commit suicide in front of her, but she struggled in an attempt to stop him harming himself and accidently cut her own throat. He again lied when claiming he threw the knife in a canal; the knife, with traces of Annette's rare blood group and strands of her hair on the blade, was retrieved from a London bus. Freedman was executed at Pentonville Prison on 4 May 1932.

* * *

Also on this day in 1943, Franciscus Johannes Winter was executed at Wandsworth Prison for treason. Winter was a steward from Antwerp who arrived in England as a refugee. He was questioned by British Immigration authorities suspecting his story to be complete fabrication. When searched, he was found in possession of a large amount of foreign currency; after further interrogation, he admitted being sent by the Nazis to spy on British convoys.

27th – Eyewitness to Murder
On the rare occasion when violent acts such as murder are perpetrated in plain view of the public, witness accounts can be disturbing but emphasise the indifference one human being can have for another. Mary Wingfield was brutally murdered by her husband John on 27 January 1880, in a public place, knowingly in front of witnesses and with a degree of violence that is truly

on College Farm, Regents Park Road, Finchley; he was employed by the Express Dairy Company. On this particular evening, Webb went out about 8 p.m. and returned a short time later complaining of being shot, blood poured from a serious neck wound and he died in the house minutes later. The doctor who attended, seeing there was a bullet hole in the deceased's neck, noted the absence of blackening around the wound ruling out that the fatal shot had been fired at close range or indeed been a case of suicide.

An inquest was held, a local woman gave evidence that she had heard two shots being fired around the relevant time but some distance away. The inquest also heard from a firearms expert, produced by the police, who came to the conclusion that the weapon had probably been a revolver fired between 150 and 250 yards from the victim and, importantly, such a weapon would only be accurate between 25 and 50 yards from its intended target. Therefore, the inquest jury concluded the incident had been a terrible accident, although the police could not trace anybody in the area who would admit to firing a gun in the vicinity at the relevant time.

30th – On Guard

On this day in the year 1800, Thomas Walton, a local beadle and constable of Paddington parish, was summoned to the Black Lion pub on Bayswater Road. The officer found a victim of murder, George Scott, and a man accused by witnesses of the killing, James Hartley; both men were from the Guards Regiment. In company with others from the regiment, they had drunk heavily until nearly 10 p.m. Following a dispute regarding payment for the last round, Scott got up to relieve himself. He approached the door to go outside when Hartley drew his short sword and stabbed Scott who fell to the floor dead.

At his trial at the Old Bailey, Hartley pleaded self-defence, claiming Scott and two others had assaulted him, and he drew his sword to defend himself. This account was contradicted by a hawker called William Davis who had witnessed the whole event – indeed striking Hartley to stop him making good his escape – and crucially, he was a civilian with no connection or allegiance to any of the participants or the guards' regiment. His evidence was damning and Hartley was convicted of the murder and hanged at Newgate on 24 February 1800. The pub still stands today.

* * *

One and a half centuries earlier, on this day in 1649, the execution of Charles I took place – the only case of regicide in British history. Charles and those loyal to the Royalist cause had been engaged in civil war with Oliver Cromwell's Parliamentarians. Following his defeat, Charles was tried on a charge that he 'traitorously and maliciously levied war against the present Parliament and the people therein represented'. Charles' trial started on 1 January 1649; he was to be tried by one-hundred and thirty-five judges at Westminster Hall, in fact only sixty-eight attended. He was found guilty and beheaded on a scaffold erected outside the Banqueting House in Whitehall.

31st – Hung, Drawn and Quartered

Charles I ascended to the throne following the death of James I in 1625. Protestant King James lived twenty years longer than a band of Catholic terrorists intended him to. The group was led by Robert Catesby who recruited his co-conspirators having hatched a plan to blow up James and his Parliament on 5 November 1605, the date of the state opening. The most infamous of the group was Guido Fawkes whose role was the safekeeping of explosives secreted in a vault under the Houses of Parliament. The group came within hours of what would have been the largest terrorist (a term we would use today) atrocity the country had ever seen. The group were in fact betrayed and searches of the building eventually (after the second attempt) uncovered Fawkes and the explosives hidden under firewood. Guy Fawkes was tortured in the Tower of London until he gave the names of his co-conspirators and signed the confession that sealed his fate. Guy watched as his co-conspirators were executed on 31 January 1606, being hung, drawn and quartered. Fawkes was the last to climb the gallows but escaped the horrors of the drawing of his intestines and the quartering of his torso when he died from a broken neck (he was only supposed to lose consciousness) at the end of the executioner's rope.

2

FEBRUARY

1st – Gang War

A Turkish gang war exploded on to the streets of North London on 1 February 2012 when gang member Ali Armagan was shot dead in Langham Parade at the rear of Turnpike Lane London Underground Station. This was the latest violent incident in a feud between two gangs in the London Borough of Haringey that had been raging since 2009. Armagan was sat in his parked Audi motor vehicle, having dropped off some friends for an appointment locally at a solicitor's office. As he waited, two men approached the car and six shots were fired through the driver's window. Armagan staggered from the car but died close by in a barber shop. Three men pleaded guilty at the Old Bailey to conspiracy to commit grievous bodily harm by giving information to the gunman of the whereabouts of the victim. A twenty-eight-year-old member of a rival gang was charged but acquitted of the actual murder in 2014.

2nd – Countryman Murders Countryman

An argument between two fellow Cypriots – cook Christos Georghiou and café proprietor Savvas Demetriades – resulted in murder. As Demetriades walked along Old Compton Street in London's Soho district on 25 October 1943, Georghiou stabbed him twice, inflicting fatal wounds. Georghiou escaped in a car identified by many witnesses, and was easily tracked down by detectives and charged with the cold-blooded killing of his fellow countryman. During his trial, he pleaded not guilty but was convicted and then executed in Pentonville Prison on this day in 1944. Contemporary records give little insight into the motive but it would appear to be a work-related dispute.

3rd – An Evil Practice

Baby farming was a despicable, and on occasion deadly, late Victorian and early Edwardian practice fuelled by the Victorian stigma attached to the birth of illegitimate babies. One infamous case involved two women, Amelia Sachs and Annie Walters, in 1902, a year after Queen Victoria's death. Sachs lived at Claymore House, Hertford Road, East Finchley (now No. 5 Hertford Road) where she professed to be a qualified midwife. Her co-conspirator Walters described herself as a 'short stay foster parent'. Both women would adopt or care for unwanted babies born, in the main, to the lower working classes whose employers would not tolerate the stigma of illegitimacy attached to their households and required a quick resolution to the problem. Sachs and Walters would persuade desperate mothers that their unwanted children would be taken care of and it was in the child's best interests not to try to see them again. This evil pair would then sell the children on to childless parents or simply murder them and dump their bodies in rivers and on waste ground.

Walters took lodgings at No. 11 Danbury Street, Islington. Her landlord was a PC called Sale who got suspicious of the rapid turnover of children in Walters' care, coupled with asking another lodger to purchase poison for her. Sale and a colleague, Detective Constable Wright, decided to follow Walters. The detective trailed her from her Islington address to Sachs' address in East Finchley and from there, now carrying a bundle, onto an omnibus to South Kensington. Wright stopped her, examined the bundle and found the corpse of a small baby that had been dead for up to twelve hours. The baby had come from Amelia Sachs' premises in East Finchley and Walters was to dispose of the tiny corpse many miles from either of their addresses. Both were convicted on specimen charges (nobody knew how many children they had actually killed) of murder and they were hanged in Holloway Prison on this day in 1903.

* * *

On 3 February 1967, record producer Joe Meek, having firstly murdered his landlady Violet Shenton at his lodgings/recording studio at No. 304, Holloway Road, North London, turned the gun on himself. Although a brilliant music producer and a pioneer in sound recording (he wrote and produced the hit record *Telstar* for the Tornadoes in this building), Meek had a serious drug abuse problem coupled with bouts of paranoia. A plaque unveiled on the building celebrates Meek's musical achievements rather than remembering the victim of the criminal act.

4th – A Clean Kill

Sarah Malcolm entered domestic service in London in the 1730s; her father moved back to Dublin following the death of Sarah's mother. Sarah, now alone, struggled financially but gained employment in a pub in Boswell Court, near Temple Bar, City of London. She also started a small laundry service for well-heeled residents living in the Inns of Court, Temple and rented a room from a Mr John Kerrel. Sarah started to mix with a rough crowd in particular Mary Tracey and her friends, brothers James and Thomas Alexander. All three persuaded the impressionable Sarah to steal small items from her clients for them to sell on. This criminal behaviour escalated to a more serious criminal conspiracy when a burglary was planned. The target was an infirm eighty-year-old lady called Lydia Duncomb who shared her lodgings with long-term companion Mrs Harrison and their young servant Ann Price.

On the night of 4 February 1733, Sarah had managed to sneak the Alexander brothers into the house where they waited until the household was asleep. They then let in Mary Tracey, leaving Sarah Malcolm on the stairs as lookout. The three thieves came out of the property with £300-worth of stolen goods, which they shared with Sarah. Later the following day, the three bodies of Duncomb, Harrison and Price were found by neighbours; Ann Price's throat had been cut, the other two had been strangled. Sarah's landlord, John Kerrel, came across a silver tankard taken from the murder scene in Sarah's room and bloodstains on her clothes. Sarah was arrested and charged with the murders. She stood trial at the Old Bailey on 23 February 1733. The trial lasted only five hours and the jury returned their guilty verdict within fifteen minutes of retiring. Sarah protested that she had been involved in the burglary (a capital offence in its own right) but was unaware of what had taken place inside as her only role was lookout. She explained the blood on her clothes as being her own menstrual blood. Sarah was hanged at Newgate on 7 March 1733. While awaiting her execution, she was visited by painter William Hogarth who sketched her portrait and sold the prints.

5th – Dumped

A most gruesome scene confronted an early morning dog walker in Southwark, South London on Sunday 5 February 1984. Two bodies lay in the scoop of a dumper truck in a small playground off Mint Street, SE1. Seventeen-year-old Michelle Sadler, who was naked from the waist down, had been garrotted with a length of wire; she lay on top of her fully clothed boyfriend Robert Vaughan, who had been stabbed in the chest and had his throat cut. It was quickly apparent to detectives that both victims had been killed elsewhere. Michelle left home at 8.45 a.m. the day before, a Saturday, in order to spend time with Vaughan who was working overtime at a local firm called Courier Displays in Union Street, SE1. Further enquiries revealed that the only other person in the workplace that day was eighteen-year-old David Carty. Detectives visited him at Peterhill House, Linsey Street, Rotherhithe, his home address, and questioned him about the previous day's events.

Carty told detectives that he had been in work earlier in the day but left to go shopping in the West End. Forensic examinations revealed blood on Carty's training shoes, the sole pattern matched footmarks found in the victim's blood at the murder scene, and he was arrested and charged. During his trial, he claimed he had returned later that day from the West End and found both victims already murdered: Michelle had been tied to shelving by a wire around her neck, Vaughan's body was in the toilet. Carty explained that he panicked; afraid that he would be blamed he cleared up as best as he could and hid the bodies. Returning later that night, he loaded the bodies onto a trolley and dumped them in the playground. Carty was convicted of the double-murder and given life imprisonment on 4 December 1984.

6th – A Hammer Blow

Proving a degree of premeditation in the case of murder is a powerful position for the prosecution to attain. There was little doubt about its presence in the murder of Margaret Williams on 6 February 1947. Margaret lived in Merton, SW19 and while walking along Parkleigh Road, she was approached by her estranged husband David John Williams. Williams had travelled all the way from Wynford Road, Finsbury Park, North London armed with the murder weapon – a hammer he struck Margaret viciously over the head with – she died where she fell. Williams appeared at the Surrey Assizes, Kingston upon Thames, on 7 March where he was convicted of Margaret's murder. He was sentenced to death and executed at Wandsworth Prison on 15 May 1947.

7th – Death a Snow Flake Away

Britain's Government of 1991, led by Prime Minister John Major, had an escape on a par with James I's in 1605. The Provisional Irish Republican Army (PIRA) had meticulously planned an attack on No. 10 Downing Street on 7 February 1991. The original target had been former Prime Minister Margaret Thatcher, who unexpectedly resigned in November 1990. PIRA sent two senior operatives to London: one an expert in the trajectory of mortars and another in their manufacture. When it became public knowledge that a War Cabinet was to assemble at Downing Street, chaired by Major, PIRA decided to act. A Ford transit van was purchased, a hole cut into its roof and three mortars – constructed by PIRA each weighing 140 pounds, 4.5 feet in length and carrying a significant amount of Semtex high explosives – were fitted securely inside. Reconnaissance had identified the exact location the van should be positioned on Whitehall; the positioning was crucial in order to attain the right trajectory.

The driver placed the vehicle in position just after 10 a.m. and jumped straight onto a waiting motorcycle. At 10.18 a.m., as a suspicious police officer approached the van, the three mortars automatically fired. The launch of the mortars was quickly followed by a timed incendiary device inside the van to destroy any forensic evidence. Two mortars landed in the grassed area by the Foreign and Commonwealth Office and failed to explode; the third landed in the back garden of No. 10 Downing Street and exploded 30 m from the target. Some damage was caused to the building; four people including two police officers were slightly injured.

It is thought that overnight snow had caused the driver to miss 'his mark' by just a few feet affecting the precise intended impact point; if the mortar had indeed struck its target John Major and his cabinet would, in all probability, have been killed.

8th – Spy Turned Robber

Dublin-born Thomas Butler was convicted of robbery on the highway at the Old Bailey and executed at Tyburn on 8 February 1720. Butler was a well-travelled man who worked as a spy in Paris and spent all his money in Holland before returning to England and a life of crime, a real rogue who admitted to robberies in London, Essex and Kent. He was rumoured to have married eight times, a fact that he denied. During his trial, he took great pleasure showing the court numerous stab wounds and other injuries on his body as badges of honour.

9th – Proud Regimental Man

As a former member of the Leicestershire Regiment, David Greenwood had fought in the Great War (1914–18), and was medically discharged after serving in the trenches. He found employment as a machinist with a manufacturing firm in London's West End. Greenwood had proudly worn his regimental badge to work and this was to be his downfall. On the night of 9 February 1918, sixteen-year-old Nellie Trew did not return home following a visit to Plumstead Library. Her worried father reported her missing; the unfortunate girl was found the following morning on Eltham Common in south-east London – she had been raped and strangled. Police discovered a Leicestershire regimental badge and a bone coat button at the crime scene, which they attributed to the killer and circulated the information to the media appealing for information. Greenwood's work colleagues questioned him about the sudden disappearance of his badge; he stated that he had sold it but went to the police to keep his colleagues off his back. Unfortunately for Greenwood, he wore the same coat he had been wearing when he murdered Nellie; a coat missing its buttons. He was questioned about the buttons but said they had been missing for some time. Detectives were able to match the wire found with the button to wire manufactured at Greenwood's workplace. The case, referred to in the press as The Button and Badge Murder, was heard at the Old Bailey in April 1918 and Greenwood was convicted of Nellie Trew's murder and sentenced to death. His sentence was commuted to life imprisonment the day before his execution; he served twenty-five years before release.

***

The Provisional IRA planted one of its largest devices on mainland UK in London's Canary Wharf on this day in 1996. The bomb – 500 kg of ammonium nitrate mixed with sugar and a high explosive charge – was loaded on a truck and parked 70 m from South Quay Docklands Light railway station. Although PIRA gave a ninety-minute warning, two people were killed during the subsequent explosion, which caused an estimated £100 million of damage and brought to an end a fragile ceasefire.

10th – Keep Your Heads Down
The residents of a quiet street in Sands End, Fulham locked their doors and windows as gunshots rang out on the evening of Saturday 10 February 1968. A gang war for control of Fulham's underworld was coming to a frightening, violent crescendo. Scrap metal dealer Anthony Lawrence and labourer Terence Elgar were paying a visit to rival gangster George Marshall at his flat, No. 51 Hazelbury Road. After a few minutes, at least six shots were heard, Lawrence and Elgar stumbled out of the premises both having been hit – Elgar fatally, and Lawrence, although hit twice in the head, survived. George Marshall and close associate Ian Horton, who were both inside the flat, were charged with the murder of Elgar and the attempted murder of Lawrence. Both Marshall and Horton gave evidence that Elgar and Lawrence had come to settle an old score, so were acting in self-defence. Horton was acquitted but Marshall was convicted of the murder and sentenced to life imprisonment; however, following an appeal on a technicality, Marshall was released in 1969.

11th – Never Underestimate the Mother-in-Law

John Donald Merrett, aged seventeen, lived with his mother in Edinburgh in the 1920s. She was found dead with a bullet in her head. Merrett was put on trial in Scotland for the murder but claimed she had committed suicide. The court returned a verdict of 'Not Proven' even though it was established he had been defrauding her for several years; it provided a motive but not proof of murder. Merrett walked away a free man and inherited his mother's £50,000 estate.

Merrett next comes to notice as Ronald Chesney in post-war West Germany 1954, where he earned a living on the black market. His prospects had taken a downturn so he hatched a plan; he would return to England in disguise (he shaved off his beard and assumed a false identity) and murder his estranged wife, thus claiming her assets. His wife Vera, from whom he had been separated for some time, ran an old people's home with her mother – Lady Menzies – in Montpelier Avenue, West London. Merrett knew his wife was an alcoholic and this featured in his plans to murder her.

On 11 February 1954, he paid a surprise visit to Montpelier Avenue, got Vera drunk on gin and drowned her in the bath, believing her death would be blamed on her intoxicated state. His plan failed when Lady Menzies (who up to this point had been unaware of his return) saw through her son-in-law's disguise and confronted him. Merrett, now fearing the game was up, hit her over the head with a coffee pot and strangled her. Detectives came to the conclusion the double murder had been carried out by somebody with access to, and intimate knowledge of, the premises and Merrett quickly became a suspect. Interpol tracked down the fugitive Merrett to a forest in West Germany and, rather than face justice and the hangman's rope in England, Merrett shot himself.

Rather macabrely, John Merrett's arms, pickled in formaldehyde are grisly artefacts in New Scotland Yard's Black Museum (or to be politically correct – Crime Museum) displaying deep defence scratch marks inflicted by his feisty mother-in-law.

12th – If the Pope Only Knew

The Apostolic Enunciator, the Vatican's official embassy in the United Kingdom, is located on the edge of Wimbledon Common at No. 54 Parkside, SW19, a building that has accommodated two popes: John Paul II in 1982 and more recently Pope Benedict XVI. It would be interesting to know if either slept well, as these premises, formerly called Winkfield Lodge, have a very dark secret. Former resident of the lodge, Captain Edward Tigue, a retired army officer, was murdered during a burglary on the night of 13 November 1917 in the most violent fashion; struck over the head with a poker eight times, smashing his skull. The gallant old soldier fought for his life over several days but alas succumbed to his injuries. The poker was recovered in the room following the assault, such force had been administered that it was almost bent in two. The captain's valet, who found the body the following morning, was able to inform the police that jewellery, a watch and a mackintosh coat had been stolen.

The police identified the killer, still in possession of the bloodied coat, as Arthur de Stanier, a former corporal in the City of London Yeomanry. He was charged with murder and stood trial at the Old Bailey. He claimed in his defence that he had met an Australian soldier called Reginald Fisher in a pub on Great Newport Street and that Fisher had persuaded him to commit the burglary in Wimbledon. Arthur de Stanier admitted being present but the fatal blows, he claimed, had been administered by Fisher when the old soldier awoke during the break-in and went for a gun under his pillow. Reginald Fisher was never traced by police, the prosecution accused de Stanier of fabricating the existence of Reginald Fisher and the jury were of the same opinion. He was convicted and sentenced to death on this day 12 February 1918; de Stanier was executed by hanging at Wandsworth Prison.

13th – Just Doing His Duty

Twenty-eight years had passed since a police officer had been shot dead in London while performing his duties; this proud record ended on 13 February 1948, along with the life of PC Nathaniel Edgar. Constable Edgar was on plain-clothes duty in Winchmore Hill, North London, engaged with colleagues in observations to detect offenders responsible for a spate of burglaries in the area. Edgar approached a man acting suspiciously near residential properties. Three shots were heard by residents who found the seriously injured officer slumped on the pavement and a man running from the scene. PC Edgar was taken to hospital but his injuries proved fatal. Before he died, he managed to tell colleagues the suspect had given him a name and address, which he recorded in his pocket book: It read, 'Thomas, Donald 247, Cambridge Road, Enfield'. Police quickly identified the suspect as Donald George Thomas, a petty villain and army deserter.

A London-wide search was mounted. Many of London's cops were armed for the duration the fugitive was sought after. Enquiries revealed Thomas had a girlfriend; she too had disappeared from her normal abode and her photograph was also circulated. This paid off quickly – the fugitives had rented a room in Stockwell, south of the river. The landlady recognised the pair and reported this to the police. Thomas was arrested following a violent struggle in which he tried to shoot the arresting officers with a Luger handgun. The police killer was tried and convicted of the murder of PC Edgar. He was sentenced to death, but this was commuted to life imprisonment as Parliament was debating the abolition of the death penalty (although such a decision would not be implemented for many years). The four arresting officers were awarded the King's Police Medal for Gallantry.

14th – Roses are Red – The Victim's Dead

A criminal trial where two killers blame each other for the act of murder, which they were both present at, became known as 'cut throat' cases, as each defendant attempted to convince a jury that the other delivered the fatal blow or shot. One such case was the Crown v. Henry Fowler and Albert Milsom, two professional criminals with a string of convictions and custodial sentences.

On the morning of 14 February 1896, the body of Henry Smith was discovered in Muswell Lodge, Muswell Hill. Smith had been seventy-nine years of age and a spritely fit man who lived alone and was known to be very security conscious. He was bound, gagged and brutally murdered in his kitchen. The intruders had dodged security measures placed in the garden, including a spring-loaded gun activated by a trip wire, and gained entry through a back window, disturbing Henry Smith – whom they dispatched with little compassion. A hasty retreat followed the killing, with those responsible leaving an identifiable toy lantern (it had been broken and repaired in several places) in the kitchen sink alongside two knives. Fowler and Milsom were immediate suspects due to their criminal records, the location of the break-in and the *modus operandi*; these suspicions were heightened when police visited their addresses to find they had decamped. The lamp belonged to Milsom's fifteen-year-old brother-in-law Henry, who unwittingly identified the exhibit from the repairs he had made to it.

Milsom and Fowler travelled around the country for several months as part of a travelling circus but were arrested in Bath and returned to London, where they were tried for murder. Both admitted burglary but blamed each other for the actual killing. Both were convicted of the murder of Henry Smith and sentenced to death. Fowler, the more violent of the two, showed his true colours during the trial when he launched himself across the dock in an attempt to strangle his co-defendant. They were both hanged at Newgate on 10 June 1896.

15th – Leave No Trace

A sequence of appalling violence that would devastate a whole family commenced on 12 February 2003, when businessman Amarjit Chohan, the owner of a successful haulage company based near London's Heathrow airport, was abducted by three men, taken to a property in Wiltshire and forced to sign over his thriving business interests before being murdered. Chohan's captors proposed to use the business as a legitimate front for a drug smuggling operation. The three men, William Horncy, Peter Rees and Kenneth Regan, persuaded interested parties, including Chohan's friends and colleagues that he had suddenly decided to pack up and return to India. The three realised that he would not simply desert his wife and children and for their evil plan to work his close family also had to disappear. Mr Chohan's wife Nancy, their two young children aged two and eighteen months, and his mother-in-law on a visit from India, disappeared from their Hounslow home on 15 February 2003. Mrs Chohan's brother Onkar Verma, who lived in New Zealand, received a call from his sister the day before she and the rest of the family disappeared; she told him that she was worried about Amarjit's whereabouts and she had been told by his staff that he had travelled to Holland on business; she knew this to be impossible as his passport was in fact at the Home Office.

Verma reported his suspicions to the police who began an investigation. Their enquiries led them to a farm in Tiverton, Devon. Horncy, Rees and Regan, probably realising the net was closing in, had allegedly returned to the farm, where the family had been buried, excavated the bodies and threw the remains into the sea. Police searched Reagan's house in Wiltshire; it had been cleaned and decorated and crime scene examiners could find no trace of Amarjit Chohan, but incredibly detected a single drop of blood belonging to one of the children on a garden wall.

The bodies of Amarjit and wife Nancy were discovered in the sea near Bournemouth, followed by mother-in-law Charanjit Kaur a few days later in a bay on the Isle of Wight. Post-mortem examinations revealed that Amarjit had been drugged and probably strangled, his wife had been hit over the head with a hammer and Mrs Kaur's body was too decomposed to identify a cause of death. The children's bodies were never recovered. Following an eight-month trial, all three men were convicted for their part in the massacre of this family; they received life sentences.

16th – Jack the ...

Name a serial killer whose first name was Jack? The obvious answer would be 'Jack the Ripper', the killer of five prostitutes in London's East End in 1888. During 1964–65, a murderer of equal savagery prowled the streets of West London claiming the lives of at least six victims; he was referred to in the press as 'Jack the Stripper'. There was to be no self-proclamation written in blood red; the murderer was given the name on merit, his first two victims were found naked in or near to the River Thames between Barnes and Hammersmith bridges. There were two earlier murders in 1959 and 1963 with very similar *modus operandi*; naked and found near the river, these murders take the total to eight at least. The case became known as the *'Nudes in the Thames Murders'*. The police enquiry expanded, as did night patrols and the stopping of vehicles in the areas the bodies had been found. This fact forced the murderer to alter his plans and dump the bodies of his next four victims inland in the Brentford and Acton areas. This did give the police more opportunity to recover forensic evidence from the victim's bodies. The last proven victim of this killer was twenty-seven-year-old Bridget O'Hara; her body was recovered from shrubbery on the Heron Trading Estate in Acton on 16 February 1965. She, like the other victims, was badly beaten. Peculiarly, all had either front teeth or dentures missing. Detectives closed in, a media release stated they had identified three main suspects, following the interviews of 7,000 men. The murders suddenly stopped.

Many theories circulated about the identity of killer 'Jack the Stripper'. World Light Heavyweight boxing champion Freddie Mills, who was believed to have committed suicide in an alleyway in Soho in 1965, was one suspect; a police officer and a security guard who worked on an industrial estate in the West London area were two others. Neither the 1888 Jack nor the 1960s Jack, collectively responsible for up to fifteen to twenty murders of women, were ever caught or positively identified, the murders remain unsolved.

17th – Hungry?

London-born Peter Bryan first came to the notice of authorities in 1987 when he was a resident of the Flying Angel hostel in Custom House where he attempted to throw a fellow resident out of a sixth-floor window. In 1993, he was sent to Rampton secure hospital for the unlawful killing of shop assistant Nisha Sheth – beaten to death with a hammer. Incredibly by 2001, he was thought mentally stable and released into the care of a psychiatrist and a social worker. In 2002, he was trusted enough to be moved to a North London hostel where he was free to come and go. By 2003, he was deemed to be of no further risk to the public. On 17 February 2004, Bryan murdered a friend called Brian Cherry with a hammer; when police caught up with him, he was cooking the victim's brain in a frying pan.

Bryan was sent to Broadmoor secure hospital where he killed his third victim, Richard Loudwell, a fellow patient. Bryan battered his victim around the head and tied a ligature around his neck; he allegedly intended to eat his flesh. On 15 March 2005, Bryan pleaded guilty to two counts of manslaughter due to diminished responsibility and was given life imprisonment. It is unlikely but not impossible this extremely dangerous paranoid schizophrenic will ever be released.

18th – London Comes to a Halt

The early 1990s witnessed an upsurge in the PIRA campaign on Britain mainland. The day 18 February 1991 was particularly bad for the population of London when republicans attempted to hold the capital and its people to ransom with scores of hoax calls camouflaging devastating bomb explosions. The first incident occurred at 4.30 a.m. at Paddington Station, when an improvised explosive device (IED) ripped through the station concourse; fortunately, due to the early hour, there were no casualties and only damage to the station's roof. But this small device set the tone for a day in which many people's lives would be changed forever. At 7 a.m. that morning, a man with an Irish accent called a London Transport travel centre warning that bombs had been planted in all of London's mainline stations and would explode in forty-five minutes. This was an impossible position for the British Transport Police. Do they close all the stations in London and cause absolute chaos or carry out a systematic search? At the same time, threats to Heathrow had closed the airport. At 7.45 a.m., a bomb concealed in a wastepaper basket at Victoria Station exploded resulting in the death of one commuter, a father of a sixteen-month-old child who died from a shrapnel injury to his chest. There were thirty-eight other casualties, the most serious resulting in leg and foot amputations; the youngest casualty was a child of twelve.

19th – A Cousin Comes Calling

A murder victim is often related to their killer. A case in point is the murder of Lucy Smith, happily married to husband Silas; they had a young daughter called Minnie. They lived in a modest house at No. 23 Venour Road, Bow, East London. The three slept in a ground-floor room next to the kitchen, other lodgers occupied the upper floors. In April 1900, Lucy's first cousin, Sampson Salmon, came to live with them sharing the accommodation on the ground floor. Over the next few months, Sampson began to drink heavily and became more and more violent towards Silas and Lucy until his behaviour became intolerable and Sampson was thrown out. On 16 December, Silas returned home from work and was met at the back door by Sampson. Silas looked passed him and saw Lucy lying on the kitchen floor in a pool of blood. Sampson admitted that he had stabbed her with her own kitchen knife in revenge for throwing him out. He didn't try to escape and waited for the arrival of the police. He was tried at the Old Bailey, convicted and executed at Newgate on this day in 1901.

* * *

Forty-seven years later, on this day in 1948, another callous killer was executed. Walter John Cross, a twenty-one-year-old local boy, entered No. 11 King Edward Road, Barking – the home and business premises of fifty-five-year-old crippled watchmaker Percy Bushby, who lived alone with his cat Toby. Cross strangled the old man for the miserly contents of his wallet and left him dead on the floor; detectives were initially perplexed as to how the murderer had gained entry. Cross was spotted leaving the house by a neighbour who heard noises from next door.

Cross was arrested the following day by police and admitted visiting the victim's shop three weeks earlier with an accomplice called Walter Bull. Cross spotted that Percy had a large amount of money in his wallet, so they hatched a plan to enter his premises and relieve him of it. When the time came, in mid-November 1947, Bull had second thoughts and pulled out leaving Cross to carry out the burglary himself. Cross claimed that Percy confronted him, shouting at him before collapsing on the floor. He took the money and left him still alive, explaining that somebody else must have entered after his departure and strangled the old man. A twist emerged during the trial when evidence was introduced implying Cross had gained entry via the backdoor using a key given to him by Bull. Cross was convicted after a three-day trial and sentenced to death. His young wife was pregnant with their first child when Cross was hanged at Pentonville Prison. Toby, Percy's faithful pet cat, couldn't be rehomed and was destroyed.

20th – A Tight Punter
Dora Alicia Lloyd, a forty-four-year-old prostitute, plied her trade in the area of Air Street and Regent Street in London's West End.

On the night of 20 February 1932, she was approached by a smart looking man aged around thirty-five years wearing a good quality coat and black trilby hat. He had already approached several other girls but was unwilling to pay their prices. The short stocky Dora wasn't so picky, and her clients were normally of a much older age; she was seen to accompany her client in an awaiting taxi. Dora lived in a flat at No. 27 Lanark Villas (now Lanark Road), Maida Vale, where she would often take her clients to. Later that night a fellow lodger – unemployed car mechanic Alexander Fraser – heard a car pull up outside and a man's voice as Dora came through the front door. A little later he heard thumping and a gurgling sound, presumably he was used to strange noises emanating from Dora's room so went back to sleep but reported the fact to the landlady the following morning. Both Fraser and the landlady knocked on Dora's door but received no reply; the door was unlocked, and on entering they discovered Dora's body on her bed, she had been severely beaten around the head and then strangled. The killer had left his gloves in the room but although extensive enquiries were carried out by detectives, Dora's killer was never brought to justice.

21st – Killed for Twenty-Six Bob

Valentine Place, SE1, was a small insignificant offshoot off Blackfriars Road, but the scene of murder on a bitter November night in 1917. Two Canadian soldiers had been lured into the darkness and ambushed by English stonemason Joseph Jones and two Australian soldiers Ernest Sharp and Thomas Maguire. Both Canadians were severely beaten and robbed, and Oliver Gilbert Imlay died of his injuries. Evidence by Jones' girlfriend Grace Mitchell was damming. She told the jury that Jones left the house that night with Sharp in possession of a police truncheon. The following morning, Jones openly told Mitchell that he and the others had dragged the two Canadian servicemen into a dark alley, hit them three or four times before stealing 26s. All three were traced by the police and stood in the dock at the Old Bailey accused of the robbery and murder of Imlay and robbery and attempted murder of the second soldier. The jury heard that the deceased died from a fractured skull having never regained consciousness. Each defendant blamed the others for administering the fatal blow. Jones was convicted of murder and executed at Wandsworth Prison on 21 February 1918. Sharp and Maguire were cleared of murder but convicted of robbery, and given seven and ten years penal servitude, respectively.

* * *

Nearly a decade later on 21 February 1927, train porter James Stratton stabbed his typist girlfriend Madge Maggs to death in a railway carriage on the North London line near Graham Street, Hackney. At his trial the twenty-six-year old pleaded guilty to the murder, but due to his mental state and a similar history in his family (one grandmother died in a mental asylum and the other suffered from epileptic fits), his defence counsel remonstrated with the trial judge about the safety of the plea. However, Stratton persisted that he was sane at the time of the murder and guilty; in the absence of any contradictory medical evidence, Stratton was sentenced to death and executed at Pentonville Prison on 29 March 1927.

22nd – Don't Talk to Strangers

Jeremy Wingfield, aged twenty-nine, was the grandson of former Admiral of the Fleet Lord Jellicoe and a successful business consultant; he lived in Lexham Mews W8. At 1.10 a.m. on 22 February 1970, his body was discovered half a mile from the safety of his home in Nevern Square, Earls Court; he had died of a single stab wound. Extensive enquiries were carried out by murder detectives to try and unravel a motive for the murder. Robbery was quickly ruled out as Wingfield appeared to be in possession of all his property. The crucial question, which when answered would probably solve the mystery, was why Wingfield had been in Nevern Square at that time of the morning. Detectives established Wingfield's movements for the previous evening apart from the hour before he was found. Door-to-door enquiries identified a likely suspect – Thomas Henry Baxter, a nineteen-year-old driver who lived in the square. The murder weapon – a dagger – that he carried everywhere for his own protection was forensically linked to the victim. Baxter was charged with the murder of Wingfield and appeared at the Old Bailey in May 1970. He was acquitted of murder but convicted of manslaughter. Baxter told the jury he believed the deceased to be a homosexual and, when he approached him in the square in the early hours of the morning fearing for his own safety he drew his dagger and stabbed him once. The jury believed Baxter's version and he was sentenced to four years imprisonment for manslaughter.

23rd – *Off with Their Heads*
The French Revolution of the 1790s inspired an Englishman, Arthur Thistlewood, to select and lead a group of ruthless men in an attempt to instigate a similar uprising in England. Thistlewood planned to murder many of the British government in a co-ordinated attack on the home of Lord Harrowby, whom he believed was hosting a dinner for Prime Minister Lord Liverpool and his cabinet at his Grosvenor Square residence. Thistlewood intended to attack the dinner party and decapitate Harrowby and Lord Castlereagh and display their severed heads to a baying crowd of revolutionaries. The dinner party was in fact a fabrication made up by a police spy, who had infiltrated Thistlewood's gang.

The conspirators met on 23 February 1820 in a loft in Cato Street, Marylebone to finalise their attack when the building was stormed by Bow Street Runners (the forerunners of the Metropolitan Police formed in 1829). Thistlewood and his gang put up a fight; one police officer was killed and Thistlewood escaped with several others. They were soon captured and all sentenced to death. They were publically executed outside Newgate Prison and then decapitated; their heads were displayed as a warning to any future revolutionists. Thistlewood became one of the first men to have his wax effigy displayed in Madame Tussauds *Chamber of Horrors*.

24th – *First of Many*
The first man to be executed in the twentieth century was Henry Grove, who murdered for a paltry sum of 1s. Henry Smith owned a sweetshop at No. 1 Notts Cottages, Parsonage Lane, Enfield; for extra income, he let out stables behind the shop for locals to stable

their horses and store their carts. Henry Grove, a costermonger, was Smith's next-door neighbour and he took advantage of the arrangement for the small sum of sixpence a week. Grove fell into arrears with his payments and owed Smith two weeks rent totalling 1s. On 24 February 1900, Smith confronted Grove about the debt and told him that he would not be able to stable his horse there until he paid up. Grove returned late that night in a drunken state and attempted to stable his horse as usual. Smith came out of his shop and told him to leave. An argument ensued in the presence of Smith's wife during which Grove threatened to kill Smith. Smith returned into the shop with his wife followed by a very angry Henry Grove, who hit Smith several times with his fists. Grove wasn't finished, following the attack he left the shop and returned with an old scythe and set about the defenceless Smith, fracturing both of Smith's legs, his right arm and inflicting vicious blows to the back of the head. Smith was taken to hospital in such a serious condition that he wasn't expected to survive. A magistrate took a dying declaration from Henry Smith about the incident that proved crucial.

Smith fought for his life but succumbed to his injuries a few weeks later. Grove was charged with murder and attempted to defend himself by proclaiming that Smith had thrown the first punch and that he only used his fists, a fact rebutted by the dying declaration and the evidence of Mrs Smith. The jury were out for only one hour before returning a guilty verdict but with a plea for leniency; this fell on deaf ears and he was hanged at Newgate on 22 May 1900.

25th – A Woman Scorned

Robert Devereux, 2nd Earl of Essex, was a great favourite of Queen Elizabeth I with whom she shared a turbulent relationship early in the seventeenth century. The debonair Devereux arrived at Elizabeth's court aged in his mid-twenties, a charming, handsome man with whom the Queen was immediately enamoured. Over the next few years he became impatient with his insignificant role in court and being ruled by a woman. As a result he plotted to seize Elizabeth and take control of the government. With only one hundred men he rode up Ludgate Hill towards St Paul's Cathedral in the City of London trying to raise support, but he failed dismally. He was thrown into the Tower of London, tried for treason and sentenced to death. He pleaded with the Queen to be executed in private and not in front of an angry mob on Tower Hill. This final wish was granted, and he was executed on 25 February 1601.

26th – 'She Made Me Excited'

Warren Street is a quiet, mainly residential street off the busy Tottenham Court Road. Lodging in the top floor flat of No. 65 was a young Cypriot waiter called Alexander Anastassiou. He was a handsome man who regularly attracted the attention of the opposite sex. One such admirer was twenty-two-year-old waitress Evelyn Victoria Holt. Anastassiou would often bring her back to his flat where they would sleep together. Holt was smitten and under the impression that they would marry, but when Anastassiou told her that he was to return to his native Cyprus, their relationship soured.

On the night of 26 February 1931, when the couple returned to the flat, having been out to the cinema and supper, an argument started almost immediately – presumably about his departure. The landlady heard screaming coming from the top-floor flat and ran up to see what had happened. She knocked vigorously on the door demanding she be let in. She saw standing in front of her a blood-drenched lodger and Evelyn Holt lying on the floor in a bloody heap. She fled downstairs and sent another to get the police. On their arrival, officers arrested Anastassiou who replied to their caution, 'I was happy with her. We had been to tea, pictures and supper. But she made me excited – I kill her.' Evelyn had her throat cut several times, but she had fought for her life suffering deep defensive wounds to her hands. At his trial for murder, Anastassiou claimed Evelyn had committed suicide and the injuries were caused when he attempted to stop her. The medical evidence did not support this version as her throat had been cut with a force unlikely to have been self-inflicted, together with the presence of the defensive wounds to her hands.

The jury convicted him of the murder of Evelyn Holt and he was sentenced to death. He did appeal against conviction; his defence suddenly changing to Holt attacking him and he acting in self-defence. Again, his version was rejected and Anastassiou was executed at Pentonville Prison on 3 June 1931.

27th – Grandfather Lend Me Some Money

Following a successful and unblemished military service, bandsman William John Holmyard was discharged in 1928. He returned to the family home at No. 39 Tatchbrook Street, Pimlico. Holmyard, and like many leaving the services, struggled to settle back into Civvy Street and find employment. In order to live, he would often borrow money from his seventy-two-year-old grandfather, a street bookmaker, also called William, who lived next door at No. 37. William discovered that his grandfather had informed his parents about the financial arrangement between them. On 5 December 1928, an angry William went next door to confront his grandfather, an argument ensued in which William struck his grandfather over the head with a pair of fire tongs, fracturing his skull. He stormed out leaving his elderly relative fighting for his life. William senior died in hospital three days later and his grandson was charged with his murder.

William Holmyard's trial took place at the Old Bailey in January 1929, during which his barrister – Venetia Stephenson – defended her client on the basis of self-defence. The jury rejected the defence put forward and convicted Holmyard of murder without any recommendations for leniency. Stephenson took the case to the Court of Appeal stating the jury's verdict was prejudiced against her client, as a court usher had taken newspaper reports into the jury room reporting legal arguments between the judge and barristers to which the jury were not privy. The appeal was dismissed and Holmyard was executed at Pentonville Prison on this day in 1929.

The trial was groundbreaking for women in the legal profession as it witnessed the first ever occasion a woman led the defence of a murder suspect. Venetia Stephenson was praised at the beginning of Judge Humphreys summing up of the evidence to the jury, as reported in contemporary news reports:

'Mr Justice Humphreys prefaced his summing up to the jury with a tribute to 'the learned counsel for the defence.'

'This case' he said 'has been defended with conspicuous ability. I am sure you will agree that a serious responsibility lies on her shoulders, but at least she may feel that she has discharged her duty to her client in a manner that reflects the highest possible credit on her carefulness and her own ability. It is a satisfaction to know that everything possible that could possibly be said for this young man, or done for him by advocacy, has been said and done'.

(*Daily Herald* 17 January 1929)

28th – Why?

Emily Wright's battered body was discovered in the kitchen of her flat at No. 4 Armadale Road, Fulham on 28 February 1945. There was no mystery surrounding who killed her – husband Arthur Edward Wright was the prime suspect from the start – but why did he kill her? Emily and Arthur had been married, seemingly happily, for over twenty years but the extent of the violence inflicted on his wife was shocking – her head had been battered to a pulp with an axe. Scotland Yard were desperate to interview the missing husband but they never got the chance. The following day, 1 March 1945, a man threw himself under a train at Earls Court station. Before he succumbed to his injuries, he confessed to medical staff that he was Arthur Edward Wright – wanted for the murder of his wife. The reason 'why' went to the grave with both victim and killer.

***

Thirty-three years later, detectives could not have a clearer motive for murder. Leo Grunhut was a very successful fifty-five-year-old diamond merchant who liked to deliver his merchandise to his various clients in person. At 6.50 p.m. on 28 February 1978, Grunhut walked along Limes Avenue, Golders Green carrying £300,000 worth of diamonds. He was ambushed by two armed men. As he attempted to escape, he was shot in the back, fell to the ground and was shot a second time; he died of his injuries three weeks later. The identity of the killers remained unknown until twelve years later in December 1990. A sixty-year-old armed robber called John Hilton was arrested following a jewellery robbery in Piccadilly. As with many 'old school' criminals, when faced with a lengthy custodial sentence, he cleared the slate clean and confessed to detectives, while in custody at Brixton Prison, the killing of Grunhut twelve years earlier. His astonishing confession included the fact that he had shot his accomplice, Ian Roberts, who subsequently died from loss of blood, and that he buried Roberts in a shallow grave on a railway siding near Dartford, Kent, a grave he led police to in February 1991. Hilton pleaded guilty to the murders of Grunhut and his accomplice in crime Ian Roberts and received two life sentences.

29th – Respect Earns Respect

'He didn't show me any respect' seems to be an acceptable basis for the initiation of frightening levels of violence often leading to serious injury or murder in twenty-first-century Britain. One such tragic case saw sixteen-year-old Ofiyke Nmezu hit violently over the head with a brick by eighteen-year-old Liam Palmer, all because of some perceived disrespectful verbal message posted on social media. On 15 February 2008, Nmezu was walking along High Street, Ponders End, North London with a female friend when a car pulled up. Palmer got out and confronted the sixteen-year old. Following an argument, he struck Nmezu over the head causing a fracture to his skull. The extent of the injury was not picked up by medical staff at two different local hospitals over the next few days. On 29 February 2008, he attended a third hospital suffering from an extreme headache and was given a brain scan, which revealed the fracture accompanied by an abscess. While being transferred to another hospital, he died of a heart attack. Palmer was convicted of manslaughter and given a four-and-half year prison sentence.

3

MARCH

1st – The Root of All Evil

Montague Road, a quiet, residential street in Leytonstone, East London, had its peace shattered when two local drug dealers, Aaron Carriere and Josiah Manful, were lured to their deaths on this day in 2014. The victim's car was blocked in by the four attackers' vehicles. What followed was described by prosecution counsel at a subsequent criminal trial as a ' ... swift, frenzied, utterly brutal attack that left Mr Manful with 13 [stab] wounds and Mr Carriere with 11' (*Daily Mail Online* 27 November 2014). Both men were pronounced dead at the scene. Cash and drugs were discovered in the car – the only item stolen was a mobile telephone that contained Carriere's 'client' list. Devonte Campbell, Omar Hussein, Casey Jones and Alex Barnard were convicted of the murders and given life sentences.

2nd – A Bizarre Law

The Treason Act 1351 was certainly a bizarre piece of legislation and completely alien to modern Britain. Under this act (abolished from the statute books in 1828), a person was guilty of *Petty Treason* if they murdered one's lawful superior. For example, a servant who killed his master or his master's wife, a wife who killed her husband or a clergyman who killed his prelate.

This was a charge Catherine Hayes found herself facing in 1726. Hayes, born in Birmingham, married husband John Hayes, a carpenter, at the age of sixteen. They moved to London and opened a shop on Oxford Road (now Oxford Street) near to the infamous Tyburn Gallows. To supplement their income, the couple took in two lodgers called Billings and Wood. Catherine started a sexual relationship with the two men and hatched a plan to murder John Hayes in order to steal his savings. In the early hours of 2 March 1726, the co-conspirators got John Hayes so drunk that he fell into a deep sleep and then bludgeoned him to death with an axe, decapitating his head, which they cast into the River Thames, the other body parts were dumped in a pond in Marylebone. When the head was eventually washed up onto the banks of the Thames, it was displayed in the courtyard of St Margaret's Church, Westminster, located next to Westminster Abbey, in order to discover the identity of the victim of this atrocious crime. Many Londoners came to examine the head up until it was positively identified by an associate of John Hayes, who had previously reported his disappearance. This led to the arrest of Catherine Hayes and her lovers.

They were tried at the Old Bailey, where Billings and Wood were convicted of murder and sentenced to death by hanging (although Wood died of natural causes before his execution date). Hayes was convicted of Petty Treason and sentenced to death by burning at the stake. Her execution took place at Tyburn, within sight of her former shop, on 9 May 1726. Catherine Hayes was the last person to be burnt at the stake in England.

Typically when a person was burnt to death, they would be tied to a post by a halter. The executioner would then pull on the halter and strangle them before the fire took hold. However, on some occasions, the execution, through neglect, drunkenness or laziness, would fail in their duty and condemning the poor person to an excruciatingly painful death.

3rd – Grocery War

In March 1902, detectives investigated a serious assault by grocer Edgar Edwards on fellow grocer John Garland. Edward's had previously shown an interest in buying Garland's business but was turned down. Garland was struck over the head with a lead weight, but he managed to escape and alert police. When Edwards was arrested for the assault, they discovered in his possession a business card in the name of a third grocer called Darby; his shop was located at No. 22 Wyndham Road, Camberwell. Officers visited the address and ascertained from neighbours the Darby family had not been seen for some considerable time. The shop was bare of any saleable goods or furniture; on further investigation, officers found a bloodstained window sash weight discarded inside the premises. Detectives were summoned and scaled up the investigation to murder. On returning to Edward's newly acquired premises in Leyton, East London, detectives spoke to neighbours in an effort to piece together what had happened. One neighbour reported seeing Edwards digging a trench in the garden. The garden was excavated and the dismembered bodies of Mr and Mrs Darby and their ten-month-old baby Ethel were unearthed – they had all been strangled. Edwards' motive was simply to build up a grocery empire across London by murdering his competitors. He was executed on 3 March 1902.

4th – A German Mystery

An intriguing tale of murder and misidentification surrounded a violent death in the top-floor flat of No. 8 Whitfield Street on 4 March 1899. The landlady of the premises had not seen her lodgers – a German called Fritz Metz and his companion Augusta Briesenick – for a number of days so went up to their room, found the door unlocked and discovered the body of a woman on the bed. A pillow had been placed on the victim's face hiding terrible disfiguring injuries; the landlady was unsure of the victim's identity, but assumed it to be her female lodger Augusta Briesenick. Detectives assumed this to be the case as well and that she had been murdered by flat-mate Fritz Metz, who had disappeared. German authorities were asked to assist in finding the whereabouts of Metz, whom they believed had returned to his homeland. British detectives got a surprising reply that both Metz *and* Briesenick, whose real name was Augusta Hnieda, had been detained. So who was the victim?

The mystery was solved when a lady, who had read about the murder, identified clothing belonging to her sister Marie Sophie Richards, who she had reported missing. The post-mortem was contradictory to say the least, with doctors giving differing evidence as to cause of death. The inquest jury came back with a verdict of wilful murder by asphyxiation. The German authorities were unwilling to extradite the couple to England but tried them in Germany. The court found there to be insufficient evidence provided by the British police against Metz and he was discharged on the proviso he gave evidence against Augusta Hnieda. The unfortunate victim's family would fail to see justice done as Hnieda was declared insane prior to her trial date and committed to a mental asylum for the rest of her life.

5th – Killed for £150

Murder of staff working on London's Underground tube system is extremely rare, but one such murder *did* take place on 5 March 1983 at Balham Tube Station, situated at the southern end of the Northern Line. The station has several entrances leading down to a central booking office. Late that evening, booking clerk Gilbert Barrett was cashing his takings up when the barrel of a sawn-off shotgun was rammed under the service window, the man holding the weapon demanded the takings be handed over. It is believed the plucky booking clerk refused and was shot at point blank range, standing little chance of survival. The murderer, grabbing what money he could, escaped down one of the many subways. Detectives conducted an in-depth investigation; robbery was the obvious motive but they kept an open-mind, and another possibility considered was Barrett, a widower, had been targeted for personal reasons. It would be several years before extensive CCTV coverage, taken for granted today, would be installed on the underground. The murder of Gilbert Barrett remains unsolved. The total takings stolen added up to just £150.

6th – RVP Charing Cross

Another example of the abhorrent Victorian practice of baby farming is recorded in the year 1899. Ada Chard Williams, a married twenty-five-year-old woman, advertised her services – the re-homing of unwanted children – in a local newspaper in leafy Barnes, south-west London. Williams ran her business under the alias of Mrs Hewetson. A desperate young, unmarried mother Florence Jones was attracted to the advertisement and met Williams at Charing Cross station in August 1899. Having earlier settled on a £5 fee, Jones was taken to a house under renovation in Hammersmith and told this would be where her baby daughter Selina would be raised. Florence wrote down the address as she had only paid Williams £3 of the agreed fee and handed over her daughter and some extra clothing. Florence was an honest girl and returned to the address in order to settle the full amount of the agreed fee – she found the house empty no Mrs Hewetson and no Selina.

Naturally, a distraught Florence reported her missing child and the circumstances surrounding the disappearance to the police, who launched a hunt for the mysterious Mrs Hewetson and baby Selina. On 27 September, the incident took a tragic turn with the discovery of the body of a female child washed up on the banks of the River Thames at Battersea; the tiny corpse was identified as Selina Jones. The investigation revealed Mrs Hewetson was in fact baby-farmer Ada Chard Williams Detectives visited an address in Barnes where Williams had been living with her husband, but they were a few days late as she had moved on. A crucial break in the case came when the police received a letter purporting to be from Ada Williams explaining she had read the details of the murder in the papers and confirmed she had been a temporary carer for young Selina before passing her onto a permanent carer called Mrs Smith in Croydon; Mrs Smith was never traced. Ada was located and arrested on suspicion of murdering the infant and by February 1900 had been tried and convicted of the child's murder. She was strongly suspected of other child murders but these suspicions were not backed up by any substantial evidence. She was executed on this day, 6 March 1900 – the last woman ever to be hanged at Newgate Prison.

A short distance along the river from Barnes is the quiet village of Mortlake. Margaret Pamphilon lived at No. 83 Second Avenue with her husband; she had recently fallen out with an admirer – baker and confectioner Charles Robert Earl. Earl, infatuated with Margaret, began stalking and harassing her to such a degree that she applied for a restraining order at the local magistrate's court. Earl swore revenge. On 6 March 1902, London was covered in a dense fog. Earl purchased a revolver and practised discharging the weapon in a nearby field before going to the Pamphilon's address with murderous intent. He shot Margaret dead as she answered the door. Margaret's husband had recognised the killer's voice and Earl was arrested and convicted of her murder. He was hanged at Wandsworth Prison in April 1902.

7th – Deptford after Midnight

PC James Hastie's beat criss-crossed the dangerous streets of Deptford. At midnight on Saturday 21 February 1846, he passed the Rodney Arms pub where he witnessed an altercation between a young woman and four men in Tinderbox Alley. The women made allegations that she had been sexually assaulted by the men. PC Hastie intervened sending the woman off home and telling her to make a formal complaint at the police station the following morning. As PC Hastie was taking the men's details, he was struck over the head with a heavy weapon and the men ran off leaving the constable badly injured and bleeding profusely. He was found by patrons of the pub and the alarm raised, another officer arrived and transported Hastie to Guy's Hospital – his injuries would eventually prove fatal and the officer died two weeks later on 7 March 1846. Four Irishmen were identified and arrested on suspicion of murder. Due to lack of any admissible identification evidence or any witnesses to the attack coming forward, the four men were released and the murder of the officer remains unsolved.

8th – Fingerprints Never Lie

George Smart was employed as a night porter at the Aban Court Hotel, Harrington Gardens, Kensington. He was on duty in the early hours of 8 March 1954 when he was murdered for the meagre sum of £2 and a few packets of cigarettes. Kenneth Gilbert, aged twenty-one and friend Ian Arthur Grant, aged twenty-four were petty thieves. They identified the small hotel with its one night porter as an easy target to make some quick cash. In the small hours of the morning they entered the hotel, intending to steal anything of value they could sell-on but were spotted by the judicious George Smart who confronted them. Gilbert and Grant had armed themselves with coshes and proceeded to beat the night porter unconscious; they bound and gagged him before escaping with their pathetic haul. George Smart was found the next morning; he died as a result of severe head injuries.

Gilbert and Grant were given up by the West London criminal underworld, shocked at the senseless violence used against such a defenceless target. They faced a prosecution case based on strong evidence. Packets of cigarettes belonging to the hotel were found in their possession, while fingerprints and forensic evidence from the crime scene sealed their fate. Their defence barrister attempted to convince the jury that the defendants had never intended to kill Smart but verdicts of guilty against both for murder were returned and they were sentenced to death. Multiple hangings had been a familiar site in England over previous centuries; Gilbert and Grant were the last pair of murderers to be executed together before this practice was outlawed by the Homicide Act 1958.

9th – Too Much Lip

Soho gangster George Cornell ran a successful pornography operation, resisting efforts by notorious East End gangsters Ronnie and Reggie Kray to muscle in on his lucrative business. Cornell increased the bad feeling between him and the Kray's by bad-mouthing the twins in public – calling Ronnie a 'fat poofter'. George Cornell pushed his luck by turning up in the Kray's local pub the Blind Beggar, Whitechapel Road on 9 March 1966. Ronnie was quickly informed of Cornell's presence and headed straight to the pub with only one intention. As Kray walked into the Blind Beggar, Cornell arrogantly sneered, 'Well look whose here.' Ronnie raised a gun and shot George Cornell between the eyes. With other patrons in the pub unprepared to testify, no charges were brought and the Kray's reign of terror continued until 1969 when Ronnie was found guilty of murdering Cornell, certified insane and transferred to Broadmoor where he died of a heart attack in 1995.

10th – An Unwanted Child

Elizabeth Ambrook, was indicted for the Murder of her male Bastard Infant, by throwing it, as soon as born, out of a Window 2 Stories high, in the House of William Ambrook, upon the Tiles covering a Shed adjoining to the said House, and thereby giving the said Bastard one Mortal Bruise on the left Side of the Head, of which mortal Bruise he instantly dyed, December 28.

(*Old Bailey Online*)

Elizabeth Ambrook was convicted of Infanticide (the unlawful killing of a child under the age of 12 months). The shocking detail of the indictment on which she was charged, produced above, tells a story either of a callous, evil woman or of one suffering serious post-natal depression. On this day in 1735, she was hanged at Tyburn with two other women and ten men from the same gallows.

11th – A Considerate Killer

Mary Summers worked as a domestic servant/companion to a well-to-do, though mentally troubled, thirty-three-year-old called Violet Granville Layard. Summers had been a loyal live-in employee of the Layard family for many years. On 11 March 1915, at the family address in Hayes Road, Bromley, Violet savagely attacked Summers with a hammer resulting in injuries so appalling she had little chance of survival. The mentally deranged Violet then attempted to kill herself but failed. She stunned detectives when she confessed she had killed Summers so she [Summers] would not be left alone should she [Violet] be committed as mentally ill and incarcerated in an asylum.

Violet pleaded not guilty at the Kent Assizes to the murder of her close companion, claiming insanity as her defence; however, she was still convicted of murder. The trial judge listened to the mitigating evidence of the medical professionals, who treated Violet before and after the offence, commiting and ordered Layard to be detained as a criminal lunatic.

* * *

Unemployed cinema actor Douglas Barrington lurked in the shadows of Park Walk, Chelsea on the evening of 11 March 1921. He was armed with a revolver and looking for an opportunity to burgle a property in this affluent area. He was approached and stopped by plain-clothed police officers who suspected, he was up to no good. Barrington made a run for it, the officers shouted out for him to stop. Barrington took out his revolver and fired at a brave passer-by, sixty-four-year-old Edwin Payne, who put an arm out to try to halt the fleeing man. Payne was hit by a single bullet and died of his injuries. Barrington continued to run and fired recklessly into a crowd of people chasing him including the police officers. At his trial, Barrington claimed, he never intentionally killed Edwin Payne and just wanted to frighten him in order to escape the clutches of the chasing police officers. The judge addressed the jury making a strong case for a verdict of guilty to murder, but to his surprise the jury believed Barrington's account convicted him of manslaughter. Barrington was sentenced to seven years hard labour.

12th – An Infamous Highwayman

Notorious seventeenth-century highwayman Jack Bird was executed at Tyburn on 12 March 1690. Bird was born in Lincolnshire, but states his criminal career in Amsterdam, Holland where he served a year of hard labour for robbery before returning back home. On his return, he stole a horse and earned his living robbing innocent travellers on the highways of southern England. During one such robbery, he held up a carriage at gunpoint. The shocked passengers included a wealthy but eccentric earl, his chaplain and two servants. The earl offered Bird a challenge – if he fought his more-than-capable chaplain hand-to-hand and came out the victor he would pay him twenty guineas. Bird accepted and after twenty or so minutes, two bloodied noses and a few broken bones the chaplain threw in the towel and Bird was duly paid his prize. Bird's exploits finally caught up with him when he was convicted of robbing a gentleman just off London's Strand and sentenced to hang at Tyburn. His body was sent to Surgeon's Hall and anatomised.

13th – Justice in the End

Emily Rosetta Murphy had endured a life of extreme poverty; she had two young children to feed and an invalid husband Thomas, who was housebound, profoundly depressed and unable to work. The family lived in squalid conditions, occupying a couple of rooms on Southampton Row, Holborn. In early March 1933, Emily was informed that she was to lose her job, which was the final straw. On 13 March 1933, while the children were out playing, Emily turned on the gas tap. The alarm was raised by neighbours, who could smell the gas. Thomas was found dead but Emily still alive; she had left a note for the children explaining her actions:

> I have tried, God knows, but fate has been against me lately. Your Dad, poor thing, I cannot leave behind, so I think I am doing the right thing so he will not suffer.
>
> (*Dundee Courier*, 20 May 1933)

Emily made a full recovery only to be charged with her husband's murder and attempting to commit suicide herself. She stood trial at the Old Bailey, but was acquitted of her husband's murder due to lack of evidence (in such tragic circumstances, maybe the police didn't look too hard, although the suicide note is pretty damning). Emily pleaded guilty to attempted suicide and was bound over to keep the peace.

* * *

Following the arrests of several local leaders of the Indian National Congress, a demonstration took place precipitating a riot resulting in the burning of British banks and buildings in the Indian district of Punjab. A few days later on 13 April 1919, a peaceful demonstration took place at Jallianwala Bagh, Amritsar. Among the crowd was nineteen-year-old Shaheed Udham Singh who, with friends, was handing water out to their fellow protestors. British soldiers were ordered to fire on the crowd without warning; hundreds were killed by the gunfire and subsequent stampede to escape and many hundreds were injured. The governor of the Punjab – Michael O'Dwyer – subsequently supported the British Army's action. Udham Singh was profoundly affected by the massacre and became a member of the Ghadar Party a revolutionary group involved in the organisation of Indians overseas with the aim of over-throwing colonial rule in India. Following a term of imprisonment, Singh arrived in London in 1934 with the intention of assassinating the man he held responsible for the deaths of his countrymen at Amritsar – Sir Michael O'Dwyer. Udham Singh had to wait six years until 13 March 1940 for his opportunity for revenge. O'Dwyer was to speak at a joint meeting of the Central Asian Society and the East India Association at Caxton Hall, Caxton Street, London. Udham Singh had gained access to the meeting with a firearm concealed in his backpack. As O'Dwyer moved to the lectern, Udham Singh fired two shots at his target, killing him instantly. Singh was convicted of murder at the Old Bailey and sentenced to death. He was hanged at Pentonville Prison on 31 July 1940 and buried in the grounds.

14th – Death in Room 14

Widow Lady White retired to her room at the Spencer Hotel in Portman Street in London's West End on the night of 13 March 1922. Lady White had taken up permanent residence in room No. 14 since the passing of her wealthy husband. She was part of the establishment and the sixty-six-year old felt safe and secure; little did she know that danger lurked within the walls of the building she called home. Henry Julius Jacoby, a simple-minded teenager, was a kitchen dishwasher with no qualifications or ambition to rise any higher than his current position in the hotel. He decided on a path of crime in order to escape the rut that he found himself in; armed with a hammer from the hotel maintenance workman's toolbox, he decided he would sneak into a vulnerable guest's room using a master key and steal high-value items that he could sell on. Lady White fitted his victim profile. Jacoby waited until the early hours of 14 March 1922, sneaked out of his room in the bowels of the hotel basement, sneaked past the night porter and went to room No. 14. Lady White, a light sleeper, awoke as the intruder entered and tried to defend herself before being bludgeoned to death. She was found the next morning with fatal head injuries and defence wounds to her arms. Jacoby placed the hammer back in the toolbox after cleaning off Lady White's blood, and returned to his room after he reported hearing noises and voices to the night porter. Detectives were initially baffled. There was no sign of forced entry and nothing appeared to be missing. Their attention soon turned to hotel staff and Jacoby in particular. Bloodstained handkerchiefs were found in his locker. When questioned he claimed that he *had* gone into Lady White's room but only because he heard the sound of raised voices. He had armed himself with the hammer but mistakenly struck Lady White. He was charged, tried and convicted of her murder. Although the jury recommended leniency with regard to execution, Jacoby was hanged at Pentonville Prison on 7 June 1922.

15th – A Frenzied Attack

Officers who were called to No. 4 Garden Cottages, Opal Street, Kennington, on 15 March 1899, met with a scene of utter slaughter. A female corpse lay under a blood-soaked sack covered by an empty orange box. The victim was fifty-four-year-old Frances Short – she had had her throat cut and been stabbed forty times with a penknife, discarded near the body. Short was widowed but lived with a man called Frederick Andrews, twenty years her junior. Short supported him by selling fruit and vegetables in nearby Newington Butts. The couple were heard arguing earlier in the day; within thirty minutes of killing Frances Short, Andrews was selling items of her clothing – a shawl and boots – to a marine store dealer in Golden's Place, Kennington for just *6d*.

Frederick Andrews was tracked down the following day to the Horse and Groom pub in Neal Street, Covent Garden. When approached by detectives, he gave the name 'Brown' but quickly revealed his true details and admitted the murder of Frances Short. He was taken to Bow Street Police Station where he made a full confession stating that:

> I killed her after I poked her eyes out with the knife and cut her throat after.
>
> (*Old Bailey Online*)

Andrews was found guilty of murder and executed at Wandsworth Prison on 3 May 1899.

16th – Taxi!

Austrian national Marie Hermann was an ageing prostitute struggling to make a living from her haggard looks; many of her clients were older men – one such punter was seventy-year-old cabbie Charles Stephens. Marie used her first floor room at No. 51 Grafton Street (now Grafton Way) Tottenham Court Road to entertain her waning list of clients. In the early hours of 16 March 1894, she murdered Charles Stephens and concealed his body in a luggage trunk. She claimed that Stephens attacked her before attempting to throttle her although a tenant heard Stephens and Hermann arguing with the cabbie appearing to demand his £5 back, presumably dissatisfied with the service provided. The next day she had possessions, including the trunk, moved to new digs at No. 56 Upper Marylebone Street. Back at Grafton Street, fellow tenants found blood in the communal sink. When they investigated further and searched the first floor flat vacated by Hermann, further bloodstains were discovered. Detectives eventually traced Marie, who had been freely spending money on drink and clothes. The battered, decomposing body of the unfortunate Charles Stephens was recovered from the trunk.

At her trial, Marie Hermann was represented by barrister Edward Marshall Hall, who was forging a reputation as a formidable defence barrister and orator. Hall argued successfully that the evidence did not prove, beyond any reasonable doubt, that his client was guilty of murder. The jury took fifteen minutes to return their verdict of not guilty to murder but guilty of manslaughter. Hall would become a star of the legal profession defending a host of infamous killers and earn the title 'The Great Defender'.

* * *

Oswald John Job was born in Bromley, south-east London of German parents but spent most of his formative years in Paris. In 1940, following German occupation, Job was sent by the Nazis to several internment camps. Because of his excellent English, the German intelligence services offered him a way out of his incarceration by returning to England as a spy. He returned with a cover story of a British subject who had escaped the Nazi tyranny. This was viewed with suspicion by British intelligence. Under interrogation, Job revealed the truth and when searched was found in possession of secret writing material (invisible ink). He was tried and convicted under the Treachery Act 1940 and executed on this day in 1940 at Pentonville Prison.

17th – If I Can't Have Her ...

Murder and suicide were the order of 17 March 1894. Lily Kate Allen was the landlord's stepdaughter at the Swan public house on Caledonian Road, Kings Cross. George Ward was a live-in barman who had fallen in love with the attractive Lily. Lily seemed attracted at first but soon lost interest and became engaged to another. On this morning in 1894, Lily and her sister were in their bedroom when Ward entered unannounced armed with a hatchet and a knife; he struck Lily over the head and cut her throat before cutting his own.

Later the same day, a second incident occurred in Boleyn Road, Upton Park in East London. Charles Passmore – a tailor of No. 90 Studley Road, Upton Park – had been involved with a married woman – Alice Burnell – who had decided to end the relationship. Gunshots were heard outside Alice's house just before 11 p.m. She had been shot and mortally injured on her doorstep by the jealous Passmore who then turned the gun on himself.

***

Jacobite James Sheppard was executed on this day in 1718 for high treason, having planned the death of Protestant King George I. James was the son of glove-maker William Sheppard from Southwark, who died when his son was five years of age. James enjoyed a privileged upbringing being educated at schools in Hertfordshire and Salisbury by a wealthy relative. He returned to London after his schooling and worked as an apprentice with a coach painter in Devonshire Street. Fourteen months into this job, he decided that it would be beneficial to the country if King George I were to be killed. Recording his intentions in a letter, delivered mistakenly to one to whom it was *not* intended, he set out his plans, requesting finance be arranged for his safe passage to Italy when the deed was complete. The letter was brought to the attention of the relevant authorities. Sheppard was arrested, placed on trial for treason and convicted. The presiding judge was damning in his comments:

James Sheppard, you are convicted according to law of the greatest offence against human authority, high treason, in compassing and imagining the death of the king. Your intent was to kill, to murder, and basely assassinate his Majesty King George, in order to place a Popish Pretender on his throne.

18th – Death of a Faithful Servant

Actor and playwright Ellis Dugnall returned to his home in Addiscombe Road, Croydon, late in the evening of 18 March 1932, to be met by a sight that would haunt him for the rest of his life. His faithful housekeeper Susan Emberton, aged fifty-six, lay on her bed near to death suffering catastrophic head injuries inflicted by a bloodied police truncheon discarded close to her body; she died of these injuries two days later. The house had been ransacked, and a cashbox had been stolen. Detectives believed Emberton had desperately fought to save her life by beating the intruders off with the truncheon. Several witnesses came forward with descriptions of men seen in the area, but no arrests were ever made and the case remains unsolved.

19th – Murder on the Tracks

Murder on Britain's railways is, thankfully, extremely rare; indeed it is safer to travel on the railways than walking some streets. But when such a murder is committed, it has a profound effect on the travelling public's confidence. One such killing took place on 17 January 1901, when passenger Rhoda King was travelling third class on the 11.20 a.m. train from Southampton to London Waterloo in order to visit a sick relative. During the journey, two other passengers joined her in the same carriage: a twenty-three-year-old ex-soldier called George Henry Parker and a Winchester farmer William Pearson. The journey was uneventful until the train passed through Surbiton station. As the train progressed towards Waterloo, Parker got up to go to the toilet and returned holding a gun. Without warning he shot William Pearson through the head. King felt, what she believed to be, blood splash on her cheek and shouted 'My God what have you done?' Parker, while searching the pockets of the dead man, told her he needed the money. He then pointed the gun at King who desperately rummaged in her bag and gave the killer some small change, begging for her life. The train slowed as it approached Vauxhall Station, and the murderer jumped from the train having ditched the murder weapon out of the window. King shouted, 'Stop that man he has killed someone.'

Parker escaped onto the street and ran towards Vauxhall Bridge pursued by four or five men; they were joined by a police officer who cornered Parker in a nearby gasworks. A search of the track led to the discovery of the murder weapon near Wandsworth Bridge, and the murdered man's belongings were found in possession of the prisoner.

Parker told detectives, 'I wish I had killed that woman then I should have got away.' He pleaded insanity due to alcoholism at his trial, which was rejected. Parker was hanged at Wandsworth Prison on 19 March 1901.

20th – A Year and a Day

British law legislated (up until 1996 when the Law Reform Act abolished it) that if a person dies within a year and a day of a violent attack, the assailant can be charged and tried for the deceased's murder. One such case was the murder of Florence Ethel Lavina Thomas. Florence and her husband Leonard married in 1932 and had one child. Leonard wanted a larger family but Florence wasn't so keen. Lack of further children caused animosity between the two causing a rift resulting in several separations. On 20 March 1949, warehouseman Leonard, who was living in Franciscan Road, Tooting (during one such separation), went to his wife's flat in Ixworth Place, Chelsea in order to try for another reconciliation, taking a new radio as a peace offering. Florence rejected his present and an argument ensued. Leonard picked up a kitchen knife and stabbed Florence thirteen times. Florence survived the attack for several weeks; Leonard was charged with grievous bodily harm and sentenced to seven years imprisonment. As he was being sentenced, news came through that his wife had succumbed to her injuries and died. A jury was sworn in and

Leonard was charged and convicted of his wife's murder. The jury added a strong recommendation for mercy. Leonard was sentenced to death but received a reprieve from execution by the home secretary a few days before his appointment with Pentonville Prison's hangman.

21st – Sunstroke in January!

Bricklayer Joseph King rented a small room in a crowded tenement at No. 19 Hart Street, Grosvenor Square. He took a fancy to a young woman called Annie Sutton, the mother of a young illegitimate son called Harry. King asked Annie out on a date several times but was politely but firmly refused. On 20 January 1887, King confronted Annie after she had accepted a similar invitation from another man. He reacted badly to what he saw as a personal slight on his character and manhood and cut Annie's throat and that of her son Harry. When tried for his crimes, King blamed an old head wound and sunstroke (in January!) for his actions. His feeble excuse didn't convince the jury who returned a verdict of guilty; he was hanged at Newgate Prison on 21 March 1887.

* * *

On New Year's Eve 1938, Peggy Pentecost and her lover booked into a hotel at No. 22 York Road, Lambeth under the names 'Mr and Mrs Armstrong of Seaford'. On the morning of 2 January 1939, Peggy was found murdered – she had a handkerchief forced into her mouth and been strangled. Police quickly identified 'Mr Armstrong' as Harry Armstrong who claimed they had travelled down to London for the New Year period but had an argument while in the hotel about Peggy seeing another man. He stormed out and spent the night with a woman he met in a café in Paddington. Armstrong's defence was this other mysterious man must have killed her. He wasn't believed by the jury who convicted him of murder; Armstrong was hanged at Wandsworth Prison on this day in 1939.

22nd – Teenage Killer

Detectives viewing CCTV coverage of a professional 'hit' by a gunman in Hackney, East London on 22 March 2010 were stunned to discover the killer was a fifteen-year-old schoolboy called Santre Sanchez Gayle who had been paid just £200 to commit murder. The victim was mother-of-one Gulistan Subbasi who, while preparing for her young son's birthday, answered a knock on the door of her mother's house only to be shot down in cold-blood. The 'hit' was sanctioned by Izak Billy, a senior member of a street gang called the *Kensal Green Boys*; the motive seemed to be both financial and status in the group. Both Billy and Gayle were sentenced to life imprisonment. Gayle will serve at least twenty years for the crime. The person who ordered the murder has never been identified so a motive as to why this particular family were targeted has never been truly substantiated.

23rd – Broken Neck – What about the Bullet Hole?

A local doctor attended No. 114 Rotherfield Street, Islington on 23 March 1915 in response to a routine call that a woman had been found dead at the base of the stairs. He concluded from a *very* cursory examination that she had simply fallen down the stairs and broken her neck. The deceased was twenty-nine-year-old Annie Josephine Wootten, the wife of Lieutenant Albert Wootten. On closer examination at the mortuary, after the removal of the victim's clothes, the doctor's negligence was revealed when a bullet hole in the victim's chest was discovered – it was now a murder investigation. Police started to look at Albert Wootten's relationship with his wife and unearthed a long-term sexual relationship he had with a woman called Alice Mary Wheatley. Albert Wootten had a cast-iron alibi for the time of the murder and police could not uncover any evidence to prove his involvement or that he wanted his wife dead, but he did inform detectives that Alice Wheatley had access to a revolver.

Wheatley worked as a barmaid at the Gun Pub in Lupus Street, Pimlico. Her relationship with the deceased's husband coupled with the revelation about the revolver (even though no such gun was ever recovered) seemed to be enough circumstantial evidence for the police to charge Alice with the murder. The prosecution couldn't prove Wheatley had possession of a revolver, was present at the crime scene or even substantiate a motive. They had no eyewitnesses and with the defence completely undermining the moral integrity of prosecution witness, Albert Wootten, a reasonable doubt in the jury's mind was established and they acquitted Wheatley, who walked from court a free woman. She earned enough money from selling her story to *Lloyd's Weekly Newspaper* that she didn't have to pull another pint for a very long time.

24th – A Husband Pushed Too Far

Russian Pole Adolf Hannella, a Soho tailor, walked into Tottenham Court Road police station on 24 March 1920 and confessed to the murder of his common-law wife Marie Everby. Police went to the small flat in Dean Street and discovered the body of the thirty-five-year old; she had been strangled. Witnesses gave evidence at the subsequent trial that the deceased was extremely aggressive towards her partner and frequent violent arguments would be fought between the two. It appeared Adolf could take no more.

25th – She Laughed in My Face

Another self-confessed killer – Michael Collins – walked into Leman Street police station on 25 March 1911, his hands and clothes awash with blood. He approached Constable John Pope and confessed, 'I have come to give myself up for murder.' About the same time, a few miles to the west, a police officer was called to a small room at No. 42 A Block, Peabody Buildings, Glasshouse Street, London where he discovered the body of Michael Collins' former girlfriend Elizabeth Kempster; she had been struck over the head with a hammer that lay next to her and had her throat cut.

Collins made a deposition to police explaining that he had moved in with Kempster the previous Christmas and things had been going okay up until the middle of March when she changed her attitude towards him, he believed she had found somebody else. A few days later on 25 March, Collins saw 'Lizzie' going into the Red Lion pub on Whitechapel Road, she caught sight of Collins and started mocking and laughing at him. Collins borrowed 2s 6d from a friend and purchased a razor in Aldgate and later that afternoon went to Glasshouse Street and confronted Kempster – she again mocked him. He hit her over the head with a hammer he picked up from the fireplace, bent down next to her and cut her throat before kissing her and saying goodbye. Insanity was offered to the court as a defence but no doctor called to the court agreed. He was convicted of murder and executed on 24 May 1911 at Pentonville Prison.

26th – Murder near the Arsenal

Avenell Road, Highbury is a distance equal to the kick of a ball from the former home of Arsenal FC. On 17 December 1946, the only shots being fired came from the barrel of a gun rather than from a footballer's expensive boot. Beatrice Greenberg lived in Avenell Mansions, Avenell Road with her husband Stanley and their fifteen-year-old son, but lived a double life with bookmaker Frederick William Reynolds, who lived in nearby Aberdeen Park. Beatrice met Reynolds thirteen years before through Reynolds' wife who worked with Beatrice at a Highbury factory; within three years of first meeting, they were having an affair. Reynolds had been putting ever-increasing pressure on Beatrice to leave her family and move in with him permanently – she had refused and in retaliation, he stopped a small allowance he had been paying her, which created even more bad feeling between them. While Stanley and their son were out of the house, Reynolds' paid a visit armed with a revolver. Following another argument he shot Beatrice on her own doorstep, dropped the gun by her side and ran. The caretaker – aptly named Robert Gallant – gave chase for over half-a-mile before losing sight of Reynolds' but was able to give the police a significantly detailed description, which contributed towards the identification of the killer.

Reynolds stood trial for the murder; he admitted the shooting but pleaded not guilty to murder on the basis that he had been very drunk at the time and fired the gun by accident. The evidence of Mr Gallant and the half-mile-chase convinced the jury he couldn't have been that drunk. He was executed on this day in 1947 at Pentonville Prison.

27th – Thumb Print

A burglary that resulted in a double-murder on 27 March 1905 has gone down in the annals of British crime detection; it would result in the conviction and execution of two men, in the case of murder, on the basis of fingerprint evidence for the first time in this country.

Thomas and Anne Farrow lived above an oil and paint shop at No. 34 High Street, Deptford – Thomas Farrow was in fact the manager. When staff arrived on the morning of 27 March 1905, they were surprised to see the shutters still down. Receiving no answer at the flat they broke in and found Thomas dead and Anne unconscious, they had both been beaten badly. A cash box with the previous week's takings lay empty on the floor, it contained about £10 (a considerable amount of money in 1905). Eventually, Scotland Yard detectives took over the case, one of whom was Assistant Commissioner (Crime) Melville Macnaghten, an officer who had promoted the use of fingerprints in crime investigation since the formation of the Fingerprint Bureau at Scotland Yard in 1901. Macnaghten preserved any possible fingerprint evidence by wrapping the box in paper and took it to the bureau. The box was examined and a mark was identified and determined to be a right thumbprint that didn't match the victim's Thomas or Anne Farrow (who had succumbed to her injuries and died a few days after her husband) or any of the officers who had attended the scene. But sadly, it didn't match any fingerprints the police had on file (approximately 80,000–90,000 at the time). The case broke when witnesses came forward identifying one of the two men who had been seen leaving the address early that morning, a man known locally as Alfred Stratton. The second description matched his brother Albert. Both were arrested, their fingerprints taken and the mark recovered from the box matched Alfred's right thumb.

The trial took place in May 1905 at the Old Bailey and the prosecution case, although accompanied with considerable circumstantial evidence, was going to succeed or fail on the fingerprint evidence. Many so-called experts were called to promote and shoot down the reliability of fingerprint evidence, but the jury were convinced of the significance and reliability of this scientific advance in crime detection, taking two hours of deliberation to return a guilty verdict. Both men were sentenced to death and executed at Wandsworth Prison on 23 May 1905.

28th – Drunken Fireman

Marylebone-born Thomas William Jesshope, the son of a coachman, married with a family, lived in South London. Thomas had a drinking problem and would often turn up at the Empire Music Hall, where he worked as a fireman, drunk. He had been suspended on a couple of occasions but was always re-instated due to his family responsibilities. On 25 March 1910, Jesshope's manager was unwilling to tolerate his behaviour anymore and dismissed him for drunkenness, employing another man to take his job. The same evening Jesshope – still drunk – approached John Healey, a carpenter and general assistant at the hall, who had played no part in Jesshope's dismissal. They had cross words, a disturbance took place, they were separated and Jesshope no doubt went and drowned his sorrows.

Jesshope again turned up outside the hall three nights later on 28 March 1910 and waited for Healy to emerge; when he did, he stabbed Healy and stood by and watched him die. When other staff members came out, Jesshope made no attempt to escape but merely commented when told Healy was dead: 'Yes I know he is, I meant it.' During his trial for murder, Jesshope gave evidence confidently and explained to the jury that he had spent some time at a lunatic asylum in a 'padded cell' and that he had been so ill that he had lost his career with the mainstream fire brigade and turned to drink. He was convicted and sentenced to death. His desperate wife wrote to King George V asking for clemency but this failed, as did an appeal to the home secretary. He was hanged at Wandsworth Prison on 25 May 1910.

29th – Death in a Coal Cellar

The life of a young clerk, working at the offices of T. H. Bartlett located at No. 2 Arthur Street West in the City of London, came to a grisly end on 29 March 1884. A trail of blood from an upper office down to the coal-cellar was discovered by a cleaner late that afternoon; police were called, followed the trail and found the body of a thirty-year-old man. The face was covered in blood and coal dust, his identity not immediately obvious but eventually confirmed as Edwin James Perkins; his injuries were shocking. Dr Thorpe, the on-duty City of London police surgeon, described the wounds as ' ... a terrible gash on the left side of the throat which had nearly severed the head from the trunk, another gash under the chin about three inches long and half an inch deep and a contusion at the base of the skull which had evidently been inflicted by some blunt instrument'. The motive seems to have been burglary as all his pockets had been turned out and his watch had been taken. No perpetrator was ever identified and the case remains unsolved.

30th – A Hero's Death

Airey Neave, the first British officer to escape from the German prisoner-of-war camp Oflag IV-C at Colditz Castle, became a Conservative Member of Parliament for Abingdon in Oxfordshire. Neave was appointed the Shadow Secretary of State for Northern Ireland in a Conservative Party in opposition under the leadership of soon-to-be Prime Minister Margaret Thatcher. On 30 March 1979, Neave parked his Vauxhall Viva car in the House of Commons underground car park. While unattended a magnetic car bomb was attached to its underside, the bomb exploding as Neave drove the car up the exit slope. Both of Neave's legs were blown off. He survived the initial explosion and was still alive when ambulance crews reached him, but they were unable to save his life. The Irish National Liberation Army (INLA) claimed responsibility for the murder issuing a statement that, with respect for Neave and his family, will not be revealed in this volume. This was the only successful attack carried out by INLA on mainland Britain.

31st – A Mad Moment in Time

The Ivanhoe Hotel was one of London's finest early twentieth-century hotels situated in trendy Bloomsbury. Harry Lawrence Kelly was the hotel's house porter; his position afforded him several perks including accommodation. During the late afternoon of 31 March 1952, Harry met up with his brother and they went on a pub-crawl, consuming several pints of cider. Kelly's brother met a lady called Joan Mauro who agreed to go back to the brother's flat No. 5 O Block, Peabody Buildings, Fulham Palace Road, leaving Harry in the pub. The brother later claimed that when they arrived at the flat they went straight to bed but fell asleep. A little later, Harry climbed through the bedroom window – as he often did following a night on the beer when unable to get back to the hotel, An argument ensued between Harry and his sibling resulting in Harry being left alone in the bedroom with the sleeping Mauro. Mauro was found dead the following day, her blouse had been torn off and she had been strangled. Harry was arrested for her murder. At a subsequent hearing, the police officer investigating the case, Chief Inspector George Jennings, informed the magistrate's court that he had attended the murder scene and seen the deceased lying on the bed with visible bruising to the throat and that the cause of death was asphyxiation by manual strangulation. On Harry Kelly's arrest, he allegedly commented in answer to the charge, 'Yes, I did kill her.' At his trial in May 1952, Harry Kelly claimed he couldn't remember the incident and had suffered an epileptic fit during which he strangled her. Kelly was convicted of the murder of Joan Mauro, but found to be insane and detained in a mental institution at HM's pleasure.

4

APRIL

1st – An Abusive Father

The sexual abuse of children in their own home is a most abhorrent crime. Bernard Alfred Cooper lived with his wife Mary Elizabeth, his fourteen-year-old daughter Sheila and two younger siblings in a house in Davisville Road, Shepherds Bush. It was alleged that Cooper sexually assaulted Sheila over a period of months, impregnating her and resulting in an abortion. Cooper later claimed that he had come clean with his wife who forgave him. However, following a blazing row between the two of them on 1 April 1949, in which the whole sordid affair re-surfaced amid fresh allegations by Mary that her husband had continued with his criminal behaviour, Cooper lost his temper and strangled her with one of her silk stockings concealing her body under a bed. He fled the scene of the murder but was arrested five days later having slept rough for four nights. During his trial, he admitted killing his wife but under provocation. The jury dismissed his claims and he was executed at Pentonville Prison on 21 June 1949.

2nd – Russian Robert

Following the end of the Second World War many consumer goods were in short supply, especially alcohol, cigarettes and other consumer luxuries such as chocolate; indeed, rationing continued in the United Kingdom for another three years. If there is a demand then somebody will profit and it was big business for black-marketers. One such profiteer was Russian Jew Reuben Martirosoff, also known as 'Russian Robert' who dealt mainly in diamonds, counterfeit currency and whiskey. On 1 November 1945, 'Russian Robert' was found in a small car in Chepstow Place, Notting Hill – he had been shot. The evidence led detectives to two Polish deserters: Marian Grondowski and Henryk (or Henry) Malinowski, strongly suspected of killing 'Russian Robert' in order to take over his criminal empire. Both were charged and convicted of Martirosoff's murder, sentenced to death and hung at Wandsworth Prison on this day in 1945.

However, a few weeks before the murder of 'Russian Robert', another murder took place with a similar *modus operandi*. The victim was black cabbie Frank 'The Duke' Everitt (don't you just love these names) who used his taxi licence as a front for his black-market dealings. He was found rammed into a small alcove on Lambeth Bridge – he had been shot with an identical calibre bullet that had killed 'Russian Robert'. Everitt's cab was recovered within close proximity to Chepstow Place where 'Russian Robert's' body would be found a few weeks later. A couple of witnesses reported to police that they had seen two smart-looking gentlemen getting into 'The Dukes' cab near the Houses of Parliament, a couple of hundred yards from Lambeth Bridge. Although detectives couldn't evidentially connect the two murders, they closed the Everitt murder investigation the day Malinowski and Grondowski were executed for the murder of 'Russian Robert'.

3rd – A Strange Tenant

Sophia and Sarah Baker were middle-aged sisters who lived at No. 5 Kingsley Avenue, West Ealing. They supplemented their living by renting rooms out in their house. In March 1912, Arthur James Benbow answered an advertisement placed in the local paper by the sisters, they agreed terms and he moved in. He seemed a little strange and would often be found just wandering around the house; this unnerved the sisters and they asked him to leave giving him short notice.

On this particular morning of 3 April 1912, Sophia served him his breakfast. At 9 a.m., Sarah went out leaving her sister with the household chores and Benbow in his room. When Sarah returned she found her sister on the floor of the kitchen. Thinking she had fainted she went for help; when she returned she examined her further and found evidence that she had been shot. Sarah asked Benbow if he had seen his sister since breakfast, he simply replied 'has she gone'. Dr George Phillips arrived and pronounced death, noting the bullet entry wound just below the deceased's left breast. Phillips sent his chauffeur for the police. Benbow was arrested and searched; in his pocket was a loaded revolver with four live rounds in a tobacco box, a sheaf knife and a flask of brandy. Police Inspector Alfred Deeks recorded a confession that Benbow signed in which he bizarrely claimed that he thought he was being operated on by Sophia Baker, aimed the gun at her and pulled the trigger but was unaware it was loaded. It was quite obvious to all those present that Benbow was not of sound mind. Indeed, he was convicted of the murder but found to be insane and detained at HM's pleasure.

4th – Murder on the Tube

Late on Sunday afternoon of 4 April 1915, a dreadful discovery was made in the ladies waiting room at Aldersgate Station (now Barbican); the body of a young girl had been dumped having been sexually assaulted with an incredible degree of violence before being killed. The victim's name was Maggie Nally, who lived in Paddington several miles from the murder scene. The crime would be described by Coroner Dr Waldo as 'an atrocious and cruel murder'. Maggie Nally was murdered one day after her seventh birthday, a handkerchief given to her as a present had been stuffed into her mouth to silence her. Her father John Nally, a lift attendant who lived at the family home in Amberley Road, Paddington, told detectives that the last time he had seen Maggie was on the corner of Carlisle Street, on the way to see her grandfather, earlier on the Sunday afternoon. When she didn't return home that evening, he and his wife raised the alarm, but it wasn't until the Monday morning that they received the tragic news that daughter Maggie had been murdered.

Inspector Groves of the Metropolitan Railway Police was the first officer on the scene a little before midnight; he gave evidence to the coroner's inquest a few days after the murder:

Aldersgate Station was exceedingly quiet on Sunday night, and there were few passengers. I unlocked the lavatory door and I had difficulty in opening it as something seemed to obstruct it. As soon as I got in there I saw the little girl's hand. The child was lying on her back her mouth was open and there was something dis-coloured in it. I formed the opinion at once that the child had been murdered – suffocated.

(*Manchester Courier and Lancashire General Advertiser* 9 April 1915)

A post-mortem examination concluded that young Maggie had been dead for at least two hours making the time of death approximately 10 p.m. on 4 April. A harrowing account of what would have been Maggie's last moments of life were given to the police by a bus conductor who, having identified the body of Maggie, stated she was the same girl he had seen with a soldier on his bus on Sunday evening, they had boarded at the junction of Chapel Street and Edgware Road, Paddington and alighted at King's Cross Station. The conductor remembers that the soldier was under the influence of alcohol and the girl seemed to be frightened of him. The last he saw of them both was as they walked in the direction of the station. He gave the police a detailed description of the soldier but he was never traced and the murder remains unsolved.

Maggie's body was preserved in a formalin preserving apparatus, the first recorded use of such apparatus for the preservation of corpses in the United Kingdom. Her body was released to her distraught parents on 22 April for burial at Kensal Green Cemetery.

5th – Journey from Hell

A generic headline 'The man who smiled at death – hanged' dominated the front pages of national newspapers in April 1923 (*Dundee Evening Telegraph* 19th March 1923). They referred to twenty-five-year-old Bernard Pomeroy. Pomeroy, a sales assistant from Hemel Hempstead, Hertfordshire, had been seeing twenty-one-year-old Alice Cheshire for a period of time. On the evening of 6 February 1923, he took Alice to the London Coliseum. Following the performance, they caught a taxi from Holborn to

Watford and then returned in the same taxi back into Central London. On the return journey, Pomeroy murdered Alice by cutting her throat. He directed the taxi driver, who apparently was unaware of the bloody carnage in the back of his vehicle, to take him to the Leicester Square area and the nearest police station. With blood dripping from his hands, he entered Vine Street Police Station, Piccadilly and informed the front desk officer that he had murdered his girlfriend who was in the taxi outside and submitted himself to his custody. Alice was found on the floor of the taxi with a deep wound to her throat; she died on arrival at hospital.

Pomeroy's trial was as peculiar as the murder itself; he pleaded guilty against the advice of the judge, refused to give evidence from the witness box in his own defence or speak at all during the proceedings or when convicted and most bizarrely smiled at the judge when sentenced to death. Pomeroy remained as indifferent to the plight awaiting him throughout his period of incarceration leading up to his execution at Pentonville Prison on 5 April 1923, often laughing and joking with visitors and talking incessantly about football. At his inquest, the prison governor told the coroner that it had taken just seven seconds from leaving the condemned cell until Pomeroy dropped to his death.

6th – Wrong Place at the Wrong Time

Hornchurch is a medium-sized town in the London Borough of Havering situated towards the eastern end of London Underground's District Line. On 6 April 2006 the whole town was in deep shock at the seemingly motiveless murder of Cheryl Moss, a nurse who worked at St George's Hospital. The murderer was nineteen-year-old teenager Stuart Harling. Harling, a local lad who had excelled at school, gave up a promising career as an accountant to stay indoors all day playing violent video games and developing a sick fascination for serial killers and paedophiles, the latter with whom he regularly communicated via online chat-rooms. On the afternoon of 6 April, Cheryl Moss was outside her building within the grounds of the hospital when spotted by the prowling teenager, who wore a wig and sunglasses and armed with a hunting knife. He stabbed Cheryl repeatedly over seventy times; many of the wounds were inflicted when she lay on the ground defenceless and obviously dead. Following the murder, he dumped his 'murder kit' containing the disguise and murder weapon in a local park. This was found by police and contained the murderer's name and address. At his trial in 2007, psychiatrists told the court that Harling was undoubtedly one of the most dangerous teenagers in the United Kingdom. He received life imprisonment with a minimum term of twenty years.

7th – A Murderous Barber

In 1888 a Pole by the name of Severin Klosowski arrived in the Whitechapel area of London's East End; a year the antics of infamous serial killer Jack the Ripper would scar the area for decades to come. Klosowski took up employment as a barber's assistant and settled in Whitechapel. He met a woman called Chapman in the early 1890s and adopted her surname, thus being known locally as George Chapman. This relationship ended after a year and he moved in with a married woman called Elizabeth Spink. Chapman used his new partner's money to start a barbers business in Hastings, Sussex and then returned with Elizabeth Spink as Mr and Mrs Chapman to run a pub in Bartholomew Square. In December 1897, Elizabeth died following a short illness with symptoms of vomiting and stomach pains. Within a year, Chapman had met Bessie Taylor, a familiar pattern emerged with them moving out of London and then back again to run a pub called The Monument Tavern in Lambeth. Bessie also suffered the same fate as Elizabeth, dying in February 1901 of similar symptoms to Elizabeth Spink. Chapman's next move was to The Crown pub in Borough High Street where he met Maud Marsh. She followed the same fate but this time the shocked and inquisitive parents of Maud suspected poisoning and when the doctor refused to sign a death certificate, a post-mortem was ordered that concluded Maud had indeed been poisoned. The bodies of Spink and Taylor were exhumed and evidence of similar poisoning was discovered. Klosowski aka George Chapman was tried at the Old Bailey and convicted of the murder of Maud Marsh, his most recent killing. Klosowski was hanged at Wandsworth Prison on 7 April 1903. Due to his presence in the East End in 1888, historians have since, naturally, speculated that Klosowski and Jack the Ripper were one and the same and that such a drastic change in his *modus operandi* was to escape detection.

8th – Oh! Brother

John Joseph Sheehan and younger brother Charles lived in a second-floor bedsit at No. 20 Hatherley Grove, Bayswater. Both were hard working men who had settled in London from their native Ireland. Like a lot of single men in their late twenties or early thirties, they liked a drink. In the early hours of 8 April 1961, both men had been drinking heavily in their bedsit. Their neighbours were used to hearing loud voices and arguing between the two brothers but on this night a difference of opinion escalated into a situation of tragic circumstance. Charles Sheehan staggered out of their bedsit desperately seeking help from a neighbour who was shocked to see the younger brother covered in blood gushing from a deep neck wound and unable to speak. An ambulance arrived and took Charles to St Mary's Hospital where he died of blood loss. When police went to the flat, they found a distraught John Joseph – he was arrested for the murder of his brother. At his trial, he admitted that he had stabbed his sibling but had not intended to kill him, he was extremely contrite as he explained to the jury what had taken place. The jury decided that John had not intended to kill his brother and was full of remorse finding him guilty of the lesser offence of manslaughter. The judge seemed to agree with the verdict as he sentenced John to a lenient four years imprisonment.

9th – Mistaken Identity

What appeared to be a tragic case of mistaken identity resulted in the murder of costermonger Joseph Wallis as he sat having a pint in his local pub *The King of Prussia* in Leather Lane, Hatton Garden on 9 April 1889. The killer was Italian cabinet-maker Guiseppe Ortelli, who entered the pub, fired two shots at Wallis and made good his escape. Ortelli was chased to a nearby address before turning the gun on himself. During a dying declaration, he admitted that he had shot the wrong man. He succumbed to a single self-inflicted shot to the head a few days later at St Bartholomew's Hospital. At the inquest into Wallis' death, police reported to the coroner that they could find no link between the killer and the victim, they appeared to have been complete strangers.

* * *

On this same day in 1925, a lovers tiff resulted in the death of a promising, beautiful young dancer – sixteen-year-old Grace Blackaller. Grace had been 'walking out' with a young nineteen-year-old valet called Ernest Rhodes who had told a close friend that Grace had been 'fooling him around' and 'teasing him about other boys' and that he intended to kill her and himself. The friend took these threats to be the ranting of a lovesick young man. Ernest took Grace out for the evening and as they returned to Grace's home (she lived with her mother), Ernest took out a razor he had bought for the purpose and slit Grace's throat. The young starlet was found in the garden of her mother's house in Challoner Mansions, Challoner Street, West Kensington; she died the following morning in hospital. Ernest was charged with the murder but declared insane and detained in a mental institution.

10th – Butchered in Bloomsbury
Taviton Street runs off Gordon Square in London's arty Bloomsbury district. It was the scene of a particularly evil murder on 10 April 1913 when butcher Henry Longden, aged fifty-two years, killed twenty-seven-year-old typist Alice More. Alice worked for the East and West Society of China on New Oxford Street and had met Longden in Leeds moved down to London in 1912. Longden was a possessive man and treated Alice appallingly, often subjecting her to violence and threats. Alice had had enough and moved out to lodgings in St Pancras. On the day before the murder, Longden confronted Alice and a new 'friend' in her life, a work colleague called Silva. Longden threatened Alice saying, 'I will deal with you later.'

The following day, Longden followed Alice from work and when she entered Taviton Street, he approached her from behind and slit her throat with a large butcher's knife. As Alice staggered down the street, her life's blood gushing from the neck wound, Longden callously followed until she collapsed before turning the knife on himself. Unfortunately for him, his butchering skills failed; he was unsuccessful in his bid to end his own life. He stood trial at the Old Bailey, his defence barrister claimed the murder to be unpremeditated even though he had armed himself with a knife and followed his victim some distance. Although details of his treatment of Alice were introduced during the trial the jury came back with a recommendation for mercy (the jury must have been all male). Fortunately, those in authority dismissed a later appeal and Longden was hanged at Pentonville Prison on 8 July 1913.

***

On this day in 1992, the City of London was targeted by the PIRA at 9.20 a.m. when a one-tonne bomb, contained in a truck, exploded outside the Baltic Exchange in St Mary Axe killing three people including a fifteen-year-old girl and injuring another ninety-one people. The bomb caused an estimated £800 million worth of damage to the surrounding buildings. The Baltic Exchange was beyond repair and pulled down to be replaced by Norman Foster's 'Gherkin'.

11th – A Long Journey to the Tower
Peruvian-born Ludovico Hurwitz-y-Zender was a well-educated man fluent in English and French who travelled to Europe via the United States where he was recruited as a spy by German intelligence. He turned up in Glasgow in 1914 via Scandinavia and stayed in Union Street. The British Security Service had intercepted telegrams sent by Zender to an address in Oslo, Norway, which they knew to be a drop point for German intelligence. Zender had naively signed the letters in his own name and given his address as No. 59 Union Street, Glasgow. Just before the Security Services arrived at the address to question him, he had departed – unaware of the Security Services' interest – to Bergen, Norway. The British bided their time and waited for Zender to return, which he did at Newcastle. He was stopped, arrested and transferred to London for interrogation.

Zender was tried by court-martial at Caxton Hall, London in March 1916, found guilty and sentenced to death by firing squad. He was executed at the Tower of London at 7 a.m. on 11 April 1916;

the firing squad composed of members of the 3rd Battalion Scots Guards. Zender was the last person from the First World War to be executed at the Tower.

* * *

Twenty-five years later on 11 April 1941, Rachel Dubinski went to meet her estranged husband who she had split from in 1920. The marriage to Harry Dobkin, a wartime fire-watcher, had been arranged by a matchmaker and they were wed at Bethnal Green Synagogue. The marriage only lasted a few days before they spilt up but it was long enough for a son to be conceived. Harry supported his son through to adulthood but community pressure meant he was expected to continue support for Rachel at £1 per week; a situation he deeply resented. They were to meet on 11 April 1941 to discuss an outstanding maintenance payment – Rachel was never seen again, and her sister reported Rachel missing the following day.

In July of the following year, demolition workers were clearing the site of a bombed out church in Oswald's Place, near to the Oval, Kennington when they unearthed a skeleton. They reported the find to police who called in Professor Keith Simpson, an upcoming pathologist and future pioneer in forensic science, who became the first appointed Home Office pathologist. He dealt with many high-profile cases in his career including the Acid Bath Murderer John George Haigh and George Cornell shot dead by Ronnie Kray in 1966. Simpson recognised that this wasn't a bomb victim but a murder victim, the head had almost been severed from the torso, the arms and legs were missing and quick lime was present in soil samples. The body was eventually identified by Simpson through dental records as that of Rachel Dubinski (Dobkin). Harry Dobkin was arrested and convicted of the murder of his estranged wife and executed at Wandsworth Prison on 27 January 1943.

12th – I'm Going Home to Mum
Dock worker Frederick Lock lived with Florence Kitching at No. 28 Coopers Road, Old Kent Road. They had been together for a number of years but the relationship was in trouble, and from a confession later recorded by police one can assume she was about

to leave him to go back to her mother. This decision seems to have led to Florence's violent death and Lock's subsequent arrest for her murder. Detective Inspector Divers informed Tower Bridge Magistrates Court:

> I saw the body lying in a pool of blood with a large wound in the throat. In a bed-sitting room adjoining the kitchen Lock was sitting in charge of several police officers. There were bloodstains on his jacket, waistcoat and both shirt-sleeves. I told him that he would be charged with murder. I cautioned him and it was alleged that he said, 'She was determined to go home with her mother so I did this. She came towards me as I was going into the kitchen. I caught hold of her and cut her throat with the razor I showed to the policeman. I kissed her. She staggered I took hold of her and carried her back to the kitchen and laid her down where you saw here.'
>
> (*Western Morning News* 10 February 1928)

Frederick Lock was executed on this day in 1928 for the murder of Florence Kitching.

13th – At the Instigation of the Devil
Charles Taylor was executed on 13 April 1791 following his trial at the Old Bailey. Before the commencement of any trial, an indictment is read to the accused informing them of offence(s) for which they are about to be tried. The following is the indictment in the case of Taylor written in a prose we have sadly lost:

> CHARLES TAYLOR was indicted, for that he, not having the fear of God before his eyes, but being moved and seduced by the instigation of the devil, on the 20th of March last, did feloniously, willfully, and with malice aforethought, make an assault on Winifred his wife , with a certain razor, made of iron and steel, value 2 d. which he held in his right hand, and giving her three mortal wounds on the lower part of her belly, of the length of eight inches, and of the depth of two inches; and also a mortal wound on the wrist, of the length of two inches, and of the depth of one inch, of which said

mortal wounds the said Winifred his wife did languish, and languishing did live, until the 21st of the same month, on which day she died.

(*Old Bailey Online*)

14th – Sex on a Bombsite – No Thanks!

For many years after the Second World War, London's derelict bombsites blotted the landscape of the capital. At the junction of Loman Street and Great Suffolk Street in Southwark, a grim discovery was made at one such site in the early hours of 10 February 1955. The partially naked body of Rose Elizabeth Fairhurst, age forty-five, lay on rubble. Her clothes had been torn from her body – she had been strangled and sexually assaulted. Rose had been seen leaving a local pub with a man the night before, who had offered her money for sex. The same man was seen about an hour later in Blackfriars Road propositioning another woman. A few days' later, police traced the man to a hostel and identified him as Sidney Joseph Clarke. The police investigation hit a snag, Clarke claimed he had been in Bristol on the night of the murder, not arriving in London until very late on 9 February; the night porter confirmed that Clarke had not booked into the hostel until midnight – several hours after the murder.

Detectives believed they had the right man and their perseverance paid off when they uncovered evidence that Clarke had in fact been staying in a Central London hostel hours before the material time and from which he moved *after* the murder, dis crediting his Bristol alibi. He was arrested and when faced with forensic evidence including semen found on Rose that matched the same blood group as Clarke (AB, of which only 2 per cent of UK population had), he confessed. Clarke said he offered Rose 10s to have sex with him, which she agreed to. He took her to the bombsite and found an old mattress, but she refused to lay down on it so they argued and she hit him. He forced Rose down onto the mattress and 'went mad' claiming he couldn't remember anything else of the incident until he was standing at a café under Waterloo Bridge. Believing he had done something wrong, he moved hostels to cover his tracks.

At his trial, he attempted to persuade the jury that he was insane, as his grandfather had died in a mental institution, but doctors decided otherwise. He was convicted of murder and executed on this day of 14 April 1955 at Wandsworth Prison.

15th – A Short Back and Death

Andrew Sams popped into his local barbers, Upper Cuts, in West Norwood, South London on this day in 2003. As the twenty-five-year old was having his hair cut, a man walked into the shop, placed the barrel of a 9 mm gun against the back of his head and shot Sams once, killing him instantly. There were many witnesses to the shooting, and as a result of the community coming together the killer was identified to police as twenty-one-year-old Rafik Alleyne, who was arrested in Brighton a few days after the killing. Alleyne was a crack-cocaine dealer and the killing was believed to be gangland related. Alleyne was convicted of the murder and sentenced to a minimum of twenty-two years imprisonment.

16th – One Good Turn Proves Fatal

Jamaican Cyrene Emmanuel Wright was a businessman who let out rooms in his house at No. 26 Beresford Road, Islington to fellow countrymen who were arriving in London to work in the public service industries in the 1950s and 1960s. Cyrene had a nephew called Selvin George Williamson who had mental health issues, so found it difficult to gain employment. His kindly uncle gave him a place to stay at the house and tried all he could to secure a job for his nephew. Selvin's mental state was more serious than his uncle had realised. This became tragically apparent on 16 April 1962 when Cyrene went up to his nephew's room after other tenants had told him that he was acting strangely; as he entered, Selvin attacked his uncle with a chair and heavy marble-topped table in a vicious unprovoked attack until he lay dead. Police were called to the house, Selvin attempting to escape by climbing out of the top-floor window and taking a huge leap onto the roof of a four-storey block of flats called Beresford Lodge. As he tried to lower himself to safety, he slipped and fell to his death.

17th – Caught in the Crossfire

This day will be remembered for two painful incidents on the streets of London. The first occurred in 1984 outside the Libyan

People's Bureau in St James' Square where a demonstration was taking place against the dictatorship of Muammar Gaddifi. This was met with a counter demonstration from occupants of the building. A number of unarmed police officers were deployed to keep public order including WPC Yvonne Fletcher. Just after 10 a.m., several shots rang out, fired from a window of the People's Bureau; several people were hit including Yvonne Fletcher, who was taken to Westminster Hospital but died of her injuries. This started an eleven-day siege between the police and the occupants of the building. A political resolution was eventually reached between the two governments in which the occupants of the People's Bureau – including the murderer of Yvonne Fletcher – were escorted from the building onto a bus, transported to Heathrow Airport and deported to Libya; all this took place on the day of Yvonne's funeral. The person responsible for the shooting has never been identified, but New Scotland Yard is determined that one day the murderer will stand trial in this country for this cowardly act. A memorial stands to the fallen officer in the square metres from where she fell.

* * *

The second incident took place on this day in 1999. David Copeland, a white neo-Nazi fascist loner with a bitter resentment of other racial groups and the gay community, took this hatred to the extreme when he planted a nail bomb deep in the heart of London's black community in Brixton. The bomb exploded; although miraculously nobody was killed, many were injured both physically and mentally. This was the start of a three-week campaign of terror during which he planted two further bombs, the next in Brick Lane, and finally the Admiral Duncan public house in Old Compton Street, the centre of London's gay community, where three people lost their lives including a pregnant woman. Copeland was identified by some dedicated police work especially in relation to CCTV, but his arrest was made just hours after the final fatal attack. On his arrest, he admitted immediately to police that he was responsible and that he had wanted to start a race-war in London. He was sentenced to six life sentences in

June 2000 and the High Court ruled he should serve at least fifty years before being considered for release.

18th – Lest We Forget

The murder of a police officer in the execution of their duty is, thankfully, rare in the United Kingdom, but as we have seen already in this volume, front-line officers who deal with societies' most violent offenders risk and sometimes lose their lives protecting us, the general public. On 18 April 1995, another Metropolitan PC, Phillip Walters, sadly became one of these statistics that we, as a society, can forget so easily. PC Walters – who had only been a police officer for eighteen months – was called to a domestic incident in Empress Avenue, Ilford, East London in company with his colleague Sergeant Derek Shepherd. On their arrival, they witnessed three men beating a fourth; as the men attempted to escape the officers courageously endeavoured to arrest the offenders. One of the men was armed and shot PC Walters in the chest, the bullet passed through his heart and he died of his injuries shortly after in hospital. His colleague Derek Shepherd luckily avoided serious injury by jamming his finger in front of the gun's hammer. The gunman, identified as Jamaican Ray Lee, was arrested at his flat in Ilford a few days later. He was tried and convicted of the lesser offence of manslaughter and was given *just* ten years imprisonment for the slaying of Phillip Walters and an additional eight years for firearms offences. Lee served twelve years of his eighteen-year sentence before being deported to Jamaica. A memorial to PC Walters, whose family will sadly endure a lifetime of profound grief, is located near to the scene of his death in Empress Avenue, a small garden of remembrance and memorial plaque can be seen in nearby Valentines Park.

19th – A Healing Touch

A most bizarre practice took place on Kennington Common in South London on 19 April 1748. Two thieves – brothers James and Walter White – were hanged on the common. As their bodies jerked with deathly spasms at the end of a rope, a nine-month-old child suffering from hideous facial tumours was handed to the executioner. He lifted the child and stroked its swollen face with the hands of the dying siblings in order to cure the child of its ills.

20th – A Lethal Mistake

The elderly in our society are often the target of ruthless criminals, one such case occurring in the early months of April 1907. Seventy-seven-year-old widow Florence Blume lived with her beloved granddaughter in a house that she owned in Fulham. They engaged the services of carpenter Richard Brinkley who soon hatched a plan to obtain the house for himself by forging a will purporting to be signed by Blume and witnesses in favour of himself. He spent some time building a trusting relationship with Florence and when at her most vulnerable tricked her into signing the will by offering her the document disguised as a list for a day trip to the seaside. He had similar success with elderly friends Reginald Parker and Herbert Heard whom he conned into signing as witnesses. When Florence died two days after the signing of the will, Brinkley claimed his inheritance. The granddaughter – although admitting the will carried the signature of her late grandmother – contested its legality with a solicitor. The solicitor immediately got to work asking Brinkley to prove the validity of the will. Its authenticity started to fall apart when Parker and Heard were interviewed. They told him they had never knowingly signed such a document and never witnessed the late Florence signing such either. Brinkley – now desperate – decided to eliminate the two witnesses who could prove a criminal case against him. On 20 April 1907, he purchased a bottle of stout from an off-licence and a quantity of prussic acid from a vet. He visited Reginald Parker at his lodgings at No. 32 Churchill Road, Croydon on the pretence of buying a dog from him. As they went into the backyard to examine the animal, Parker's landlord Richard Beck, his wife and daughter entered Parker's room, saw the bottle of stout –unbeknown to them laced with acid – and sampled some. Mr and Mrs Beck fell ill and died, but their daughter survived. Brinkley was arrested and charged with the murders. The off-licence assistant and the vet were both traced and gave evidence at his trial. Brinkley was convicted in July and executed at Wandsworth Prison on 13 August 1907. The conviction begged the question: did Brinkley murder Florence who died so conveniently after she had signed the will? Detectives had the same train of thought and exhumed the body expecting to find evidence of murder – but none was found. It appears she died of natural causes.

21st – *Violence in His Blood*

Frank Burgess had a difficult start to life when his mother was incarcerated in a mental institution during his formative years. He was educated at an approved school and gained a reputation for being aggressive. Frank joined the Royal Armoured Corps as a trooper at the age of seventeen and served in North Africa. He was discharged from the army after several violent incidents and ended up as a voluntary patient in a mental institution, from which he discharged himself. Following a stint on probation for a knife attack on a taxi driver, he gained employment at the Elgin Court Hotel in Elgin Road, East Croydon as a porter. On 21 April 1952, his violent tendencies surfaced again with tragic consequences when he strangled a young housemaid called Johanna Hallahan, who had been employed at the hotel for only six weeks. Following his arrest, he was charged with Johanna's murder and appeared at East Croydon magistrates court, a letter written in Burgess' handwriting discovered in his room following his arrest was read out: 'I don't know why I killed Joan ... but it was in quite a fit of laughter I killed her.'

Strong representations were made by his defence team regarding his sanity but Burgess was declared mentally fit to stand trial, found guilty of murder and executed at Wandsworth Prison on 22 July 1952.

22nd – *A German Deserter*

German-born Franz Joseph Munch was facing conscription to the German army when he decided to abscond and emigrate to London and settled in Bermondsey. He gained employment as a baker at a small independent bakery at No. 49 Lucey Road. This bakery was run by a Mrs Konrath for whom Franz developed a deep affection. However, a few months later in March 1891, Mrs Konrath's brother James Hickey came to London from Ireland, a powerfully built man compared to the diminutive Franz. Friction developed between the two about

Franz's relationship with Mrs Konrath. On 22 April 1891, Franz waited in a dark alleyway near to the Palmerston pub in Lucey Road where Hickey was drinking. As Hickey left, Munch shot him at point-blank range. Two PCs, Craske and Hamilton, were within twenty yards of the location and arrested Munch with the gun in his hand. Hickey was taken back to the pub, given a brandy but died of his injuries. Munch was convicted of murder. He appealed to the German embassy for help but was offered little assistance when found to be an absconder. He was hanged at Wandsworth on 21 July 1891.

23rd – *One Woman Not Enough*

Those close to William and Caroline Tuffen assumed their two-year marriage to be a happy one especially as they had moved into a new home at No. 12 Alexandra Road, Thames Ditton. Things were not what they seemed; William started to seek other female company and began an affair with a young lady called Mary Stone, who rather bizarrely moved into the marital home with William and wife Caroline. On 23 April 1903, William and Mary beat Caroline to death and hid her body in the house. Caroline's brother became suspicious when he couldn't contact his sister. He asked his brother-in-law of her whereabouts and was told that she had died of natural causes and was buried in a Thames Ditton churchyard, but refused to show him exactly where. The brother went to the police who searched No. 12 Alexandra Road, discovering the mutilated body of Caroline in a locked room together with the murder weapons, a bloody axe and hammer. Both William and Mary were charged with Caroline's murder and convicted. William was executed on 11 August 1903 at Wandsworth Prison, but Mary's sentence was commuted to a term of imprisonment.

24th – *A Shattered City*

Following the devastating PIRA bomb outside the Baltic Exchange (see 10 April) in the City of London, PIRA returned with another destructive and murderous attack. At 9 a.m. on this day in 1993, an Iveco truck laden with a huge one-ton bomb was driven onto Bishopsgate and parked on the junction of Wormwood Street and Camomile Street outside No. 99 Bishopsgate – the

Hong Kong and Shanghai Bank. Coded telephone calls were received from County Armagh, Northern Ireland warning of the impending explosion that duly occurred at 10.27 a.m. as police were evacuating the area. The bomb caused considerable damage to many buildings including the NatWest Tower. It also destroyed the ancient church of St Ethelburga's, which stood only several metres from the blast. Despite gallant efforts to evacuate the area, forty-four people were injured and *News of the World* reporter Ed Hendy lost his life when ignoring police warnings to leave. Following this devastating attack, a 'ring of steel' – armed police checkpoints – was placed at strategic entry and exit points around the City of London and is still present today.

25th – Foiled by a Goat

Shopkeeper Frederick Gosling had occupied his premises in Clay Corner, Chertsey, Surrey, for forty-four years. On 12 January 1951, two men, later identified as Joseph Brown and friend Edward Smith from Ashford, Middlesex, entered the shop with the intent to steal cash from the safe, while a third stayed in a getaway vehicle parked close by, but they were disturbed and fled. Seventy-nine-year-old Gosling reported the attempted robbery to local police who came and took a statement from the proprietor including descriptions of the offenders. All three men surprisingly returned later the same day; Gosling was bound and gagged and the safe emptied. The elderly shopkeeper was discovered by his milkman the following morning – he had died of asphyxiation. The police had an early break in the investigation when a witness came forward and told them he recognised the man sitting in the car. Fred Brown was arrested and gave up his brother Joseph and Edward Smith. Fred was given immunity from prosecution on the proviso that he gave evidence against Joseph and Smith. Forensic evidence also proved crucial, goat hair found in the getaway car matched a goat rug present in Gosling's bedroom. Both men were hanged at Wandsworth Prison on 25 April 1951.

26th – Finished with a Bayonet

Irishman Patrick Carroll joined the Royal Fusiliers aged twenty-two; he served with them for seven years before transferring to the Royal

Marines and a posting to Woolwich. His local pub was the *Britannia*, which he frequented regularly. He was attracted to the landlady Mrs Browning whom he asked to marry him. She refused Carroll's advances as he was often drunk and would abuse her on a regular basis when so intoxicated. On 26 April 1835, Browning burst into a private tea-party Browning was holding for friends. Carroll was offended he had not been invited and had cross words with her. He later returned and demanded a chance to speak to Browning. When refused, he took matters into his own hands, burst into the bar and struck Browning with his hand before drawing his bayonet and fatally stabbing her. Carroll was tried at the Old Bailey (this was the first trial the court was referred to as the Central Criminal Court, as it is known today, following a jurisdiction change). Carroll was hanged outside Newgate on 18 May 1835.

27th – Anarchists on the Met Line
The terrible events of 7 July 2005 remind us of the vulnerability of London's transport system to terrorism. During the late 1800s in Victorian London, the threat came from a group of anarchists' intent on destroying the lives of the citizens of several European liberal democracies. One such attack occurred on the London Underground. On Monday 27 April 1897, a bomb exploded on a crowded Metropolitan Line train as it stood with its doors open at Aldersgate Station; the time was 7.10 p.m. towards the end of the evening rush hour. Many passengers were injured, several losing limbs, and remarkably only one fatality – Harry Pitts a thirty-six-year-old manual worker on his way home from work. Nobody was ever arrested for this cowardly attack.

28th – No Help for Our Heroes
Soldier Henry Perry returned from the Great War mentally scarred following his capture in Turkey and subsequent torture. Like many such soldiers, Henry found it difficult integrating back into ordinary society following such horrendous experiences. On 28 April 1919, Henry was passing the home of Alice Cornish, his stepfather's sister who lived at No. 13 Stukeley Road, Forest Gate, East London. He had previously lodged at the address, where Alice lived with her husband Walter and two children aged fourteen and five years, but

was asked to leave due to his erratic, aggressive behaviour. Alice saw Perry outside and called him in and enquired about his health, but within minutes they started arguing. Henry lost his temper, picked up an axe and sank it into Alice's head. Perry sat in the house waiting for each of the remaining members of the family to come home, murdering each in a similar manner before stealing money and other items of value. At his trial, Henry offered insanity as his defence blaming the treatment he had endured during the war including shrapnel injuries to his head, beatings and hearing voices when carrying out the murders. His claims were not backed up with any medical evidence; the jury found him guilty and he was executed on 10 July 1919 at Pentonville.

***

Another crime that ended in murder was a burglary in Harlington Road, Hillingdon on 31 December 1958. Joseph Chrimes and an accomplice broke into the home of sixty-year-old Nora Summerfield. They disturbed the old lady who was subsequently beaten over the head with a tyre-lever. The accomplice gave evidence against Chrimes at his trial; he was convicted of murder and executed on this day in 1959 at Pentonville Prison. The total haul from the burglary was a clock, cigarette case and a couple of spoons.

29th – *Violence Breeds Violence*

Gertrude and Walter Fairlie married during the First World War; Walter had enlisted in the army as an officer in 1914. The couple produced one child, then aged three, but the marriage hit trouble when Walter began drinking heavily, becoming abusive and violent to his wife. On 29 April 1920 – having been separated for several weeks – Walter approached his wife at a lunch engagement with a friend in Cheapside in the City of London and asked to speak to her outside. Walter pulled out a revolver and shot his wife dead before turning the gun level to his right ear and firing two shots; he died later in hospital. In the subsequent inquest, evidence was given of Fairlie's violent behaviour and drunkenness during his army service.

30th – Put That Light Out

During the early hours of 30 April 1942, a police patrol was called to a pawnbroker's shop on Hackney Road, Shoreditch, a passer-by having reported a light shining from a window contravening the strict blackout regulations. They found the proprietor Leonard Moules on the floor suffering from serious head injuries. A palm print belonging to a known criminal called George Silverosa was recovered from inside the shop's empty safe. Following a witness appeal, a member of the public came forward and informed detectives that he had overheard two men talking about the robbery in a café, one had brazenly waved around a gun; they referred to each other by the names George and Sam. George and close associate Samuel Dashwood were traced by detectives to Pitsea in Essex where they were arrested. Each man blamed the other but both were convicted of Leonard Moules murder; he died nine days after the attack. Silverosa and Dashwood were executed at Pentonville Prison on 10 September 1942.

5

MAY

1st – Gang Warfare

As brave young men and women fought for their country during the Second World War, often making the ultimate sacrifice, terrorists continued planting bombs and criminals fought turf wars to increase their power and profit. Italian criminal gangs were making considerable inroads into drugs, prostitution and gambling in London's Soho, often pushing more traditional villains out of the area. One such gang was led by Antonio 'Babe' Mancini whose gaming machines could be found in over half of the clubs and pubs of Soho. Inevitably, territories would overlap. No. 37 Wardour Street was one such example. Mancini had gaming machines in part of the building that also housed a club and restaurant run by brothers Harry 'Little Hubby' Distleman and his big brother (yes you've guessed it) 'Big Hubby' Distleman. A lot of bad blood and threats came to a climax on 1 May 1941 when a large fight broke out between the two gangs. Mancini stabbed 'Little Hubby' Distleman in the shoulder, which proved fatal. Self-defence was a logical defence to place in front of a jury. The defence claimed Distleman initially attacked Mancini with a chair, and, they suggested, if one intended to kill somebody else you probably wouldn't stab them in the shoulder. However, the jury were convinced of Mancini's *malice aforethought* and found him guilty of murder and, after a failed appeal to the High Court and the House of Lords, Mancini was executed on 17 October 1941. Although the conviction seemed harsh and the sentence excessive, few residents of Soho would have been shedding many tears at the loss of two such menacing characters.

2nd – *The Barnes Common Mystery*

Local butcher James Wells escorted his two daughters safely home late in the evening on 1 May 1894. On his return journey in the early hours of 2 May, he decided to walk via Barnes Common. As he crossed the public land, he was hit on the head with a piece of lead piping and left to die. Police found him badly injured but conscious, managing with difficulty to tell the officers that his attacker's name was either Arthur West or Welch; he died a few hours later. Detectives arrested a close associate of the butcher's whose name was indeed Arthur West. He was questioned and charged with the murder. He admitted seeing Wells earlier that day but explained he had been home by 10 p.m. and therefore not in the vicinity of Barnes Common. His alibi was backed up by his family and a lodger who swore West had been home at the material time and the door had been bolted after him. The prosecution offered no evidence before the commencement of his trial and Arthur West was released. The murder remained unsolved for several more years when a man called Welch gave himself up and confessed to the murder of Wells. His confession turned out to be a complete fabrication and a waste of police time – the murder of James Wells remains unsolved.

3rd – *Poor Nellie – Slit from Ear to Ear*

We stay in West London for our next case, the savage murder of a street prostitute – eighteen-year-old Nellie Pearce. Nellie's murderer was not a stranger-attack in a dark alleyway but a man whom she trusted: her landlord, twenty-five-year-old Rowland Duck. French polisher Duck, his wife and three children lived in a reasonable-sized house in Cambria Street, Fulham. On 3 May 1923, Rowland Duck confided to a friend that he had murdered Nellie earlier that day. He then confessed to his wife, sought out his children and said his goodbyes before walking into his local police station in Walham Green. He informed a rather shocked desk officer that 'I have killed a woman called Nellie Pearce at Cambria Street by cutting her throat. You will find her under the bed. I did it with a razor.' Police did indeed find the unfortunate Nellie; she had been wrapped in a military blanket together with the bloodstained murder weapon. Duck was arrested and charged with her murder. His explanation to the police was calm and quite chilling:

> About three weeks ago, my wife was good enough to take Nellie Pearce in and give her lodgings. One morning she was in bed and I visited her after my wife had gone to work. About a week ago I asked her if there was anything the matter with her, and she told me she had suffered from a certain disease for a long time. She also told me I deserved everything I got. This morning I done no more than got a razor and cut her throat, put a blanket round her head, and put her under the bed. Afterwards I washed and dressed the children and came out with them and left them in the care of my wife's mother. I had been drinking all day. That is all I have to say.
>
> (*Hull Daily Mail* 11 May 1923)

At his trial, Duck wasn't quite so forthcoming claiming that he had cut Nellie's throat while in an epileptic state but could not remember killing her, and when he returned to his senses Nellie was in his arms and wondered if he had been responsible. The defence produced expert witnesses who stated that it was possible for Duck to be in an epileptic state, kill the girl and not remember. The jury took only thirty minutes to dismiss such a notion and convicted Duck. He was executed on 4 July 1923 at Pentonville Prison.

4th – What is That Smell?

The aroma of rotting human flesh clings to clothes, seeps into lungs and lingers in nasal passages for days. On Monday 9 May 1927, railway staff at Charing Cross Railway Station smelt such a stench of death escaping from a large trunk deposited at the station luggage office for transportation to the south coast. Police were called and took the offending trunk to Bow Street Police Station. On opening the lid, they discovered five brown paper parcels of various sizes, tied up with string, a ladies handbag and shoes. Each parcel contained human body parts; the largest parcel was that of a torso and head of a woman, the head had been wrapped in a duster. The smaller parcels contained the four limbs that had been removed from the torso and wrapped separately in female's clothes. The woman had been badly beaten before death and then strangled. Pathologist Sir Bernard Spilsbury estimated the woman had been dead for at least a week.

The trunk was traced to No. 86 Rochester Row, Victoria – the business address of John Robinson – via a taxi-driver who had transported it and Robinson to Charing Cross Station. Robinson had not been seen at the premises for a few days. The items of clothing led to the identification of the victim as Mrs Minnie Alice Bonati. Detectives eliminated the dead woman's estranged husband from suspicion and concentrated on finding John Robinson. They persuaded a former partner of Robinson's to assist them in a sting to flush him out. She set up a meeting with Robinson in the Elephant and Castle pub; when he showed up the police moved in and made their arrest. Initially detectives struggled to prove Robinson's involvement until Bonati's blood was found on a wastepaper basket in Robinson's office. Robinson – faced with mounting evidence – made a statement to police claiming Bonati had propositioned him at Victoria Station on 4 May 1927; he had taken her back to his office for sex where she became violent and abusive and demanded money; a struggle ensued in which Bonati fell and hit her head. He did not admit killing her but never denied dismembering the body and transporting it to Charing Cross. Spilsbury's evidence of pre-mortem injuries and asphyxiation were crucial and the jury dismissed the defence case of accidental death. Robinson was executed on 12 August 1927 at Pentonville Prison.

5th – Just a Bad Egg

Thomas Cooper was disturbed committing an armed robbery by PC Charles Moss in the Finsbury Park area of North London on 5 May 1842. Cooper shot and wounded the officer before making his escape. Members of the public heard the shot and chased the assailant. The gallant pursuers were joined by another constable, Timothy Daly. As Daly closed in on Cooper, the robber fired another shot this time killing the officer instantly. Cooper was over powered by two gardeners and detained. He faced trial at the Old Bailey and was convicted of the murder of PC Timothy Daly and executed outside Newgate Prison on 4 July 1842.

6th – The Woman in Red

The body of Winifred Mulholland was discovered on the steps of No. 18 Finborough Road, West Brompton. The deceased wore a red dress and a fur coat; the media imaginatively nicknamed the killing the *Woman in Red Murder*. The occupier of the house was forty-one-year-old engineer Cyril Epton. He was arrested and charged with the murder after making a statement to the police claiming to have met Mulholland in Piccadilly on the evening of 6 May 1948; she had smiled at him and they had got talking resulting in her accompanying him back to his Finborough Road flat. After a couple of hours, he discovered she had stolen £9 from his trouser pocket, they argued, and he hit her and she fell striking her head on the mantel piece. He went and had a cup of tea (as you do) and when he returned she was dead. He kept the body in the flat for three days before throwing the corpse out of the window in order to make it look like she had jumped. The jury rejected his defence and convicted him of murder; he was sentenced to death. The home secretary decided to give Epton a reprieve from the hangman's rope commuting the sentence to life imprisonment.

7th – The World's Wickedest Man

The murder of a twelve-year-old boy on 7 May 2000 followed a very disturbing sequence of events. Diego Pineiro-Villar lived in the Covent Garden area of Central London and would often play in an area known as Phoenix Gardens located in the grounds of St Giles Church. The gardens were also used by local drug dealers and the homeless. Diego had been befriended by fifty-two-year-old homeless male Edward Alexander Crowley the previous year. This relationship had developed over a period of months with Crowley spending money on Diego – buying him presents and food. The relationship became of concern to Diego's mother and eventually a restraining order was taken out against Crowley following an investigation by the police; no evidence of any sexual assault was ever uncovered. On the evening of 7 May 2000, Diego and his elder brother, Roberto, were sent on an errand, and the route took them past Phoenix Gardens. As they approached the gardens, Crowley confronted both boys armed with a knife, slashed at Diego's brother, inflicting a nasty wound, and then attacked Diego who had managed to ring 999 on his mobile; the operator could only listen on the open line as Diego was brutally stabbed twenty times.

Crowley was arrested and charged with the murder of Diego. Crowley's antecedents unravelled a disturbing picture of a man with serious mental health problems and an unhealthy obsession with the occult. He had changed his name by deed-poll from his birth name Henry Bibby to Crowley in honour of early twentieth-century occultist Aleister Crowley, once dubbed the 'world's wickedest man'. He was sentenced to life imprisonment in February 2001.

8th – A Killer with a Conscience
A few days before Christmas 1958, twenty-five-year-old scaffolder Ronald Marwood went out drinking with a good friend, Mick Bloom, to celebrate his wedding anniversary (Mrs Marwood had preferred to stay at home). Marwood and Bloom travelled to Tottenham and had several drinks before going on to Gray's Music Hall on Seven Sisters Road. A fight broke out between two groups of 'Teddy Boys' involving several weapons. Marwood and Bloom got involved; at one point Marwood saw Bloom being held by a lone police officer, PC Raymond Summers, who was attempting to break up the mass brawl. Marwood went over to help his friend, later claiming he had his hands in his pockets. As he approached the police officer, he claimed that he removed a hand to help Bloom and found himself holding an underwater swimmer's knife with which he accidently stabbed the officer who fell to the floor and subsequently died of his injury. Marwood and Bloom left the scene before the arrival of police reinforcements and detectives struggled to identify the pair described by witnesses.

The murder would probably have remained unsolved to this day without Marwood's conscience profoundly troubling him. He attended Caledonian Road Police station and admitted to his role in the officer's death. He was tried at the Old Bailey in March 1959 and the jury were invited by the defence to convict on the lesser charge of manslaughter but returned a guilty verdict on murder. Marwood was sentenced to death and executed at Pentonville Prison on 8 May 1959. Over one thousand people demonstrated outside the prison – many with 'Save Marwood' banners. Following Marwood's execution, a public debate raged in which very vocal politicians and religious leaders demanded an end to the barbaric practice of capital punishment in a civilised society. But of course, the murder of PC Raymond Summers, bravely carrying out his duty, and the suffering of his family were rarely mentioned by those who sit safely and securely in their ivory towers conveniently forgetting who they will call when it all goes wrong.

9th – I Can't Remember a Thing Officer
No. 5 Elton Road was a tiny cottage situated in leafy Kingston upon Thames. On 9 May 1954, police officers acted on information from a member of the public and forced entry to find the body of forty-four-year-old waitress Nellie Officer. Her killer, a very intoxicated fifty-three-year-old storekeeper called Rupert Geoffrey Wells, lay semi-conscious on the floor. Wells was taken to hospital under police guard and arrested on suspicion of Nellie's murder when he sobered up. Wells' defence was thin to say the least, claiming he had been under the influence of drugs and alcohol and couldn't remember anything about the incident so therefore could not be guilty of the offence of wilful murder. This was dismissed by the jury and following a failed appeal, Wells was executed at Wandsworth Prison on 1 September 1954.

10th – A Child's Last Journey
The village of Shefford is located in the county of Bedfordshire and home in 1879 to forty-one-year-old, married, picture framer and part-time postman James Dilley. While on his postal rounds, Dilley met twenty-nine-year-old domestic worker Mary Rainbow, who lived in the nearby village of Baldock in the adjoining county of Hertfordshire. Their affair produced an unwanted illegitimate child on 22 April 1879. On 10 May 1879, Dilley spent the night with Rainbow and his child. The next day they set off for London, by train with a package, which they deposited at St Pancras Station, before casually going for a drink in a local pub. A little later that afternoon, a workman, suspicious of the odour emanating from the package, opened it and discovered the remains of Dilley and Rainbow's child, the infant having been beaten and poisoned. Both stood trial for murder and were sentenced to death. Rainbow received a pardon two days before she was due to hang; Dilley was executed in Newgate Prison on 25 August 1879.

11th – A Premier Assassination

The only British prime minister to be assassinated was Spencer Perceval, shot in the lobby of the House of Commons at 5.15 p.m. on 11 May 1812. The assassin was a man called John Bellingham. Bellingham was a merchant who had, in his view, unjustly been imprisoned in Russia. On his return to England in 1808, Bellingham petitioned the government and Perceval insisting he was entitled to compensation – the petition fell on death ears. His wife appealed to him to drop his grievance with the government and get on with his life. He seemed to adhere to her wishes until 1812 when he renewed his efforts for compensation with a visit to the Foreign Office. A civil servant reportedly told him that he was allowed to take *whatever* measures he thought fit to further his claim – a piece of advice he took to the extreme. On 20 April 1812, Bellingham purchased two pistols from a gunsmith, had a tailor sew a covert pocket into the lining of his coat, in which he placed one of the pistols. Following a visit to an art gallery with a friend on 11 May 1812, Bellingham nonchalantly made his way to the House of Commons, a place he was regularly seen so had easy access to. He waited patiently for Perceval to leave the Commons Chamber before shooting the prime minister through the heart at point blank range and then sat defiantly on a nearby bench until detained by parliament security staff.

Bellingham was tried and sentenced to death. His case evoked a lot of passion from the ordinary working man. Rene Martin Pillett, a Frenchman who recorded accounts of many incidents he witnessed during his ten years in England, wrote:

> Farewell poor man, you owe satisfaction to the offended laws of your country, but God bless you! You have rendered an important service to your country, you have taught ministers that they should do justice, and grant audience when it is asked of them.
> (*Views of England, During a Residence of Ten Years; Six of Them as a Prisoner.* Rene Martin Pillett 1816)

On his death, Parliament suddenly realised that no portrait of Spencer Perceval existed, so a hastily arranged sitting was made five days after his murder, with the corpse of the late prime minister supported in an upright position fitted in a fine suit. The artist managed a very good likeness under the circumstances but had trouble painting the lifeless eyes. He overcame this problem by substituting Perceval's eyes for those of his sisters.

12th – I Panicked but Didn't Kill Her

Harding's furniture warehouse was located on the corner of Islington Green in North London. Early on the morning of 13 May 1937, the smooth running of the company was thrown into turmoil when employee Fred Murphy reported the discovery of a decomposing body of a young lady behind a tin box in the basement of the building. By the time police arrived, Fred Murphy had disappeared. A couple of days later Murphy walked into Poplar Police Station and explained that he had found the body of the woman on the morning in question, panicked and moved the corpse behind the tin box but denied killing her. He was arrested on suspicion of murder and detectives began to piece together a case against Murphy. They had by now identified the victim as prostitute Rosina Fields, who lived a short distance away in Duncan Terrace; Murphy lived in an adjacent street, No. 57a Colebrooke Row. Witnesses came forward following appeals for information. One witness remembers seeing Murphy and a woman going into the furniture warehouse on the evening of 12 May; she identified Murphy but couldn't identify Fields but recollected the woman wearing a distinctive blue coat. Other witnesses recall the pair drinking in a local pub earlier in the evening and one witness later seeing Murphy alone. Murphy was charged with the murder of Rosina Fields.

While awaiting his trial, detectives discovered that Murphy had previously been arrested on suspicion of the murder of another prostitute in Aldgate whose throat had been cut. The case was discontinued when the main witness, who had seen Murphy in the victim's company, disappeared. This time the evidence stood firm and Murphy was executed at Pentonville on 17 August 1937.

13th – Justifiable Homicide

Policing the streets of London in the years following the formation of the Metropolitan Police Force in 1829 was a dangerous business.

Today's modern service police the law of the land by public consent; this certainly was not the case in the 1830s when the police were seen as little more than agents and spies of the government. The first major test between the police and the mood of the general public came in 1833 when the National Union of the Working Classes organised a rally against the Great Reform Act of 1832. The meeting was arranged for 2 p.m. on 13 May 1833 on the Calthorpe Estate, Cold Bath Fields, Clerkenwell. The meeting, which had been declared illegal by the government, had been advertised for at least a week in advance and many hundreds attended. Tensions were high between the crowd and the large detachment of police present. The violence started soon after with each side blaming the other for its instigation. Numerous allegations from different sources claimed the police were heavy-handed, charging the crowd with their batons. *The Times* recorded that:

> The police furiously attacked the multitude with their staves, felling every person indiscriminately before them; even the females did not escape the blows from their batons – men and boys were lying in every direction weltering in their blood and calling for mercy.

Three police officers were stabbed, Police Sergeant John Brooks and PC Redwood as they tried to wrestle a flag from demonstrators; the third was PC Robert Culley, who staggered into a nearby pub with blood oozing from his chest – he died shortly after.

The inquest into the death of PC Culley produced a shocking verdict of 'Justifiable Homicide'. The jury believed the crowd had not been ordered to disperse under the Riot Act and that the conduct of the police was 'ferocious, brutal and unprovoked by the people'. The jury received huge congratulations from all areas of the general public, each member received a medal from an anonymous donor made from pewter, which was inscribed:

> In honour of the men who nobly withstood the dictation of the coroner; independent and conscientious discharge of their duty; promoted a continued reliance upon the laws under the protection of a British jury.

14th – PIRA Go South

The south-east London suburb of Eltham was targeted by the PIRA on 14 May 1990. The Directorate of Army Education was bombed resulting in seven people being injured. The 5–10 lb device was concealed in a nearby flowerbed before exploding, causing extensive damage to the building's foyer and overturning a nearby car. The injury toll would have been much higher, with possible fatalities, if the building's security features hadn't been upgraded just a few weeks before. The windows had been covered with protective laminate covering and withstood the blast thus protecting workers within the office space from shrapnel and flying glass.

15th – Life for a Life

John Gavan fatally stabbed his father William on 15 May 1893 in Lambeth, South London. He was arrested and tried at the Old Bailey within three weeks. Holloway Prison's medical officer Phillip Francis Gilbert gave evidence to the court regarding observations of Gavan since the day of the murder and informed the jury that the eighteen year old had claimed, 'It was a life for a life.' He added that the defendant had claimed his father and brother had been trying to poison him in a variety of different ways including putting lice in his food, mixing phosphorous with paraffin and putting it on his bed and poisoning his towels. Gilbert added that Gavan's mother was at present detained in a lunatic asylum. Gavan was declared insane and detained in an asylum.

16th – Cowardly Attack

Another PIRA bomb placed under a minibus at the rear of the Army Recruitment Office on the High Street, Wembley exploded on 16 May 1990 killing Sergeant Charles Chapman of the Queen's Regiment and injuring four others. The thirty-four-year-old soldier, who was based at the Inglis Barracks in Mill Hill, was the father of two young children and served for eighteen years in HM's Armed Forces having completed a tour in Northern Ireland months before his murder. Nobody has ever been charged in relation to Sergeant Chapman's murder.

17th – A Fatal Kiss

Magistrate Henry Edgell lived at No. 21 Cadogan Place, Chelsea and employed several domestic staff, one of whom was eighteen-year-old William John Marchant. In early May 1839, a new member of staff took up a position, a beautiful under-housemaid named Elizabeth Paynton. Marchant instantly fell in love, becoming obsessed with the young girl. On 17 May 1839, he could no longer keep his ardour in check and attempted to kiss Elizabeth when they were alone in the kitchen. Elizabeth resisted his advances and a struggle ensued in which she threatened to report his attack to the master of the house and get him transported for his crime. Marchant picked up a razor and slashed Elizabeth across the throat, slicing through the carotid artery before letting her drop to the floor. The young footman made good his escape but gave himself up to the authorities in Hounslow a few days later. He appeared at the Old Bailey on 21 June 1839 and pleaded guilty to the charge of murder and was sentenced to death; the media reported in detail the young man's final moments at Newgate before execution:

> While the executioner was pinioning the prisoner's arms and wrists he stood with astonishing firmness and conversed freely with those around him. When the prison bell sounded the first knell he shuddered, but the effect was momentary. The procession was shortly moved through the avenues to the fatal scaffold, the ordinary reading portions from the burial service.
>
> The executioner performed his awful duty with celerity and the culprit had not been exposed to public gaze more than a minute before the bolt was withdrawn and after a few struggles he ceased to live.
>
> (*Windsor and Eton Express* 13 July 1839)

18th – Not Destined to Die

James Allison and wife Alice were landlord and landlady of a popular public house, The Rising Sun, on The Strand. Sometime in March 1896, Allison's wife developed a medical condition, which made her bed-ridden. This had a profound effect on James who took to the bottle spiralling downwards into a deep depression. In the early hours of 18 May 1896, shots were heard by the pub's staff after James and his wife had retired for the night. A police officer was on patrol in the vicinity of the pub and responded to their cries of help; the officer found Alice shot through the head and James with three self-inflicted gunshot wounds caused by the same firearm. Both were taken to hospital; Alice died at 2 a.m., James survived and was released into police custody some days later and charged with his wife's murder. He was found to be of sound mind to stand trial and convicted of Alice's murder; however, the jury recommended mercy due to the extenuating circumstances and he received a reprieve from execution in July 1896.

19th – An Angry Lot

A group of British anarchists operating under the name of the Angry Brigade carried out twenty-five terrorist attacks in the United Kingdom between May 1970 and August 1971. They ran their operation from No. 359 Amhurst Road, Stoke Newington; their target was generally the British establishment – in particular the Tory government of Edward Heath. The attacks, which included small explosive devices and firebombs, were directed towards politician's homes, government buildings, embassies and high profile media-grabbing public events such as the Miss World competition. The group were an embarrassment for the government and the police who seemed unable to catch those responsible. One of the very first attacks in this campaign was the firebombing of the Conservative Party Association building in Wembley on 19 May 1971. This was followed by bomb attacks on targets including home secretary Robert Carr's house and the home of the director of the Ford Motor Company's Dagenham plant – William Batty.

Metropolitan Police Commissioner Sir John Waldron formed Scotland Yard's 'Bomb Squad' in January 1970 in order to bring to justice members of the Angry Brigade. The raid at the Amhurst Road address by Bomb Squad detectives took place on 20 August 1971, a number of the group – who were to become known as the 'Stoke Newington 8' – were arrested and charged with causing explosions. Police recovered an armoury of firearms and explosives including a Browning revolver, a Beretta, sixty rounds of ammunition, thirty-three sticks of gelignite and detonators. Four men were convicted and sentenced to fifteen years imprisonment, reduced to ten on appeal. The 'Bomb Squad' went on to form the basis of Scotland Yard's elite Anti-Terrorist Branch – SO13.

20th – A 'To Do' List

At the conclusion of a long voyage from Australia, two sea-weary sailors arrived in London on 15 March 1909; alcohol and sex were on the top of their 'to do' list. Having drank to excess, they were picked up by two prostitutes who escorted them back to No. 3 Rupert Street, Whitechapel where two brothers, Morris and Mark Reubens, who ran the girls, were waiting to burst into the room when the men were at their most vulnerable and either blackmail or rob them. The scam, in which they were well versed, didn't on this occasion go according to plan as the sailors William Sproull and Charlie McEachern put up a good fight. The brothers managed to eject Charlie out the front door but William fought tooth and nail before being stabbed with a clasp knife. Sproull staggered after Charlie leaving a trail of blood until he collapsed in the street dying from his injuries. Detectives had a relatively easy task of following the bloody trail back to the address and arrested the Reubens brothers and the two prostitutes.

During their trial, the brothers blamed each other for the murder. The two prostitutes gave evidence against them pointing the finger of blame at Mark who they accused of actually stabbing Sproull. A defence of accidental stabbing was dismissed as one has to actually pull the blade out of a clasp knife before utilising it; the jury saw this as a pre-meditated act. The judge directed the jury that as the two brothers had planned to rob and inflict grievous bodily harm jointly, the resulting death of William Sproull meant both men were as guilty as the other of murder. Both brothers were convicted and executed together on 20 May 1909 at Pentonville – ironically by two brothers – Henry and Thomas Pierrepoint.

21st – Common Thieves

Infamous highwaymen, Royal Mail robbers and murderers John Hawkins and James Simpson had a long criminal career, mostly holding up the rich at gunpoint in locations as far apart as Hounslow Heath and Finchley Common. They were eventually caught and executed by being hung in chains on Hounslow Heath on 21 May 1722.

22nd – *Lock the Cell Door and Throw Away the Key*

The murder of Fusilier Lee Rigby on 22 May 2013 was a despicable and cowardly act. Lee was a member of the Royal Fusiliers; he had fought for Queen and country in Afghanistan. Lee returned home safe and sound only to be brutally murdered on the streets of London. This afternoon Lee Rigby was off duty in civilian clothes walking back towards his barracks in Woolwich, south-east London. He was specifically targeted as a member of HM's Armed Forces, struck by a car at high speed and subsequently hacked to death by two British men of Nigerian descent whose names will not be mentioned, even in a volume of this nature. The men claimed this cold-blooded murder was in revenge for the deaths of members of the Taliban in Afghanistan. Bystanders showed extraordinary courage in protecting the body of Lee Rigby from further desecration from his attackers. Both men, who were shot by police at the scene, survived to stand trial during which they failed to demonstrate any courage and admit their guilt, they were found guilty and sentenced to forty-five years imprisonment. This fine soldier is remembered by a number of memorials to him; one at the location at which he was slain. His name has been added to the Armed Forces Memorial at the National Arboretum.

23rd – *A Trooper's Spur*

Royal Academy exhibitor Archibald Wakley was found murdered by his charwoman Mrs Mercer in his studio at No. 76A Westbourne Grove, West London; he had been battered around his head and body with a hammer. It would appear that the artist had a penchant for young soldiers especially from the Royal Horse Guards barracked nearby. The police traced one such acquaintance, Trooper J. Walker who explained to detectives that he had met Wakley in Hyde Park about four months before his murder. Wakley had invited him back to his studio for a drink but he left promptly when Wakley propositioned him. The trooper provided the police with a solid alibi for his movements for the late evening of 23 May 1906, the likely time of death, that cleared him of any involvement. Detectives believed that a soldier was responsible for the murder mainly due to the findings of forensic pathologist Augustus Pepper who discovered a series of small puncture wounds on the victim's thighs and concluded they were made by a trooper's spurs. This was backed up by a crucial witness – salesman George Miles who saw Wakley enter 76A Westbourne Grove on the evening of 23 May followed by a uniformed soldier. Police believed that Wakley had subsequently picked up another soldier as before, but this time rather than leaving promptly, as Walker had, this soldier had decided to teach the artist a lesson by beating and kicking him to death. The investigation came under the scrutiny of the press, in particular the *Daily Mirror* who rather tongue in cheek suggested Sherlock Holmes would have been more successful in finding the culprit. Nobody was ever charged with Wakley's murder, which remains unsolved.

***

Another murder that caused the Metropolitan Police some embarrassment was the case of Daniel Good. Good murdered his common-law wife Jane Jones and dismembered her body before burning it over a period of time in the Putney stables where he worked. Good rather foolishly stole a pair of trousers witnessed by two shop boys who followed him to the stables and then informed the local police. PC William Gardner spoke to Good in the stable and started to search for the trousers but found the torso of Jane Jones. Good fled locking the PC in the stable. The subsequent search for Good can at best be described as un-coordinated with uniformed police from different divisions crossing over each other and an investigation that was at best inadequate and unprofessional. Good was eventually captured by an ex-police officer who spotted the killer working as a bricklayer's mate in Tonbridge, Kent. Good was executed on 23 May 1842. The demand for a Detective Branch to investigate serious crime following this debacle resulted in the establishment of such a department on 15 August 1842 based at Scotland Yard; this evolved into what we know today as the Criminal Investigation Department (CID).

24th – Death of Lady Teresa

A lift attendant at London Transport's Gloucester Road Tube Station heard the desperate shouts of a lady screaming 'bandits' during the late evening of 24 May 1957, went to her assistance and found the passenger bleeding profusely from a number of stab wounds to her chest and back. The victim was taken to St Mary's Hospital but died from her injuries after informing police that she had been attacked on the platform. A post-mortem examination revealed the victim had been stabbed five times; two of the blows had penetrated her heart. Tattooed on her forearm was the number 44747. The deceased was identified as Lady Teresa Lubienska, a woman who had led an incredible life. Lady Teresa was born into aristocracy and spent her childhood on her family's large estate in Eastern Poland. She moved to Warsaw prior to the Nazi invasion of 1939. When her son was killed fighting for the Polish army, Teresa joined the resistance but was captured and sent to Auschwitz where she received the tattooed number. She was released midway through the war and fled to London. Prior to her murder, she lived in a flat in Cornwall Gardens, Kensington. The motive for the murder was never established, her possessions were intact ruling out robbery. Detectives interviewed many thousands of people including train and bus drivers and conductors, searched all trains on the Piccadilly Line for the murder weapon and forensically examined every knife found on the system for several months after, but the killer was never identified.

25th – No Loyalty Just Greed

German couple Carl and Matilda Rasch owned a restaurant at No. 167 Shaftesbury Avenue in Central London; they lived above the premises with their four children. The Rasch's had live-in employees including fellow German's Paul and Susan Koczula, who were married and shared the bedroom on the second floor. The Koczula's were employed as waiter and general servant respectively. Mrs Rasch was in the habit of keeping the restaurant takings in her bedroom wardrobe with the key on her person at all times. A regular patron of the restaurant was a man called George Schmerfeld also a German who had arrived in London a few months earlier.

In the Early evening on 25 May 1894, Schmerfeld asked Carl Rasch to accompany him on a walk to Hyde Park; Matilda always had a sleep between 7 and 9 p.m. and would normally be woken by one of the children. Carl returned to the restaurant about 10 p.m., asked the children where their mother was and told that Susan Koczula had asked that she be left to sleep. Carl went upstairs to find their bedroom ransacked, his wife Matilda was bound tightly with cord and quite dead. Carl ran out of the house shouting 'murder' and returned with a PC. The cord that bound Matilda was the same cord kept in their garden shed; the Koczula's had disappeared as well as their belongings. They were traced to No. 181 Hampstead Road, arrested and charged with the murder of Matilda. George Schmerfeld was charged as an accessory to murder by distracting Carl away from the restaurant so that the crime could be perpetrated. He was arrested attempting to board a ship going to Holland. At the Old Baily trial on 23 July 1894, Paul Koczula was found guilty of Matilda's murder but his wife was acquitted. Schmerfeld was convicted of being an accessory before the fact. Paul Koczula was executed at Newgate on 14 August 1894. George Schmerfeld's death sentence was reduced to penal servitude.

26th – Is Jack Back?

The mutilated body of a young female discovered in a dingy lodging house at No. 35 Dorset Street, Spitafields, resulted in a wave of panic and hysteria in London's East End thirteen years after *Jack the Ripper's* last known killing. The victim was Mary Austin, last seen alive on the evening of 26 May 1901 as she entered her lodgings with a man whom the landlord was unable to later identify. Her husband, William Austin, who stayed with his wife at the lodging house three nights a week, identified the body as that of his wife. William produced an alibi for the evening of the murder – he had been in at his lodgings in Battersea several miles away. Detectives, however, arrested William Austin and charged him with the murder of his wife based on a sighting of the killer entering the lodging house by a second witness. She described the suspect as being short and dark – William Austin was in fact over six feet tall. The identification was paper-thin as the witness only identified William Austin as the person she had seen when he gave evidence at the coroner's inquest a few days after the murder. No further evidence was forthcoming and the public prosecutor threw in the towel, declaring the identification evidence wholly unsatisfactory and the case against him was discharged. No other suspects were ever identified and Mary Austin's murder remains unsolved – could she have been another *Jack the Ripper* victim?

27th – A Watch Full of Blood

Two workers at Euston Railway Station fell out over a drugs deal, both ended up dead. Joseph Aaku had rooms at No. 10 Oakley Square near Camden Town. On the night of 4 January 1952, neighbours heard shouting coming from the premises and saw a black man running away towards Euston. When they further investigated they found Joseph in his room with stab wounds to his neck and face, he died of these injuries later that night. Friends informed detectives that a distinctive watch that Joseph always wore was missing. A forensic examination of the scene found two blood groups, one obviously the victims; the second likely to be the killers. Detectives trawled through personal associates and work colleagues of the deceased in order to establish a motive. One man they interviewed, who worked with Joseph, was Backery Manneh. Manneh had a bandaged hand, which he told detectives was as a result of a mugging a few days earlier. Detectives could prove nothing more at this stage and released him. Manneh's story started to fall apart when it came to the police's attention that Manneh had told a friend not to talk to the police if asked about his injury. Another vital witness came forward with information that would crack the case wide open. He had bought a watch from Manneh a few days after the murder, on removing the back of the watch he found the movement caked in what would prove to be the deceased's blood. Manneh was arrested and charged with the murder of Joseph Aaku, convicted and executed at Pentonville Prison on 27 May 1952.

28th – From Wallington to Wandsworth

David Ballie Mason strangled his wife Dorothy and three-year-old son David John at their home at 12A Haslemere Close, Wallington, Surrey on 28 May 1946. Mason stood trial at the Old Bailey for his crimes and was convicted and sentenced to death; he was executed on 6 September 1946 at Wandsworth.

29th – Body in the Elephant

Marie Ellen Bailes failed to return home to Prebend Street, Islington on 29 May 1908; police were informed that the diminutive six year old was missing and a major search commenced. The following day, eight or so miles from Islington, a man nervously entered a public toilet situated on the junction of St Georges' Road and Elephant and Castle; he was carrying a neatly tied, weighty, brown package in his hands. He was noticed by an alert lavatory attendant who saw the man acting nervously before entering a cubicle, and never saw him leave. A little later, while cleaning out the cubicles, the attendant came across the brown paper package he had seen the man carrying earlier. He cut the string and opened the package to reveal a tiny human hand and then the mutilated torso of missing Marie Ellen Bailes. The head was almost decapitated where the throat had been cut; the child's legs and arms had been broken and fastened to the torso. Clothes had been torn from the body, a garment forced into the child's mouth. Detectives carried out extensive enquiries in both the Islington and Elephant and Castle areas tracing all London Transport staff at the local underground stations to try and find further witnesses that could remember the man with the brown paper parcel. The killer of this poor child was never identified.

30th – I Needed a New Suit

George James Newland, a twenty-one-year-old metal-caster who lived with his mother at Cogan Avenue, Walthamstow, needed a new suit. So he travelled down to Grosvenor Road, Orsett in Essex on 30 May 1953 to visit an elderly married couple he had previously befriended – Henry Tandy and his wife. Newland battered sixty-five-year-old Henry to death before stealing articles of property from the house. Detectives learnt of the 'friendship' between the Tandy's and Newland; when they visited Newland to ask him some questions regarding his relationship with the murdered man Newland admitted his guilt, allegedly telling the arresting officer, 'Yes, I did it. But I don't want mum to know. I was in a bit of trouble and I wanted some money badly to buy a new suit.' Newland was executed at Pentonville Prison on 23 December 1953.

31st – Killer With an Inferiority Complex

Former Greek soldier George Aspergis came to London, changed his surname to Anderson and met a young lady called Pauline Barker. The couple set up home at No. 184, Belsize Road, West Hampstead, where they lived together for ten years. By 31 May 1942, the relationship had deteriorated, George had been suffering from depression. He went into a local pub and told the landlord that he was going to commit a murder. He went back to Belsize Road and shot Pauline dead. He returned to the pub a while later and told the same landlord that he had done it and offered the revolver to him. George pleaded guilty to murder but while insane, his barrister adding in mitigation that the stress of a failed business in Ireland had left him with an inferiority complex. He was executed on 21 July 1942 at Pentonville Prison.

* * *

Exactly eleven years later on 31 May 1953, Alfred Charles Whiteway murdered two teenage girls on a towpath of the River Thames near Teddington Lock. The victims were sixteen-year-old Barbara Songhurst and eighteen-year-old Christine Reed. The two girls were last seen riding their bikes down the towpath about 11 a.m. Barbara was found the next day and Christine several days later. Both girls had been raped, beaten to death and thrown into the Thames. At the end of June 1953, Whiteway was arrested for the rape of one woman and the attempted rape of another on Oxshott Common. Whiteway carried a concealed axe in his coat, which he somehow managed to ditch in the police car as he was being driven to the police station. The axe wasn't discovered until weeks later when an officer cleaning out the car found it. The axe was forensically examined and linked not only to Whiteway but had traces of blood belonging to Songhurst and Reed. When confronted with the evidence he broke down and confessed to the murders. At his trial, he pleaded not guilty and said his confession had been a fabrication put together by the police. The jury took an hour to decide Whiteway's guilt and he was executed at Wandsworth Prison on 22 December 1953.

6

JUNE

1st – Stealing Another Man's Food

Scratchwood in Mill Hill, North London, lent its name to the
M1 motorway's most southerly services for many years. Long
before the M1 was built, Scratchwood was the scene of a
particularly nasty murder. Several wooden shacks stood deep in
the woods and were utilised by the homeless. On 1 June 1931, a
walker noticed a human body part extending from a smouldering
pile of rubbish: closer examination revealed it to be a charred
human arm. The arm was attached to the torso of a man who
had been brutally murdered. The victim was identified as Herbert
William Ayres, nicknamed 'Pigsticker', by a tattoo on his body.
Another occupant of the shacks informed detectives that he had
seen two men whom he knew only as 'Tiggy' and 'Moosh' beating
up 'Pigsticker' on the date in question. 'Tiggy', sixty-one-year-old
Oliver Newman, and 'Moosh', fifty-seven-year-old William Shelly,
were arrested by police and charged with the murder. The shacks
occupied by the two accused were searched – a bloodied axe was
concealed under the floor-boards of Newman's shelter. The axe
blade was consistent with the injuries inflicted on Ayres body. Both
admitted the murder, claiming they had caught Ayres stealing food
and gave him a good beating; when they realised they had killed
him they tried to destroy the evidence. Both men were executed on
5 August 1931 at Pentonville.

2nd – A Last Resort

Thirteen-year-old Nellie Else escaped being killed at the hands of her own father by the smallest of margins after he had cut the throats of Nellie's mum and younger sibling. William Else – a cab driver of No. 11 Jeffreys Street, Kentish Town – couldn't work after a career-changing accident in February 1891 in which he broke a leg and was unable to walk without the aid of sticks. He had some savings but with a wife and two children to support these soon ran out. On 2 June 1891, with the bodies of Nellie's mother and sister lying downstairs Else went into the room of his oldest daughter asking to feel her throat; luckily Nellie was wide awake and saw the bloodstained knife in her father's hand, slipped from his grasp and escaped to raise the alarm. Police searched the house and discovered the bodies of Else's wife and their youngest daughter Alice. William Else had committed suicide in the back garden.

3rd – Taking Flight

Pilot John Hall walked into West Ham Police Station on 3 June 1961 and told a police officer on the front desk that he had come to give himself up as he had seriously assaulted his wife, his mother and stepsister. The police officer asked Hall to empty his pockets and as he did so he produced a revolver and fired at the policeman, missing him narrowly, before running out of the police station pursued by several unarmed officers. Police Sergeant Frederick Hutchins patrolling in a car with another officer spotted the fugitive in Tennyson Road. Hutchins jumped out and wrestled Hall to the ground but Hall wriggled free and shot both officers – Sergeant Hutchins died of his injuries. Minutes later Police Inspector Philip Pawsey, on his way into work, saw Hall with the revolver in his hand and courageously attempted to arrest him but was also shot and killed. Hall continued his murderous spree, shooting at a police motorcyclist who dodged the bullets and escaped injury. The last sighting of Hall was as he turned onto Romford Road before disappearing. Later that night Hall contacted the *Sunday Express* newsroom from a call box on Wanstead Flats. The reporter managed to keep Hall on the phone and obtain his whereabouts, which he passed onto police. As police surrounded Hall, he shot himself and died of his injuries soon after.

4th – Pay Your Debts

On 4 June 2003, thirty-six-year-old You Yi He, a Chinese money-lender living in Mare Street, Hackney, visited China Town – an area of London he was very familiar with. Mr He was sitting in the BRB bar in Gerrard Street, Soho when a man, described by witnesses of oriental origin, entered the bar and shot Mr He twice. The victim was struck in the chest and hand and died of his injuries. Nobody has been convicted of You Yi He's murder. The murder was probably connected to an unpaid debt.

5th – A Woman Scorned ...

By 1913, the Women's Suffragette movement had progressed to a direct action phase with attacks on targets such as St Paul's Cathedral. On 5 June 1913, an arson attack on a cricket pavilion in Muswell Hill caused £1,000 worth of damage. The word 'Suffragette' first appeared in the *Daily Mail* newspaper on 10 January 1906 to distinguish the women who used direct action to campaign for the vote from the peaceful 'Suffragists' who used constitutional methods. The Suffragettes' leaders were Mrs Emmeline Pankhurst and her daughter Christabel.

6th – Memory Spots a Deserter

Miriam Deeley joined the Women's Auxiliary Air Force (WAAF) in 1942 and she was posted to the No. 1 Balloon Centre at RAF Kidbrooke, south-east London. Miriam obtained a weekend pass for 12–13 February 1944, which she spent with her fiancé at her family home in Wanstead, East London. Her fiancé worked at the Science Museum and escorted Miriam to Charing Cross Station on the Sunday night in order to return to her unit. Miriam missed her direct train to Kidbrooke and boarded an alternative service to Lewisham. Miriam's body was found alongside the track at Well Hall Station the following morning. She had been raped and strangled with her own scarf. Detectives traced witnesses who had seen Miriam in the company of a talkative soldier with an impressive set of medal ribbons. A description of the suspect was circulated and a sharp-eyed PC, Charles Memory, spotted a soldier of similar appearance in the company of a WAAF. He questioned the soldier and, not satisfied with his replies, detained him. The man's name was Ernest James Harman Kemp, a deserter from the British Army. When searched, he was found in possession of personal property belonging to Miriam Deeley and his boots matched boot marks found close to the crime scene.

Ernest Kemp was tried at the Old Bailey and found guilty of Miss Deeley's murder and executed on 6 June 1944 at Wandsworth Prison.

***

Also on this day in 1952, a short taxi ride ended in murder. John Godar and his girlfriend Maureen Cox got into a cab at Uxbridge Station, and within minutes the cab driver heard screams from the back of his vehicle. He stopped and found Cox lying on the vehicle floor – she had been stabbed by Godar in a frenzied attack resulting in over sixty wounds to her head, neck and chest. Godar rather bizarrely informed the cabbie, 'I think I have hurt her' and asked the driver to take him to a police station. During that initial short journey from Uxbridge Station, Cox told Godar she wanted to end their ten-month relationship as she had met somebody else. He was executed on 5 September 1952 at Pentonville Prison.

7th – Murder Kit

London's gay community has often been the target of disdain, intimidation and violence (*see* David Copeland 17 April). Colin Ireland targeted members of this community in 1993 and became one of London's most infamous serial killers. His first victim was theatre director Peter Walker – found strangled at his home in Vicarage Crescent, Battersea in early March 1993. Ireland carried a 'murder kit' that included a rope, handcuffs and a change of clothes. The day after each murder, he would contact the Samaritans or the media to inform them of his latest killing. He murdered again on 28 May, his victim librarian Christopher Dunn, and again on 4 June, an American sales director Peter Bradley. Both these men were picked up by Ireland in the Coleherne (renamed the Pembroke), a gay pub on Old Brompton Road. On 7 June 1993, his fourth and penultimate victim was housing supervisor Andrew Collier, who took Ireland back to his

Above: 32 Westbourne Terrace, where Ruby Bolton was murdered whilst her pimp husband slept – 13 Jan 1956. (Author's collection)

Below: 4 Bolton Crescent, where Rachel Samuel was beaten to death – 11 Dec 1878. (*Illustrated Police News*, 28th Dec 1878)

MURDER OF AN OLD LADY IN BURTON CRESCENT

Above: 75 Star Street where Harry Tuffney sank an axe into Edith Longshaw's head – 30 June 1934. (Author's collection)

Below: Walham Green police Station (now Fulham) where Rowland Duck gave himself up having slit his girlfriend's throat – 3 May 1923. (Kind permission of Peter Kennison)

Above: 'The Pentonville Murder' Lloyd Square – 19 Jan 1899. (*Illustrated Police News*, 28 Jan 1899)

Below: The Mitre Pub, Holland Park where the plot to rob Pope-Hennessey was hatched – 25 Jan 1974. (Author's collection)

Above: 9 Ladbroke Grove where Pope-Hennessey was battered and stabbed to death – 25 Jan 1974 (Authors collection)

Left: 'The Black Museum' showing the murder weapons used by retired Head teacher Rev Selby – 8 Oct 1871. (*Illustrated Police News*, 1890)

Above: 66 Redcliffe Square where Marilyn Bain killed lover Jean McVitie – 13 Sept 1962. (Author's collection)

Right: Vine Street Police Station where murderers George Barton – 22 Jan 1925 – and Bernard Pomeroy – 6 Feb 1923 (Executed 5 Apr 1923) gave themselves up. (Kind permission of Peter Kennison)

Above: View of Nevern Square, Earls Court where Thomas Baxter stabbed Jeremy Wingfield – 22 Feb 1970. (Author's collection)

Below: The first occasion fingerprint evidence secured a conviction. (*Grantham Journal*, 29 Apr 1905)

FINGER-PRINT EVIDENCE.

At the Tower Bridge Police-court, London, on Tuesday, Alfred and Albert Stratton, brothers, were committed for trial charged with the murder of Mr. and Mrs. Farrow, at an oilshop at Deptford. Inspector Collins, of the Finger-Print Department, Scotland Yard, said he took a photograph of the imprint of a digit found on the cash-box belonging to Mr. Farrow. At the police-station witness took digital imprints of Alfred, including the right thumb. Afterwards he compared the latter with the impression on the cash-box, and found it to agree wherever it was clear in eleven points.

Metropolitan Police
Assistant Commissioner
Melville McNaughton.
(*Police Encyclopedia Vol:V*,
Hargram Adam. Published
1920, Blackfriars)

Witnesses give evidence at
the coroner's inquest into
the death of William Terriss
(*Lloyds Weekly Newspaper*,
26 Dec 1897)

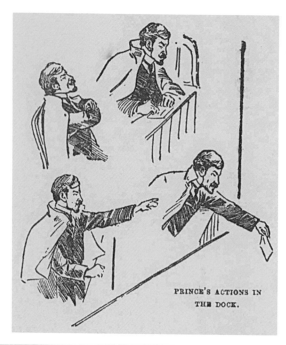

PRINCE'S ACTIONS IN
THE DOCK.

Left: Richard Prince in the dock of the Old Bailey for the murder of William Terriss. (*Lloyds Weekly Newspaper*, 16 Jan 1898)

Below: Memorial plaque to William Terriss above the Adelphi stage door. (Author's collection)

CITY OF WESTMINSTER

WILLIAM TERRISS
1847 - 1897

HERO OF THE ADELPHI
MELODRAMAS

MET HIS UNTIMELY END
OUTSIDE THIS THEATRE
16 DEC 1897

THE ADELPHI THEATRE CO. LTD

Above: The Coleherne Pub (now called Pembroke), Old Brompton Road where Colin Ireland selected two victims. (Author's collection)

Below: Broad Court Covent Garden where PC William Fitzgerald was savagely beaten to death – 23 Jan 1866. (Author's collection)

Above: The White Horse Pub where barman Paddy O'Keefe was slain – 14 June 1964. (Author's collection)

Below: The former business premises of Cartmell and Schlitte at 84, Shaftesbury Ave where Frederick Schlitte was shot and stabbed to death – 6 Jan 1908. (Author's collection)

Right: PC Comley who captured the Infamous 'Lambeth Poisoner' Dr Neil Cream. (*Illustrated Police News*, 1890)

Below: Montrose Place where Detective Jim Morrison was stabbed by a thief. (Author's collection)

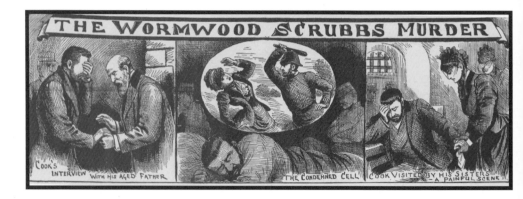

Above: PC George Cooke murders Maud Merton with his police truncheon on Wormwood Scrubs – 25 July 1893.

Below: Caxton Hall where former Governor of the Punjab, Michael O'Dwyer, was shot by Udam Singh – 13 March 1940. (Author's collection)

Above: Libyan People's Bureau, St James' Square, from which a bullet killed unarmed WPC Yvonne Fletcher – 17 April 1984. (Author's collection)

Below: Memorial to Yvonne Fletcher unveiled by Margaret Thatcher in 1985. (Author's collection)

Left: Field Marshal Henry Hughes-Wilson, gunned down by the IRA – 22 June 1922. (Author's collection)

Below: No. 36 Eaton Place where Henry Hughes-Wilson lived and was murdered. (Author's collection)

Above: Arlington Road Camden where Eugene de Vere battered Polly Walker to death on New Year's Day 1926. (Author's collection)

Below: The Angry Brigade Motif. (Author's collection)

Above: Banqueting Hall, Westminster, where Charles I was executed on 30 Jan 1649. The only case of regicide in British history. (Author's collection)

Below: No. 50 Onslow Square, Kensington, where Det Sgt Purdey was murdered by Gunter Podola – 13 July 1959. (Author's collection)

flat in Dalston; Ireland tied him up before strangling Collier with a noose. He then killed the victim's cat, placing the pet's mouth over Collier's penis and inserted its tail into his mouth. This sadistic behaviour followed newspaper reports that the killer was an animal lover when the telephone call following the first murder included concern for the welfare of the victim's dogs. Ireland left a single fingerprint mark at the Dalston crime scene. The final murder took place on 12 June – the victim a Maltese-born chef called Emmanuel Spiteri.

Detectives were able to trace the last movements of Spiteri, spotting him on CCTV at Charing Cross Station with his killer. The image was circulated throughout the media but, to the frustration of detectives, failed to generate the name of the killer. On 21 July 1993, Colin Ireland walked into a Southend solicitor's office asking for legal representation. He was transported to Kensington police station and admitted being the man in the CCTV image but denied being involved in the killings – unaware at this time of the single fingerprint the police had discovered in the fourth victim's flat. He was charged with and pleaded guilty to all five murders in December 1993 and received a sentence of life imprisonment with a recommendation that he never be released.

8th – An Evil Nephew

Printer William Standley and his wife Elizabeth lived in a flat above commercial premises at No. 13 Blackstock Road, Finsbury Park. The couple took in two lodgers to supplement their income. On the morning of 4 March 1933, William and the two lodgers left for work as usual. One of the lodgers returned at dinner time hoping to cadge a meal from Elizabeth. When he entered the flat he could find no sign of her and she failed to answer to her name when called. Now quite worried, he knocked on her bedroom door. Receiving no answer, he peered in and saw a pair of legs protruding from under the bed. He pulled the body out and saw it was Elizabeth: she had savage injuries to her head and a piece of wire flex tied securely around her neck. There was no sign of a break-in so police concentrated on the remaining lodger and husband William, both had solid alibis for the estimated time of death. The murder received extensive media coverage resulting in a bus conductor, Louis Zackis, coming forward with information that proved to be crucial. On the day in question, his bus was passing the murder scene when he saw a young man run from No. 13 Blackstock Road and jump onto his bus. Detectives by this time had turned their attention to Elizabeth's thirty-one-year-old nephew Jack Samuel Puttnam, who often quarrelled with Elizabeth over money and had stolen from her before. Jack was put on an identification parade and picked out by Zackis as the man he had seen leaving the house. Jack was charged with the murder of his aunt. He was tried at the Old Bailey and convicted and hanged for his crime at Pentonville Prison on 8 June 1933.

9th – A Bomb at a Student's Party

The headquarters of the Honourable Artillery Company on City Road became the target of a PIRA bomb on 9 June 1990; nineteen people were injured – but miraculously no fatalities. The year 1990 was an exceptionally prolific year for PIRA attacks on the mainland; leading up to this assault, they had already carried out six deadly attacks. This device targeted a student's twenty-first birthday celebrations; his father was a Territorial Army (TA) Captain. The bomb was placed on the function hall roof, left on a short timer of only one hour. Fatalities were avoided due to the roof structure withstanding the blast. Prime Minister Margaret Thatcher made a scathing attack on the terrorists:

> This is the IRA. They deliberately shoot women and children. They put bombs under a school bus. They detonate bombs at a cenotaph memorial service. They bomb Christmas shoppers and now they bomb a student's party. This should evoke contempt for the IRA throughout the whole of the United Kingdom and Republic of Ireland.
>
> (*The Times* 11 June 1990 p.1)

10th – A Dabbler in Stolen Property

Retired umbrella manufacturer John Goodman Levy lived at No. 31 Turner Street, Commercial Road, Whitechapel, with his faithful housekeeper Mrs Anna Sarah Gale. Levy was known to dabble a little in stolen property. On 4 April 1896, Levy himself became a victim of crime when his house was broken into, he and Anna Gale were murdered; their throats cut with such force resulting in near decapitation. Police had been called following reports of a stranger seen in the house. They discovered the bodies of the two occupants. Hearing a noise from the top floor they rushed upstairs saw a hole in the ceiling leading into the loft and out onto the roof. Shouts from outside the premises informed them somebody was indeed on the roof desperately attempting to escape arrest and were looking to jump. The man was William Seaman; he leapt 50 feet to the ground landing partially on a young female passer-by. Seaman was severely injured and taken to the London Hospital. When discharged, he was transferred directly to court appearing in front of magistrates confined to a chair as he couldn't walk. He admitted to police that he had killed Levy because the victim owed him £70. If he had paid up, he stated, he wouldn't have killed him; he did not appear to mention Sarah Gale. There was little doubt that Seaman would hang and the hangman duly obliged on 10 June 1896 in Newgate Prison.

11th – The Stink of Blood

Tobacconist Herbert Blades occupied his shop at No. 18 Hillside, Stonebridge, Willesden for many years. Nineteen-year-old Donald Brown of Chaplin Road, Wembley was a regular customer. On 11 June 1955, Brown was seen in the shop by a witness between 12.30 and 1.15 p.m. Sometime between the witness leaving the shop at 1.15 p.m. and Brown arriving at friend Tony Castle's house at 2 p.m., he stabbed Herbert Shields seven times in the back and the nape of the neck. When Brown arrived at Castle's house his friend noticed a nasty cut on this left hand covered by a rag, he asked how he got the injury Brown explained that he had 'done the old man in'. He instantly laughed, as if telling a joke, and retracted the admission explaining to Castle that he had cut his hand opening a bottle of beer with a knife. The two friends went to the cinema later that afternoon, on the way Brown again boastfully repeated that he had 'stabbed the old man and I have got plenty of money'. When leaving the cinema, Brown told Castle he had to go and buy some new clothes as the ones he had on 'stink of blood'. Castle went to the police and reported his suspicions, by this time Herbert Shields' body had been discovered with £30–£40 missing from the till. Staff at the cinema found the murder weapon – a bloodstained sheath knife – concealed under a seat in the auditorium. The rag on Brown's hand that he had discarded before leaving Castle's house was forensically linked back to the crime scene. Brown disappeared but tracked down two days later to a lodging house in Folkestone. He had swallowed over one-hundred aspirin, telling the doctor on arrival at the local hospital that he might as well die as he was 'going to be hanged anyway I stabbed a man in the back on Saturday'. Brown was tried for the murder and sentenced to death but was reprieved at the last moment. He committed suicide in prison in 1964.

12th – 'Murder'

'Murder' cried Alice Garrett from her home at No. 126, Old Church Road in Stepney, East London. Garrett lived with common-law husband William John Cronin. Cronin was an aggressive, violent man previously tried for murder in September 1897, but, due to the skill of his barrister, avoided the rope when convicted of the lesser charge of manslaughter. He served seven years penal servitude in Australia. By June 1925 – now aged fifty-four – Cronin was back in London working on the ships and boats of the Thames and living with Garrett. They had a volatile relationship and were often heard fighting and casting verbal abuse at each other. On the night of 12 June 1925, neighbours William and Rose Blanks heard Garrett's desperate screams of 'murder!'. William ran into the house and found Alice with 'her head hanging off'. Rose saw Cronin running from the house with a razor, dripping with blood, in his hand. No obsequious barrister was going to convince a judge and jury this time. Cronin was hanged at Pentonville Prison on 14 August 1925.

13th – A Loyal Housekeeper

The death of Eileen Mann is clouded in mystery. Eileen was a loyal thirty-three-year-old housekeeper for an elderly gentleman called Herbert White; they lived together at No. 189 Hampstead Road, London for a number of years. On 13 June 1956, Eileen Mann murdered her employer. Little of the murder features in the media of the day and Eileen does not appear on any subsequent record of trial or execution so one can only presume she was never charged with the inexplicable killing of Herbert White.

14th – It Went Off Accidently Officer

The White Horse Hotel (now the White Horse pub) on the junction of Archer Street and Rupert Street was a popular venue in the busy red-light district of Soho. Employed behind the bar was experienced Irish barman Paddy O' Keefe. On the night of 14 June 1964, O'Keefe was in the wrong place at the wrong time when a member of the Parachute Regiment, intent on making a few quid to take home, entered the bar shouting, 'This is a holdup. I want the money.' Armed with a revolver, purchased from another soldier for this very purpose, the robber pointed the weapon aggressively at anybody who looked like challenging him. Having watched the robber help himself to £47 from the till, O'Keefe confronted the armed man who without hesitation shot the barman at point-blank range before making his escape. The soldier was tracked down quickly by detectives. His name was Private Lawrence Winters. Winters claimed at his trial that the weapon had gone off accidently, an unlikely story from an experienced soldier competent in the handling of weapons. Winters escaped the rope for this cold-blooded killing just a year or so before the abolition of the death sentence in the United Kingdom. A medical examination from a psychiatrist confirmed the soldier suffered from violent psychopathic tendencies. Winters was found guilty of manslaughter on the grounds of diminished responsibility and sentenced to life imprisonment.

15th – A Terrible End for a True Heroine

Incredible acts of bravery by women can easily be forgotten in the male-dominated theatre of war. The actions of women, in particular those members of the Special Operations Executive (SOE), are often relegated to the back pages of history and few are household names. Christine Granville (born Krystyna Skarbek in Poland in 1908) was one such woman. Following the occupation of Poland by Germany, Christine offered her services to British Secret Intelligence Services (SIS) who sent her back to Poland and then onto Hungary and lastly France as an intelligence gatherer and organiser of resistance movements. She was captured by the Gestapo on a number of occasions but used skill and ingenuity to survive. Granville survived the war (sadly many of the SOE operatives didn't) having been awarded the George Medal, an OBE and a French *Croix de Guerre* for her valour. She was treated pretty shabbily by the British Government who offered her a 'desk job'. When she refused, she was dismissed with one month's pay.

Granville decided to take a job on an ocean liner as a stewardess where she met forty-one-year-old bathroom steward Dennis Muldowney who fell in love with Christine; these feelings, however, were not reciprocated. On returning to London, she took up rooms in the Shelbourne Hotel (now the Lexham Gardens Hotel) in Lexham Gardens, Kensington. On 15 June 1954, Granville was returning to the hotel and ascending the stairs to her room when Muldowney, waiting in the shadows, stabbed her in the chest with a long-bladed knife. She died where she fell. Muldowney was executed at Pentonville Prison for the murder of a woman he professed to love on 30 September 1954.

16th – Don't Dump Him During the Football
Latvian Anna Kurlilaityte told her Polish boyfriend, forty-four-year-old Henryk Piezynski, a former professional footballer, that she wanted to end their relationship as he watched a Germany v. Holland European football match in room 202 at the Britannia Hotel in London's Bayswater on 16 June 2005. Piezynski picked up a knife and stabbed her eight times. He was jailed for life.

17th – Just Six Minutes
On the morning of 17 June 1974, the Press Association received a short message from a man with an Irish accent stating that there was a bomb in Houses of Parliament; the message was not specific regarding an exact location but authenticated by a recognised PIRA code word. Police were in the process of evacuating the vast building when the bomb exploded in the oldest part of Parliament – the eleventh-century Westminster Hall – just six minutes after the coded warning had been received. The bomb injured eleven people and caused extensive damage to the fabric of the historical site. The year 1974 proved to be one of the bloodiest years during

PIRA's mainland campaign including the M62 coach bomb (eleven dead including eight soldiers and two children), Tower of London (one dead, forty-one injured), Guildford (two bombs in pubs – four killed), Brooks Club (three injured), Woolwich (two dead), Birmingham pub bombs (twenty-one killed, one-hundred and eighty-two injured). This year recorded the death of the 1,000th victim of 'The Troubles'.

18th – I Never Stopped Loving Her

Dressmaker Jane Youell was bored of lover Joseph Canning, a young soldier from Jersey. Unable to accept being rejected, Canning cut Jane's throat on 27 April 1895 in Bermondsey, South London. His confession proclaimed jealousy as his motive and that he had never stopped loving her and hoped to meet her again in heaven. Canning was executed on 18 June 1895 at Wandsworth Prison.

19th – Murdered at the Wheel

Michael Onkonko Zwoso, a minicab driver from Plumstead, was working the graveyard shift on 19 June 2010; he was murdered in his cab. The forty-nine-year-old father of two was found with head injuries in Cookhill Road, Abbey Wood. Robbery didn't seem to be the motive as valuables were still in the car. The case remains unsolved.

20th – A Highly Strung Thespian

Paul Acheton and his common-law wife Elizabeth Stoffel occupied a couple of rooms at No. 53 Whitfield Street, Tottenham Court Road. They had lived as husband and wife for little more than three months. Acheton was a part-time actor. Their relationship, according to neighbours, was a volatile one. They were often heard arguing loudly at all times of day and night. On 20 June 1891, Acheton had been out all afternoon drinking before returning home the worst for wear. A little later that evening Acheton knocked on the door of a neighbour and beckoned him into his bedroom to check on his wife. The neighbour, concerned for Elizabeth's safety, did so and saw Elizabeth lying motionless on the bed. Acheton had followed the neighbour into the bedroom armed with a lump of wood and was clearly drunk. Acheton then ushered the neighbour out of the room before he could examine Elizabeth more closely, not knowing if she were dead or alive, and immediately summoned a police officer. An officer attended the address but decided all seemed quiet apparently having not entered the bedroom to check on the welfare of Elizabeth.

The following morning a laundryman arrived at Acheton and Stoffel's flat. When he received no answer, he spoke to the neighbour who informed him of the previous night's events and his concern for the safety of Elizabeth. After failing to rouse either of the occupants, the laundryman summoned the police again who this time broke in. Stoffel was found lifeless on the bed where she had lain the night before; she had been badly beaten around the head and body. The murder weapon, a wooden table leg, lay beside her. A letter purporting to be from Paul Acheton lay near the body. He explained that he had a vague memory of fighting with his wife the night before and that he had been mad drunk but did not kill her and would give his life if it would bring her back. He made clear his intention to kill himself as he could not live without her. His body was found floating in the River Thames.

21st – A Terrible Death

Up to the year 1790, women convicted of high treason and petty treason faced the dreadful prospect of being burnt at the stake. There were many offences that constituted high treason, including clipping gold and silver coins in order to make other coins (a practice often called 'coining'), counterfeiting coins, colouring a silver coin to look gold or having possession of equipment to carry out any of these offences. Coining was considered an extremely serious offence (as a similar offence today would) where the very integrity and confidence in the coins of the realm could be compromised.

Phoebe Harris was arrested at her home in London's Covent Garden in February 1786 following the discovery of counterfeit coins and related equipment. She was charged and appeared at the Old Baily, convicted within one day and sentenced to death by burning at the stake. On 21 June 1786 at 8 a.m., Harris became the first woman to be executed at Newgate Prison in such a barbaric way. A crowd of over twenty thousand people witnessed her gruesome end.

22nd – *Survived the War, Killed by Terrorists*

Sir Henry Hughes Wilson, a courageous, highly decorated soldier, survived the First World War only to die at the hands of terrorists. On 22 June 1922, Sir Henry attended Liverpool Street Station, in full uniform including a ceremonial sword, to unveil a memorial to those fallen in the Great War. Sir Henry then travelled back to his home at No. 36 Eaton Place, Belgravia. As he stood at his front door with his back to the pavement, he was shot seven times by two members of the Irish Republican Army: Joseph O'Sullivan and IRA Commander Reginald Dunne. Gallant to the end, Wilson tried to fight his attackers off with his sword but fell mortally wounded on his own doorstep. The reason for his death was attributed to the fact he had recently been elected MP for North Down in Ulster and been anti-republican. O'Sullivan and Dunne were finally cornered by a mob, having shot two police officers, and would have been publicly lynched but for a large police response. They were executed at Wandsworth Prison later the same year. Their bodies were buried in the prison grounds until the 1990s when they were repatriated back to Ireland. Hughes-Wilson's memorial can be seen at Liverpool Street Station next to the one he unveiled on the morning of his cowardly murder.

23rd – *Never Trust a Lodger*

Caretaker Louise Bertha Gann trusted Allan James Grierson enough to allow him to lodge with her and her daughter Maxine, with whom he was romantically involved, at No. 19 Gloucester Place near London's Regents Park. On 7 June 1935, Grierson betrayed that trust by stealing items from the flat. He didn't return for a number of days but wrote a letter to Mrs Gann expressing remorse for his crimes; she forgave him and he was allowed to return. A few weeks later Grierson told Maxine and Louise that he had at last got a job as a car salesman and wanted to take them on holiday to thank them for their understanding and support. On 23 June 1935, he arranged to meet Louise and Maxine at Marble Arch after the latter had finished work. His real intention was to get both out of the flat and steal anything of value before disappearing for good. However, his plan nose-dived when Louise decided to stay at home to prepare for the trip.

Grierson, surprised by her presence in the house, beat her viciously before disappearing. Louise was found unconscious by Maxine who returned home when Grierson failed to pick her up. Louise Gann died the following day.

The murder investigation revealed Grierson had a history of conning young women in the past. A nationwide hunt for the killer was launched with the assistance of the media who circulated Grierson's description. Several days later Grierson was identified as the wanted fugitive by a local man working for a lady called Mrs Church in Weybridge, Surrey. Mrs Church, it seems, was to be the killer's next victim. Grierson was charged with the murder of Louise Gann and tried for his crime. He was executed at Pentonville Prison on 30 October 1935.

*　*　*

Former Belgian army officer Pierre Neukermans was invalided out of the forces in 1938. He settled in Brussels, working for his father-in-law. When the Germans invaded Belgium during the Second World War, Neukermans was recruited as a German spy and sent to London via Lisbon in July 1943. He was interviewed on entry to Britain claiming he had escaped from Belgium, with the help of others, and wanted to do his bit for the allied cause. Six months later the British Security Services established that the man who helped Neukermans escape was a SS spy. Neukermans was interrogated and admitted sending details of British convoys back to German intelligence. He was convicted of spying and executed at Pentonville on 23 June 1944.

24th – A Murderous Temper
Married couple Jacob and Emma Hill were in the White Lion pub on the afternoon of 24 June 1893. Jacob was a porter who worked in nearby Covent Garden. They lived in rooms in Clare Market, Portugal Street, Holborn. During the afternoon drinking session Emma, who had a sharp temper, unleashed a verbal tirade against her mild-mannered husband. When they reached home later that evening, they had further words. Jacob, knowing his wife's foul-temper could not be abated, decided to leave the building, but

that wasn't going to stop the spousal wrath; Emma followed. A passer-by, Thomas Williams, witnessed what happened next:

I am a plasterer's labourer, and live at 10, King's Place, High Street, on 24th June, about quarter to seven; I was walking along Portugal Street, near King's College Hospital. I noticed the prisoner and a woman together, the woman was in the roadway and the prisoner was standing on the pathway. They were about four paces apart, walking along talking; I could not hear what they said. They were not talking sharp to one another; I did not hear any quarrel. I saw him lift up his right hand, take two paces in front, and stab her in the left side of her breast with a clasp knife; he had the knife up his sleeve all the time. He said, 'Now I have done it, you b——cow, give me in charge.' The woman had nothing in her hand—I did not see her raise her hand at all before the blow was struck. I ran to the Law Courts for a constable, when I came back they had moved on fifty or sixty yards; when the constable came up the prisoner ran through the archway—I helped the woman to the hospital.

(*Old Bailey Online*)

Other witnesses gave evidence of a furious argument between the two with Emma hitting Jacob several times and an exchange of filthy language. Emma was taken to nearby Kings College Hospital and died from her injuries the next day. During his trial, Jacob Hill produced witnesses to the fact that his wife had been extremely violent to him for many years. Hearing that Jacob was a man of previous good character, the jury found him guilty of manslaughter; he was sentenced to six months hard labour.

25th – Another Ripper

The pseudonym 'Ripper' has not only been synonymous with infamous and undetected nineteenth-century killer 'Jack' but also other killers of a similar ilk: 'Yorkshire Ripper' (Peter Sutcliffe) and Gordon Frederick Cummins the 'Blackout Ripper' who murdered four women in war-torn London in 1942. Cummins was a Leading Aircraftsman in the Royal Air Force on a short-term training course based in Regents Park in February 1942. Cummins took advantage of the blackout in London to murder four women and attempt to murder two more over a period of just six days. The first killing was pharmacist Evelyn Hamilton, discovered in an air-raid shelter in Montagu Place; she had been strangled. The following day, the body of Evelyn Oatley was discovered in her flat on Wardour Street: she had been strangled, mutilated and sexually abused with a can-opener. The following day, Cummins returned to Marylebone and murdered prostitute Margaret Lowe whom he strangled with a silk stocking and abused with a candlestick. The following night, 12 February 1942, his final victim was married Doris Jouannet in a flat that she shared with her husband. His reign of terror would come to an end on Friday 14 February when he attempted to murder Greta Hayward in a doorway near Piccadilly Circus but was disturbed in the act. A short time later, obviously frustrated by his earlier failure, he attacked a second woman, a prostitute called Kathleen King, in her flat near Paddington Station but she fought him off. During his haste to escape from the first failed attack he left his RAF gas mask, which had a unique issue number imprinted on the inside rim. Detectives discovered the identity of Cummins through the gas mask and arrested him on 16 February 1942, seizing personal tokens belonging to the victims that he had kept as trophies. Cummins' fingerprints were found at two of the crime scenes and on the can-opener used to abuse the second victim Evelyn Oatley.

Cummins' trial was concluded in one day, the jury took thirty-five minutes to convict him and he was sentenced to death. Cummins was executed on 25 June 1942 at Wandsworth Prison, ironically during an air raid.

26th – Dodgy Dumplings

Housemaid Elizabeth Fenning was convicted of the attempted murder of three members of the same family, by poisoning their dumplings. In 1815, Fenning was housemaid to the Turner family: Oribar, his wife Charlotte and their son Robert. Fenning had been severely reprimanded by Charlotte over a small misdemeanour. A few days later, Fenning cooked up some strange looking dumplings, which she served for dinner; all the family ate the dumplings including Fenning herself. All four became very ill but survived. When the dumpling mix was tested, it was found to contain arsenic. Fenning appeared before the Old Bailey on 11 April 1851 charged with feloniously administering arsenic with the intent to murder. Of course, her defence focused on the fact that she had eaten the dumplings herself and indeed suffered serious illness. A number of character witnesses appeared on her behalf but the judge's summing-up swayed strongly towards the prosecution and against Fenning. She was found guilty and sentenced to death. An appeal followed a large swell of public support for Fenning, but she was hanged on 26 June 1851. She swore her innocence until her very last breath.

27th – Also Known as Percy

Single parent Amy Eugenie Russell had a fourteen-year-old child; they both lived in lodgings at No. 33 Railton Road, Brixton. Amy was courting Ernest Walter Wickham, also known as Percy. Wickham would often return home to the lodgings drunk and disorderly. At 1.15 a.m. on 27 June 1901, Police Sergeant William Goode saw Wickham and Russell arguing in Josephine Avenue, Brixton Hill. Goode went up to them and advised them to be quiet and go home. A few minutes later, a witness, living at No. 60 Dalberg Road, Brixton, heard a shout for help. He looked out of his window and saw a man running away from a woman bleeding profusely from a wound to her throat that had been savagely cut. The witness and his wife tried to stem the flow of blood from the victim but Amy Russell died on the street. Wickham approached a small coffee shop on the corner of Atlantic Road and Brixton Road, five minutes from the murder scene. When serving Wickham with a coffee, the proprietor noticed that his hands and clothing were covered in blood. Police officers were in close pursuit, following a blood trail the short distance from Dalberg Road via the coffee shop where they spoke to the proprietor and onto Santley Street where they found Wickham asleep. Wickham's hands were bloodstained, and his discarded blood-soaked outer clothes and boots lay nearby, together with the murder weapon, his brother's cut-throat razor. Wickham was executed at Wandsworth on 13 August 1901.

28th – Swallow This!

Jewish umbrella maker and salesman Israel Lipski was the only suspect in the murder of a young woman forced to swallow nitric acid. When police arrived at No. 16 Batty Street, Commercial Road, East London on 28 June 1887, alerted by neighbours who heard the screams of the victim, they discovered the body of Miriam Angel. Hidden under the bed was the upstairs lodger, Israel Lipski; he too had acid burns around his mouth but not to the same degree as the deceased. Lipski always denied the murder of Miriam but crucially, for the prosecution, the police could prove Lipski had purchased nitric acid prior to the murder. The motive was thought to be sexual.

Lipski had little chance of a fair trial or escaping the hangman's noose; the judge, Mr Justice Stephen, was openly anti-Semitic throughout the course of the trial. He was convicted and, while awaiting his appointment with the hangman, cleared his conscience by admitting he *did* kill Miriam but the motive was robbery rather than rape. He was executed on 21 August 1887.

* * *

Frederick Robinson, his wife and three children moved into the lower floor of a maisonette at No. 12 Saratoga Road, Lower Clapton in early June 1913, appearing to be a very happy family. Within three weeks, Robinson's wife was admitted to the Homerton Infirmary suffering from a mental breakdown. The children – twins Frederick Ernest and Nellie Kathleen and their baby sister nine-month-old Beatrice Maud – were left in the care of their father. Occasionally, the upstairs neighbour kept an eye on the children. On the afternoon of 28 June 1913, Frederick went out, while the children played outside for most of the afternoon. When Frederick returned, he told the neighbour that the children would be going to the Salvation Army, the following morning, to be cared for as he couldn't cope anymore.

Within a couple of weeks, Frederick moved out of No. 12 Saratoga Road. Towards the end of July, the neighbour complained to the landlord of a foul smell emanating from the lower floor still unoccupied since Robinson's departure. When the landlord checked the property, he found the bodies of the three Robinson children concealed under the floorboards behind some recently constructed brickwork. This was the beginning of a difficult prosecution for the

Crown. Robinson told the court at his trial that the children had all died of natural causes, blaming meningitis. The pathologist stated that the bodies were in such an advanced stage of putrefaction that he could not conclude, without doubt, the cause of death but believed it to be violent asphyxia. The jury listened carefully to the inconsistencies of Robinson's story: the children were in perfect health when last seen by the neighbour and Robinson hadn't at any time enquired with or handed over the care of the children to the Salvation Army. Robinson was convicted of the murder of his three young children and executed on 27 November 1913.

29th – Armed with a Bayonet Just in Case

Raymond Jack Cull, twenty-two, married his childhood sweetheart, Jean, when she was just sixteen. Three months into the marriage, problems emerged. Raymond heard rumours that Jean had been seeing somebody else, an affair that had started before the marriage took place. Jean packed her bags and moved back to her father's house. Cull went around to Shadwell Drive, Northolt on 29 June 1952 to talk to Jean. He armed himself with a bayonet in case Jean's father interfered. When he arrived, Jean told Raymond that she couldn't abide jealousy (even if there was some element of truth to the rumours) and that she wasn't going to go back with him. Raymond lost control and stabbed his wife with the bayonet. Raymond Cull was executed at Pentonville Prison on 30 August 1952.

30th – Not a Happy Ending

Harry Tuffney, a thirty-six-year-old motor mechanic, and his girlfriend, twenty-eight-year-old Edith Longshaw, lodged in a flat at No. 75 Star Street, Paddington. Harry had ideas of a perfect wedding, a family and living happily ever after. Edith, however, wasn't like-minded, still wanting to enjoy herself; she liked to date other men and had no intention of settling down to married bliss. The final straw was the discovery of a letter to another man, written by Edith, suggesting she may leave Harry in the near future. During the late evening and early morning of 29/30 June 1934, Harry sat in their lounge drowning his sorrows in the bottom of a bottle of whiskey, Edith had retired to bed. Harry decided if he could not have Edith then no other man would, picked up an axe and sank it into his sleeping girlfriend's head. He would later tell police that he tried to gas himself following the murder before walking into Marylebone Lane Police Station and confessing he had 'killed my girl'. The only chance to save Harry from the rope was a defence of insanity. The defence relied heavily on his medical history during his military career, informing the court that he received shrapnel injuries to his head during direct action and another incident in which he killed three Egyptians during an uprising. There were conflicting medical reports: the Harley Street specialist for the defence found Harry far from sane but the prison doctor could find no such insanity. The jury took little time in convicting Harry and he was executed at Pentonville Prison on 20 September 1934.

* * *

Frederick Field was questioned in relation to the death of prostitute Nora Upchurch, murdered in the basement of an empty shop at No. 173–9 Shaftesbury Avenue on 2 October 1931. The police had insufficient evidence to charge him until he made a full confession to the murder in a newspaper. He was arrested and interviewed but his description of the murder, including his professed *modus operandi,* did not tally with the facts. Detectives, keen to clear a case of murder from their books, charged Field. He stood trial but withdrew his confession, with little other evidence the judge directed the jury to acquit the defendant. In 1936, Field decided to join the Royal Air Force but soon deserted; when he was detained he confessed to a second murder of a prostitute. Beatrice Sutton had been found strangled in her flat at Elmhurst Mansions, Elmhurst Road, Clapham on 4 April 1936. This time detectives made sure the confession was much more substantive, asking Field to describe the method of death, the inside of the flat and what the victim looked like. At his trial, he again attempted to withdraw the confession but the case was put to the jury to decide and, they convicted Field. He was executed at Wandsworth Prison on 30 June 1936.

7

JULY

1st – Substitute Shot

Engineering student Madan Lal Dhingra was born into an affluent family in British-ruled India. He was sent to England to study during which time his extremist, revolutionary views came to the fore. He studied his subject by day and by night mixed with activists in London's India House, receiving instruction on the use of firearms and explosives. On 1 July 1909, the Indian National Association had organised a gathering of many Indians and Anglo-Indians at the Imperial Institute in Kensington. The Secretary of State for India, John Morley, was expected to attend but withdrew at the last moment, replaced by Sir Curzon Wylie, a former Indian army officer and an official of the British Indian Government. As Wylie entered the hall, he was shot four times by Dhingra – killing him instantly. Two further shots fatally injured a young Parsee doctor called Cowasji Lalkaka, who had bravely attempted to wrestle the gun from the assassin. Dhingra made no attempt to escape. He was arrested and charged with murder, appearing at the Old Bailey within two weeks of the incident. He refused any legal aid, representing himself; the trial lasted just one day, where he was sentenced to death. Dhingra left a message to be released following his execution on 17 August 1909:

> I believe that a nation held down by foreign bayonets is in a
> perpetual state of war. Since open battle is rendered impossible

to a disarmed race, I attacked by surprise. Since guns were denied to me I drew forth my pistol and fired. Poor in wealth and intellect, a son like myself has nothing else to offer to the mother but his own blood. And so I have sacrificed the same on her altar. The only lesson required in India at present is to learn how to die, and the only way to teach it is by dying ourselves. My only prayer to God is that I may be re-born of the same mother and I may re-die in the same sacred cause till the cause is successful.

2nd – *Murderers with Style*

In the early 1950s, Clapham Common gang 'The Plough Boys' – named after the nearby Plough Inn at No. 196 Clapham High Street – would often loiter in the area wearing the latest Edwardian style clothes: typically, long jackets, white shirts, ties, tapered trousers and shoes with thick crepe soles known as creepers; the look was completed with greased back hair and long sideburns. They were known as Spivs, Cosh Boys or Creepers – the cult term, Teddy Boys was yet to be coined. On 2 July 1953, a large number of The Plough Boys were on Clapham Common enjoying some live music. Nearby, four youths from another area sat antagonistically on benches with their feet outstretched talking to each other, they were John Beckley (17), Frederick Chandler (18), Brian Carter and one other. A fifteen-year-old Plough Boy called Ronald Coleman walked through the group provocatively. One of the group reacted to Coleman's action by telling him to 'Walk around the other way you flash c*nt.' Sensing that there may well be trouble and the fact they were outnumbered, the four decided to make a move but were chased by the Plough Boys and attacked. One of the pursuing Plough Boys was heard to shout 'Get the knives out'. Two of the fleeing group escaped the other two. Beckley and Chandler thought they were safe jumping on a No. 137 bus. As the bus inched forward into traffic, several members of the Plough Boys caught up and pulled Beckley and Chandler off and stabbed them repeatedly. Chandler, stabbed in the groin, managed to scramble back onto the platform of the bus. Beckley, badly injured, ran a few yards towards Clapham Old Town, slumping down on the pavement outside an apartment block called Okeover Manor.

Beckley was again attacked and received further stab wounds that would prove fatal.

Six men were charged with the murder of John Beckley (who had received seven stab wounds to his back and neck) including the gang leader Ronald Coleman and Michael John Davies. Lack of evidence against the other four led to just Coleman and Davies standing trial at the Old Bailey. The jury could not reach a unanimous decision and were discharged. The Crown decided not to proceed with the case against Coleman but went for a retrial against Davies. A witness on the top deck of the bus described Davies as being the main protagonist wearing a gaudy coloured tie and wielding a green handled knife. A similar tie was seized from Davies with the rest of his clothing on the night of his arrest. The identification was weak, the main witness only identifying Davies from the witness box at the magistrate's court. Davies was surprisingly convicted and sentenced to death. A public outcry surrounding the reliability of the identification evidence and the possibility of a miscarriage of justice forced the home secretary's hand, Davies was reprieved ninety-two days after sentence and given a custodial term; he was released in 1960.

During the media coverage of the investigation and trial, Ronald Coleman was referred to as the leader of the 'Edwardians', a teenage gang who wore eccentric suits. Shortly after the word Edwardians got shortened by the *Daily Express* to 'Teddy', giving birth to the generic name 'Teddy Boys'.

3rd – *You Have Your Wish George*
George Marshall, a forty-five-year-old barman, and Alice Anderson lodged at No. 70 Mina Road, Walworth. On 3 July 1915, following an argument, George stabbed Alice with a knife. Alice managed to escape but collapsed in a corridor of the property where she was found in her blood-soaked nightdress; she died of her injuries. In a statement, made at the police station just after his arrest, George Marshall told police that 'my misery is finished. I took out the knife and slashed her. I did it properly and am ready for the scaffold. I want to pay the penalty.' And so he did; George Marshall was executed at Wandsworth Prison on 17 August 1915.

4th – A New Life

Grocer John Thomas Gregory separated from his wife in Devon and came up to London to start a new life running a wine store/off licence at No. 62 Colindale Avenue, Hendon, North London. Gregory lived in Ealing but commuted daily to his place of work. Before licensing laws changed pubs as well as off licenses had to close between 2.30 and 5.30 p.m.; this was an opportunity for Gregory to relax in a backroom.

On 4 July 1919, a little after 5.30 p.m., two young ladies were passing the store and heard what they described as a fight taking place in the premises, they peered through the window and saw a young man viciously assaulting John Gregory. They described a bloodbath with splashes of blood dripping down the window pane through which they peered. Police were called and on their arrival broke into the premises to find Gregory lying on the floor with severe injuries to his head; he died shortly after. A number of blood-covered weapons were recovered including a poker and two bottles. Detectives also found a suitcase inscribed with the initials 'J. W. B'. A description of the killer was circulated; robbery was soon dismissed as a motive as the takings from the morning's business were still in the shop's till. A number of witnesses came forward following the appeal, one stating they had seen a man matching the description on a bus in Golders Green – covered in blood. Another witness informed detectives that on a previous day he had seen Gregory with the described man boarding a bus and travelling south; Gregory alighted at Edgware Road, with the suspect carrying onto Tottenham Court Road where he entered the YMCA. Police followed up the enquiry with the YMCA and identified a suspect whose initials matched those on the suitcase left at the crime scene. This man was eliminated from the enquiry but informed detectives he had lent his suitcase to an associate called Arthur John Biggin. Biggin was traced and arrested and charged with the murder. When he appeared for his trial, he admitted being responsible for the attack, but only in self-defence as Gregory had propositioned him for sex, he fought him off fearing for his own life. Much was made of the fact that Biggin had received no injuries during the struggle and things were not looking good for the young man until a police officer from Devon gave evidence, on behalf of the defence, that John Gregory had been a suspected predatory homosexual in Devon before moving to London. This revelation obviously gave more credence to Biggin's story and saved him from the rope, the jury found Biggin guilty of manslaughter; he was given twelve months hard labour.

5th – Death in the Park

Second World War Reserve PC Jack William Avery served less than one year with the Metropolitan Police before he was murdered in Hyde Park on 5 July 1940. The twenty-eight-year-old officer was patrolling his beat when approached by a member of the public who reported a suspicious-looking man in the vicinity. As Avery approached the suspect, he was stabbed in the groin and died of his injuries in St Mary's Hospital, Paddington. The killer, Frank Stephen Cobbett, was of no fixed abode. He was charged and convicted of Avery's murder but following an appeal, the conviction was downgraded to one of manslaughter, for which he served fifteen years penal servitude. A belated but welcome memorial to Jack Avery was unveiled by Commissioner of the Metropolitan Police Sir Ian Blair in 2007 at the spot the constable fell.

6th – Your Mug is Everywhere Mate

Cecil Court, Covent Garden is an intimate, pedestrianised shopping paradise for collectors of militaria, medals, books, prints and antiques. The small shops may have changed name and ownership over the years but not purpose. In 1961, No. 23 Cecil Court was an antique and curio shop owned by Louis Meier and managed by Marie Gray. On the morning of 3 March 1961, both Meir and Gray were at auctions purchasing further stock, leaving the shop in the capable hands of part-time employee Elsie May Batten, who took the job to fill her lonely weeks – her husband was renowned sculptor Mark Batten who spent most of his working week in his Sussex studio. Elsie opened the shop at the usual time and was seen arranging a display outside. When Louis Meier returned to the shop at midday, he found it insecure and Elsie missing. Concerned, he searched the premises and found Elsie Batten's body in a back stockroom. She had an 18-inch dagger jutting from her chest, another from her neck, and had initially been hit over the head with a vase that lay bloodstained near her body.

The crime scene yielded clues to the murderer, a bloody partial footprint from a man's shoe stained the carpet nearby. Questioning of other shop owners provided a description of a young Indian -looking man seen entering the shop just after Elsie had opened up – in fact he had visited other shops previously that morning enquiring about dress swords. The police used, for the first time in an active investigation, a technique called an *Identikit* where a likeness of a suspect could be compiled by a witness using different pictures of facial features. The *Identikit* picture was circulated to all police officers in the area. A local officer, PC Cole, while patrolling along Old Compton Street five days after the murder, armed with his copy of the *Identikit* image, noticed a young man who appeared a good likeness. The suspect's name was Edwin Albert Bush described at the time as Eurasian. Bush was picked out on identification parades by witnesses. Of course, that would put him at the murder scene at the time in question but not convict him of murder. Detectives resorted to more traditional methods to prove the suspect's guilt, matching his shoeprint to that found near the body in a part of the shop customers would not have access to. Bush admitted the murder, which he committed in order to steal a sword.

At his trial at the Old Bailey in May 1961, he tried to suggest that Mrs Batten had made inappropriate racial remarks against him about the colour of his skin, to which he had reacted. He was found guilty and after a failed appeal on 6 July 1961 became the last man ever to be hanged at Pentonville Prison.

7th – A Waiting Game

Grace Newing lived with her mother at No. 28 Stevens Road, Chadwell Heath. Newing, a shop assistant, was pregnant with boyfriend Robert Kirby's baby. Late evening on 6 July 1933, Kirby came around to Stephens Road to wait for seventeen-year-old Grace to come home; he sat in the kitchen with Grace's mother, Rosina, and her young son, Grace's brother. At 10.45 p.m. Rosina retired to bed leaving Kirby downstairs. When Grace returned home at 11.30 p.m., the couple talked into the early hours of the morning of 7 July, when it seems Kirby wanted sex and Grace refused. Rosina was awoken by a disturbance and the front door slamming shut, she went downstairs to discover her daughter had been strangled with a piece of cord. Kirby went to his parents' house a few streets away in Valence Circus, Dagenham and confessed to his brother and mother that he had murdered Grace. Kirby made a statement to police that Grace had pleaded with him to kill her and he obliged. He was convicted of her murder and executed on 11 October 1933.

* * *

Another spy executed on this day in 1942 at Wandsworth Prison was Jose Estella Key, who spied for the Germans. He had been tasked by German intelligence to record and pass on movements of British land troops, warships and aircraft in and around Gibraltar.

8th – It's the Removal Man

We return to Dagenham for our next crime. John and Florence Pearce had been happily married and lived with their young children at No. 131 Crescent Road, Dagenham, until an illness changed John for the worse. He became paranoid that his wife Florence was having an affair with a local removal man. He would accuse her of seeing other men and often come home at unusual times in order to catch his wife out. With little trust, the marriage approached breaking point. Florence's sister-in-law, a frequent caller at the address, visited on the afternoon of 8 July 1954. She heard her brother making spurious accusations against Florence. After dinner that evening, the children had been put to bed. Florence's sister-in-law was upstairs when she heard screaming coming from the kitchen: she rushed downstairs but found the kitchen door locked. She summoned neighbours who rushed around to the back garden to find Florence slumped up against the garden fence – she had been stabbed several times. John had locked himself in the kitchen where he attempted suicide by cutting his wrists and throat. Florence's injuries proved fatal but John survived. He was later found to be insane and detained in a mental institution.

9th July – Got Him the Second Time

Iraqi military officer and former premier Abdul Razzaq Al-Naif was assassinated outside the Inter-Continental Hotel, Park Lane, Mayfair on 9 July 1978. The hotel doorman courageously chased and caught the killer. Al-Naif was a former general who became prime minister for two weeks in 1968 following a bloodless coup; when ousted he fled the country in 1971 and was tried and sentenced to death in *absentia*. A previous assassination attempt in 1972, in which his wife was injured, failed. His killer Salem Ahmed Hassan was tried at the Old Bailey and convicted of the murder and imprisoned for life in 1979.

10th – No Title, Just a Rope

Canadian professional boxer Raymond Henry Bousquet, who fought under the name of Del Fontaine, arrived in England to further his fighting career. Although married with a family back in Canada, he started a relationship with a young girl called Hilda Meeks. On 10 July 1935, Bousquet walked in on a conversation at Meeks' family home in Aldred Road, Kennington, and found she was making arrangements with another man. He ripped the phone from her hand, threatened the man on the other end of the line, slammed the phone down and removed a revolver from his pocket. He shot Meeks in the back as she fled onto the street before turning the gun on her mother, who had run into the room to protect her daughter. When Hilda's father Sam returned home, he saw Bousquet carrying the body of his daughter back into the house telling Sam that 'I've done for her and done for the old woman'. In fact, Hilda's mother survived the attempt on her life. During his trial for murder, he attempted to convince the jury that he was 'punch drunk' from his boxing career, therefore not guilty of murder due to diminished responsibility. The jury dismissed this and convicted him of murder.

When the date of execution was fixed, many people, including members of Parliament, protested against the sentence, demanding it be commuted to life imprisonment. On 29 October 1935, Bousquet was executed at Wandsworth Prison as hymns were sung and speeches made by the great and good of society. No reference was made to victim Hilda Meeks, shot in the back as she ran for her life.

11th – A New Life in the South

Ronald Bertram Mauri, a powerfully built thirty-two-year-old lorry driver from Nottingham, was a married man but separated. In 1945, he met a woman called Vera Guest, who was a lot younger. They decided the age gap was irrelevant and started a new life in the south of England, lodging with Mauri's sister in Denecroft Crescent, Hillingdon. A few weeks later, Vera Guest was strangled. Mauri was the main suspect; he was arrested and charged. During his trial, he came up with a most bizarre defence. He told the jury that on the morning of 11 July 1945, he confessed to Vera that he had been arrested for the theft of a quantity of cigarettes but was in fact innocent. Because of the shame he felt he would bring to her and her family, he wanted to kill himself. Vera, he claimed, had pleaded him to take her with him, but he refused, so she began throwing herself around the kitchen in order to cause self-harm and hit her head on the gas stove, falling to the ground in a heap. Mauri thought her dead but wasn't sure. Rather than call for help he tied a scarf around her neck, dragged her into the front room, where he left her. He told the jury he had never intended to kill her. Mauri was convicted and executed at Wandsworth Prison on 31 October 1945.

12th – A Belgian Wheeler Dealer

Before the Nazi invasion of Belgium in May 1940, Joseph Van Hove was a wheeler and dealer of black-market products in Belgium's criminal underworld and well known to the police. When the Germans invaded, many Belgians fled their country, a number escaping to the United Kingdom, but Van Hove decided to stay and take advantage of the business opportunities the situation offered him. He was recruited by German intelligence; his assignments included the gathering of intelligence on French and Belgian labourers working for German occupation forces in the airfields of Northern France. In 1944, now well established in the German intelligence network, he was tasked to enter the United Kingdom on spying missions; he travelled to England via Sweden. British Security Services had received information about Van Hove and were expecting him; he was allowed to enter Britain but immediately arrested and charged with spying. He was tried at the Old Bailey in May and executed at Pentonville Prison on 12 July 1944.

13th – Last Man to Hang for Killing a Cop

Following a burglary in Kensington in July 1959, the female victim received a telephone call in which the caller purported to be the burglar. He claimed to have several compromising photographs of the victim, which he would make public unless she paid him a substantial amount of money. The victim notified the police at Chelsea and a trap was set for the offender. Detectives identified the calls were being made from a public telephone box outside South Kensington Station. The victim was asked to keep the caller on the phone as long as she could the next time he rang. She was again contacted on 13 July 1959 and kept the offender on the line for a long enough period for two detective sergeants, John Sandiford and Raymond Purdey, to arrive at the phone box and arrest the blackmailer. As they marched him away towards Chelsea Police Station, the man wrestled free and ran into Onslow Square; taking refuge in the lobby of an apartment block at No. 50 Onslow Square. The detectives followed him in and again took him into their custody but failed to search him. Sandiford went to get assistance leaving Purdey to guard him, the offender drew a revolver from a jacket pocket and shot Purdey through the heart, who died instantly.

Detectives had no idea of the identity of the fugitive who had killed one of their own until they received an enormous slice of luck wrapped up in the tragedy. When Purdey's personal belongings were returned to his wife she discovered a diary, and informed detectives that her husband never carried one – the diary belonged to the killer. Purdey, following the arrest of the blackmailer in the phone box, had picked up the diary, in which the offender had recorded the number of his victim in, and placed it into his own pocket. From details in the diary, police were able to identify the killer as German-immigrant Gunther Podola. He was eventually arrested in a local hotel. He was tried for the murder of Raymond Purdey; his execution on 5 November 1959 would be the last execution to take place in the United Kingdom for the murder of a police officer.

14th – Divine Info

A local vicar informed Hampstead police of a man soliciting young men to commit acts of gross indecency in the area. From the description given, officers identified the culprit as former army captain Richard Howard Gorges. Aware of his military antecedents, two local detectives – DC Alfred Young and DS Arthur Askew – gained entry to Gorges' house, No. 1 Mount Vernon, Holly Hill, Hampstead, on 14 July 1915, in order to take possession of a legally registered firearm while Gorges was drinking in a local pub. The officers seized a service revolver and 197 rounds of ammunition. Later that evening, Gorges returned home having been drinking heavily all day and discovered his firearm missing. Young and Askew returned to the address to interview the former army officer regarding the allegations made against him, confident that he had no access to a firearm. As they entered the address, Gorges took out a second revolver from his back pocket and shot DC Young at point-blank range. Askew managed to overpower Gorges and detained him. DC Young, who died of his injuries, survived a similar life-threatening situation earlier in his police career in 1909 receiving the King's Police Medal for bravery. He lost his wife a few years earlier; his death orphaned his six-year-old daughter.

At his Old Bailey trial, Gorges was acquitted of murder on the basis that he was so drunk he could not have formed the *malice aforethought* – the intent to kill – required to prove the offence of murder. He was sentenced to twelve years imprisonment, released in 1925 to enjoy the rest of his life – an opportunity he denied Young and his daughter.

15th – A Senseless Killing
Henry Mappin, a forty-seven-year-old blacksmith, was a man in the wrong place at the wrong time. As he walked along Oakley Street, Waterloo Road on the night of 15 July 1898, he was stabbed in the neck by a local hooligan for no apparent reason, an injury that proved to be fatal. The killer identified as nineteen-year-old John Darcy had been drinking in a nearby pub and decided on the spur of the moment he would go and speak to Mappin, a complete stranger to him. It was suggested at his trial that he tried to rob the victim but with a lack of any other witnesses this was never proved. Darcy was tried at the Old Bailey and convicted of the murder but the jury bizarrely recommended mercy. He was sentenced to death as the law required for an act of murder but his sentence was later commuted to life imprisonment.

16th – A Thespian in Love

Liverpool-born theatrical actor Thomas Weldon Atherstone was a familiar face on the English stage during the second half of the nineteenth century. He left his wife and four children after meeting a significantly younger actress called Elizabeth Earle in 1899. They fell in love and eventually moved into her mother's ground floor flat at No. 17 Clifton Gardens, Prince of Wales Road, Battersea, in 1902. When Elizabeth's mother died, she inherited the flat and started teaching the dramatic arts to private students – she was very successful. Weldon Atherstone's career began to decline and he became envious of his partner's success.

By 1905, Weldon Atherstone's relationship with Elizabeth hit rock bottom; he instructed her not to have any male students at the flat, when she disobeyed him he struck her across the face before ending the relationship, storming out of the flat and moving to another address. Several years later in 1910, Elizabeth Earle, now thirty-five-years-old, was having a relationship with Weldon Anderson's son Thomas from his first marriage. During the late evening of 16 July 1910, Elizabeth and Thomas were sitting in the flat at No. 17 Clifton Gardens when they heard what sounded like gunshots from the back of the house. A little later, a policeman came calling making enquiries with local residents about reports of gunfire and enquired if they had heard anything that may have been construed as such, Earle informing him of the earlier incident. Thomas showed the police officer down into the backyard where they found the body of a man who had gunshot injuries to his face, rendering him almost unrecognisable. When the officer searched the body for identification, he found such in the name of Weldon Atherstone – Thomas' father. Nobody was ever arrested for the murder; the police had a theory that Weldon Atherstone may have been spying on his former partner and his son and been shot at by a neighbour who thought him a burglar. The murder still remains unsolved.

17th – A Cancelled Wedding

An August date in 1900 was set for the marriage of brewery worker Alfred Highfield and his fiancée, nineteen-year-old Edith Poole. Over the Easter period leading up to the planned wedding later that year, Edith started to get cold feet. Following an argument, Edith decided to call off the wedding to Alfred and told him she no longer wished to see him. Both families were devastated. Edith's sister tried to play peace-maker inviting Alfred – who had tried to reconcile their relationship on several occasions – to tea at the Poole family home on 22 May. Following tea, the family went for a stroll near Lincolns Inn Fields in Holborn, and the troubled couple drifted at the back of the group deep in conversation. As they were walking down Great Queen Street Edith let out a scream. The family ran back to find her on the floor with a gaping hole in her throat, where she had been slashed with a razor; Alfred stood over her with the murder weapon in his hand. In his defence, he claimed that Edith had once again told him their relationship was over and he took out the razor to kill himself in front of her. Edith tried to stop him and she was fatally injured. The jury rejected his version and convicted him. He was executed on 17 July 1900 at Newgate Prison.

18th – While the Husband is Away ...

At the start of the First World War, Arthur Baker enlisted in the local Poplar and Stepney Rifles and was posted to the Western Front in 1915, leaving his family with little support. His wife Annie got a job as a waitress in a cafe where she met docker Richard Luck; they started a relationship and fell in love, but to Annie's dismay she fell pregnant. Annie was shunned by both her husband's and her own family and forced to move in with Luck who occupied a fourth-floor flat in Whitechapel. Annie had the baby, a daughter they named Annie Elizabeth, in June 1918.

Six weeks later, she received a letter from her husband that he was coming home on leave. Annie and Richard decided that the only way out was a 'suicide pact'. On the morning of 18 July 1918, Richard Luck attempted to kill himself under the wheels of a London Transport underground train at Aldgate East Station but failed. He was detained for his own safety and told police that Annie and their daughter would be found dead in his flat. When the police arrived, they indeed found the bodies of Annie and her daughter lying on the bed – both had been poisoned. In her diary, Annie's last entry simply read, 'Well there are plenty like me, I shall not be missed for long.' Luck was charged with murder; the law simply decreed that when two people enter a suicide pact and one survives the survivor would be guilty of murder. Luck was found guilty of murder but with a jury's recommendation for mercy, he was imprisoned for the remainder of the war and released in 1921. Arthur was notified of his wife's death via a very blunt telegram stating 'Wife and baby dead – Suicide'. When Arthur returned and learnt the true story he was understandably distraught and never really recovered, turning to the bottle. He died in 1940.

19th – Sarah and Sarah – an Evil Pair

What follows is a tale of the most horrendous act of child brutality imaginable. In 1768, Sarah Metyard was a milliner in Bruton Street; her daughter, also named Sarah, assisted her in the running of the business. They employed a number of young girl apprentices whom they treated with insufferable cruelty, working them to exhaustion with little food and rest. One particular girl named Ann Taylor was of a sickly disposition and missing a finger from one hand so was unable to work as hard as the other girls, which made her a target for extra abuse from the odious Metyards. It got so bad that Ann took her chance to escape. She was quickly caught and confined to an upper room of the premises and given only a small piece of bread and dirty water to drink once a day. She managed to escape again and begged members of the public to help her, but Metyard junior dragged her back, beat her severely with a broom and then secured her with cord around her waist and hands to a door knob so she was unable to sit or lie down. Ann was kept in this manner without food or water for three days. Now totally exhausted, young Ann died on the fourth day. When Metyard junior told her mother she thought Ann was dead, Sarah Metyard beat the diminutive child over the head repeatedly with a shoe. When they were sure the poor child was dead, they took her down into the basement where her corpse was kept for two months, telling the other girls that Ann had in fact been successful in her latest escape bid.

It got to a point when the smell of the decomposing body of this poor child could not be masked anymore. The evil pair decided to cut the body up and dispose of the body parts in the local area apart from the hand with the missing finger, which they burnt to hide any possible identification. The body parts were found, but a surgeon came to a misleading conclusion that they had probably come from a grave robbery – no further investigation took place. The murder was only uncovered when Metyard junior had a violent falling out with her mother, went to the authorities in a fit of anger and confessed everything. Both were tried and sentenced to death and executed at Newgate on 19 July 1768. Following execution, the bodies were sent to Surgeons Hall for medical dissection; a truly fitting end for this vile pair.

20th – A Week Long Binge

Unemployed bricklayer Robert Ward had turned to the bottle as he struggled to find work and support his family. The family home was in Boundary Road, Camberwell, to which he returned on the afternoon of 20 July 1899 having been drinking heavily for over a week. His devoted wife and mother of his two children, Florence, worked as a charwoman and any other employment she could find to keep the family fed and clothed. Ward asked his wife to prepare him some food; she left the children in the care of their father while she went out to buy some provisions. While out Ward called both his daughters, Mary and Violet, back into the house from the street where they had been playing and told them to go upstairs; he followed. He then set about both of them with a blunt knife causing terrible, crude, fatal injuries to their throats before attempting to kill himself with the same weapon. The landlady heard the children screaming out 'Don't Daddy' and summoned the help of a police officer, who found both girls dead but Ward still alive. Ward survived and faced a trial for the murder of his children. He pleaded insanity in order to escape the rope but was hanged at Wandsworth Prison on 9 October 1899.

21st – Bumps in the Night

A murder hunt commenced on the morning of 23 July 1990 when the bodies of two women were found slumped in a gold Toyota Corolla motor vehicle on Spears Road, Holloway. The vehicle was registered to an address in Grenville Road, Holloway. The victims were flatmates Patricia Morrison, the car owner, and Elaine Forsyth, both had been strangled, Patricia with a handbag strap and Elaine throttled with a curtain tieback cord. The pathologist's post-mortem report concluded the girls had been murdered at least thirty-six hours earlier on Saturday 21 July 1990; this was backed up by evidence from neighbours who heard shouting and screaming from the flat and a bumping sound as the murderer dragged each body downstairs. The flat, bloodstained and missing a carpet, was the obvious crime scene. Detectives appealed to the public for sightings of the unusual gold-coloured vehicle, and a number of people came forward having seen the vehicle being driven erratically along Junction Road, Upper Holloway by a distinctive looking driver. Detectives were now looking for a black male with a long-permed hairstyle. The former boyfriend of Elaine, Michael Shorey, matched the description and was arrested on suspicion of murder and questioned but bailed due to lack of evidence. Following the news of his release, a friend of Shorey's approached detectives with crucial information; Shorey had asked him to look after a piece of carpet wrapped in plastic. Forensic examination showed the carpet was stained with blood and saliva belonging to both girls. The victim's blood was also found in the tread of a training shoe belonging to Shorey. He was convicted of murder at the Old Bailey in July 1991 and received a mandatory life sentence.

22nd – No Luck for Amy
Amy Judge had never been lucky in love. She had previously been married to a rogue sent to prison on a number of occasions for violence and distributing indecent images. She tried a second time when she met a man called Thomas Smithers, they set up home together at No. 30 Cross Street, Battersea. Amy didn't help her cause and was the architect of her own downfall at times as she was no angel and liked to play the field; couple this with Smithers' profound jealously, the relationship was always going to be explosive. However, against all odds, they stayed together for three years until Judge met up with an old boyfriend, who had emigrated to New Zealand a number of years before. Smithers found out about the new competition, couldn't cope and cut Amy's throat on 22 July 1878. He disappeared but was tracked down and placed on trial at the Old Bailey. Smithers was convicted and sentenced to death, becoming the first man to be executed at Wandsworth Prison on 8 October 1878.

23rd – A Reign of Terror

South London criminal Kenneth Erskine, whom the media tagged 'The Stockwell Strangler', murdered seven elderly victims between April and July 1986. Erskine progressed from petty crime as a juvenile to burglary, serving time in Feltham Young Offenders Institution. His criminal career continued into his early twenties; burglary progressed to serious sexual attacks and murder. His first victim was seventy-eight-year-old Nancy Emms, whom he attacked on 9 April 1986 in her Wandsworth home. At first, her death was treated as non-suspicious, until her home-help spotted her television had been stolen; a post-mortem examination revealed she had been raped and murdered. Further victims followed: a woman on 9 June in Wandsworth, two victims on 28 June in Stockwell, both men and both sexually assaulted, another man on 8 July in Islington, back to Stockwell on 21 July and the murder of William Downes and finally on 23 July 1986 the murder of eighty-three-year-old Florence Tisdall in Fulham. His reign of terror ended when arrested at a social security office on 28 July. Forensic evidence at some crime scenes and identification by seventy-four-year-old Fred Prentice, whom Erskine had attempted to strangle weeks before his arrest, sealed his fate. He was convicted and sentenced to life imprisonment with a recommendation to serve at least forty years. His convictions were reduced to manslaughter due to diminished responsibility in 2009, following a diagnosis of chronic schizophrenia and antisocial personality disorder. He was suspected of four other murders but never charged.

24th – His Last Commission

Belgian artist Ernest Castelein was found unconscious in his Kensington flat, No. 52A Cromwell Road, on the morning of 25 July 1945. The painter of beautiful women was found slumped naked in front of his latest commission. Detectives traced Castelein's last movements the night before 24 July 1945 when he was seen entering his flat in the company of a soldier. Detectives believed the soldier attacked Castelein, stole the artist's clothes and left him for dead. Castelein was admitted to hospital but never regained consciousness and died of his injuries a week later. The murder has never been solved.

25th – Not Above the Law

Instead of the murder *of* a police officer, we turn to murder *by* a police officer. In 1893, PC George Cooke was stationed at Bow Street Police Station in London's West End where he met prostitute Maud Merton. A sexual relationship took place between the two before Cooke lost interest and put an end to the affair. Maud threatened to report Cooke to his superiors; she carried out her threat, and Cooke was suspended from duty subject to an investigation before eventually being posted to 'X' Division, West London. But Maud did not intend to let it end there; she heard Cooke was engaged to a young servant girl. She waited and confronted Cooke while walking his beat on Wormwood Scrubs in the vicinity of the North Pole pub. A heated argument took place and George beat Maud to death with his police issue truncheon. Cooke was arrested and charged with the murder of Maud; he claimed at his trial that Maud had been stalking him for some time and persisted with such behaviour following his disciplinary hearing and transfer to West London, a fact corroborated by several of his police colleagues. Cooke was found guilty of murder accompanied with a recommendation for mercy by the jury. The judge sentenced Cooke to the mandatory death sentence for murder adding that the degree of violence used was so excessive he believed the sentence of death would stand, which proved to be correct. Samuel Cooke was hanged at Newgate Prison on 25 July 1893.

26th – A Killer with Long Hands

Mrs Stephanie Marie Small, a 'really beautiful woman with that rare Anglo-Indian complexion and poise' (*Yorkshire Post and Leeds Intelligencer* 29th July 1952), was murdered, stabbed twenty-four times in the back, in her flat in Melville House, Blackheath Hill, Blackheath on 26 July 1952. She had five daughters, one of whom was married to John Kenneth Livesey. Livesey, his wife Pam and their nineteen-month-old daughter shared the accommodation with Small and another of her daughters. Livesey became the police's main suspect as he vanished shortly after the murder. He was described in a police circulation as having 'long hands, a soft voice and two lower teeth were missing'. The murder weapon was believed to be a dagger or stiletto knife with a 3- to 4-inch blade.

By the middle of the following week, Livesey was found in Ramsgate, Kent wearing just a shirt. He was recognised as the fugitive wanted for murder and when questioned by detectives, claimed his clothes were stolen while swimming that morning and they were 'barking up the wrong tree' if they thought he had anything to do with the murder even though he initially admitted knowledge of his mother-in-law's death. He was tried at the Old Bailey and following a dismissed appeal hanged at Wandsworth Prison on 17 December 1952.

The man who hanged Livesey, Assistant Executioner Syd Dernley, was removed from his position in 1954 amid allegations that he had made an inappropriate crude remark on the size of Livesey's manhood and gaining a conviction for publishing obscene material.

27th – A Rough Diamond

Serial womaniser and bigamist Arthur Andrew Goslett was a former diamond trader in South Africa before coming to England at the beginning of First World War. He married his first wife and joined the Royal Naval Air Service. In 1919, he married again followed by a further wife, Daisy Holt, later the same year. By this time, Goslett had a very good position as an aircraft engineer but was feeling the financial strain of keeping three women and three homes. But this did not stop him marrying again; his fourth wife was called Evelyn. Goslett impregnated both Daisy and Evelyn. Daisy wanted Goslett to herself and threatened to tell Evelyn (who was unaware that he was already married). Goslett placated Daisy by passing her off as his brother's widow and moving her into the same address as Evelyn – Armitage Mansions, No. 85A Golders Green Road.

Following the birth of Evelyn's child, Goslett decided to reduce his burden by 25 per cent. On 1 May 1920, he lured Evelyn to a secluded spot, Brentmead Place, Western Avenue, next to the Brent River, on the pretence of showing her a house that he wished to buy for her and their new arrival. The callous Goslett struck Evelyn over the head several times with a tyre-lever, knocking her unconscious and rolling her into the river where she drowned. The following day, when the body was discovered, Goslett was questioned by an astute detective, who noticed the trousers worn by him did not match his jacket and asked him where his trousers were. When Goslett produced them, they were damp and covered in bloodstains. After sitting in a police cell for a couple of days, Goslett came clean claiming that Evelyn had begged him to kill her and that he had struck her with a tyre-lever, which the police could find in his toolbox. He was tried and convicted and executed at Pentonville Prison on 27 July 1920.

28th – Take it in Turns

Prostitute Lucy Nightingale ran her business from a room she rented at No. 13 Prah Road, Finsbury Park. Her landlord was a man called Henry Ball, who was fully aware of Lucy's occupation. On 28 July 1919, Ball was having a drink in a local pub with two seamen – Harold Morgan and Frank Warren; Morgan had spent the previous night with Lucy at Prah Road and tonight it was Warren's turn. All three men went back to the house, Morgan and Ball stayed downstairs while Warren went up to Lucy's room. A little later, the two men heard a scream followed by Warren running downstairs and telling Morgan they needed to leave. Ball found Lucy tied up with strips of linen and her own lingerie – she had been strangled. Ball reported the murder to the local police in the early hours of the following morning. Morgan and Warren were soon apprehended. Detectives retrieved jewellery stolen from Lucy that had been gifted to Warren's girlfriend. Morgan and Warren were charged with Lucy's murder and Ball as an accessory. By the time of the trial at the Old Baily, Ball had become a prosecution witness and no further evidence was offered against Morgan who was acquitted. Warren was found guilty and executed at Pentonville on 7 October 1919.

* * *

Exactly seven years after the murder of Lucy Nightingale, another killing took place several miles to the west in a small grocer's shop on Leinster Terrace, Bayswater. When grocer Edward Creed failed to come home on the evening of 28 July 1926, his wife became worried and raised the alarm. At 10 p.m., a local beat constable was walking past Creed's shop and noticed that the padlock was not in place on the front door and a light was on inside the premises. As he investigated he smelt gas, broke the door down and discovered Edward Creed lying at the bottom of the stairs – he had been murdered. The constable could see Creed's head was covered in blood; there were further bloodstains on and around the shop counter with blood smearing on the floor where the body had been dragged to its final position. The till had been emptied with some coins spread over the floor. Some evidence had been left by the killer: a brown coat button and a pair of discarded gloves but no fingerprints. Nobody has ever been charged with Edward Creed's murder and it remains unsolved.

29th – A Mother-in-Law from Hell

Mother-in-laws can be ferocious creatures (my mum-in-law is wonderful) but surely the most evil in criminal history is Styllou Pantopiou Christofi. In 1954, Greek Cypriot Stavros Christofi and his family occupied two floors of a large house at No. 11 South Hill Park, Hampstead. Stavros worked long unsociable hours as a wine waiter at the *Café de Paris* in Leicester Square. Stavros' wife was called Hella, who originated from Germany; she was a loving, conscientious wife and mother to their children. A year earlier in 1953, the family were joined by Stavros' mother Styllou Christofi, who could only speak her native language and was obstinately unwilling to learn English in order to fit into her new home or communicate with her daughter-in-law. Over the next year, Styllou – who was truly a cruel, evil woman – made her daughter-in-law's life intolerable whom she hated her.

On the evening of 29 July 1954, after the children had been put to bed and Stavros had left for work, Styllou's hatred of Hella reached a violent crescendo. She smashed Hella over the head with a cast-iron ashtray and then strangled her unconscious daughter-in-law to death. She wasn't finished; she dragged the body out into the garden and burnt the corpse, a neighbour giving evidence at her trial that she thought Styllou was burning a shop dummy. She then attempted to cover her tracks by making out it was all an accident. Forensic evidence formed the basis of the prosecution with blood pattern analysis and other evidence revealing the truth. She was tried at the Old Bailey and found guilty in October of that year and hanged at Holloway Prison on 13 December 1954. Following Styllou's death, it was revealed that she had been tried in her homeland for the murder of her own mother-in-law; allegedly ramming a burning torch down her victim's throat, but was acquitted. Christofi was the penultimate female execution to take place in England; the last, Ruth Ellis, shot David Blakeley in April 1955, nine months after this murder, in the very same street!

30th – Double Traitors
In 1915, as war in Europe took hold, two men travelled to England separately, masquerading as cigar salesmen. Their names were Haicke Petrus Marinus Janssen and Willem Johannes Roos. They were here to send intelligence back to the Germans on British ships and ship movements from British ports. The secrets were sent in a code deciphered by British intelligence services. Both men were arrested and tried at Middlesex Guildhall (now the Supreme Court in Parliament Square) convicted and sentenced to death by firing squad. They were executed at the Tower of London on 30 July 1915 by a detachment of Scots Guards; Janssen first at 6 a.m. followed by Roos at 6.10 a.m. There were eleven executions by firing squad at the Tower during the First World War – the first executions here for 150 years. In fact, more people were executed at the Tower of London in the twentieth century then in Tudor times. Only two or three of the firing squad would be issued live bullets, the rest issued blanks in order that no individual soldier or those presiding over the execution would know who fired the fatal shots.

31st – Sane Enough to Hang
Heavy-drinking, spouse-beating, forty-six-year-old Thomas Foster lived with his wife Minnie and their six children in Stainsbury Street, Bethnal Green. Foster was a former soldier who had survived the First World War and was a chair-maker by trade. The couple had been married for fifteen years but their marriage had recently suffered due to his excessive drinking. Minnie tried to take a restraining order out against her husband but relented when Foster swore he would give up drinking and work at their marriage – unfortunately, his turning of a new leaf would last a very short while. On the morning of 11 June 1919, a violent row

erupted in the Foster house, which was followed by a frightening scream and Foster running from the front of the house. He was detained by a number of neighbours who had come out of their houses to see what the commotion was. When police arrived, they discovered Minnie on her bed with her throat cut from ear to ear and still protectively clutching her youngest child; a bloodied razor lay on the floor nearby.

At his trial, Foster tried to blacken the name of his hard-working wife by telling the jury that she was a prostitute, a fact refuted by a number of witnesses who knew Minnie well. Foster then tried a defence of insanity, claiming to be mentally unstable at the time of the murder and his family had a history of mental illness – several previously incarcerated in mental institutions. The jury dismissed his claim after hearing evidence of his stable mental state from a prison doctor. He was found guilty and executed on 31 July 1919.

8

AUGUST

1st – Slaughtered

The Lion pub, Caledonian Road was one of several pubs in Islington that served the thirsty slaughtermen of the Metropolitan Cattle Market built in the mid-1850s to take the pressure off Smithfield meat market in the City. It was a busy pub with a large turnover of staff. Its upper floors were used for private dining with a few rooms available for overnight accommodation. Unbeknown to any staff members, including landlord Fred Keeble, a romance had been blossoming between twenty-two-year-old chambermaid Jane Geary and twenty-three-year-old waiter Charles Bicknell. But the attraction started to fade after a while and the pretty Geary started to date other men. Bicknell took this badly – his peers noted a change in his personality around this period. On the evening of 8 June 1864, a scream was heard from one of the upper floors and Keeble ran upstairs to discover Jane Geary lying on the floor with Bicknell standing over her body with a knife, dripping blood, in his hand. The police were called, and an officer recorded Bicknell's reply to caution on his arrest: 'She is the only girl I ever loved, and poor girl she has got it, and I hope she will die.' His dismally weak defence of being emotionally distressed at the time held no water with the jury and he was executed outside Newgate on 1 August 1864. The Lion pub still stands today at No. 98 Boundary Road but has been converted into flats. The market has also long gone too, but it is remembered in street names such as Market Road and the Market Estate.

2nd – Death of a Pink Panther Villain

Celebrated British actor Peter Arne played character roles in fifty-plus films and television productions during a career that spanned forty years; his best-known role was as a villain in three of the *Pink Panther* films. His life came to a violent end on the night of 1/2 August 1983 when he was viciously beaten around the head. His body was discovered face down on the floor in his flat at No. 54 Hans Place, Knightsbridge when a child-minder of a neighbour discovered bloodstains in the hallway leading from Arne's flat. Detectives pieced together the crime and concluded that Arne had first been attacked in his living room with a log from his fireplace. He managed to stagger into the hallway in an attempt to escape his attacker. He was struck again but managed to open his front door leading out onto communal hallway before being struck a final time, dragged back into the flat and having his throat cut. The investigation revealed that Arne, who was homosexual, had befriended an Italian male seen in the vicinity of Hans Place waiting for Arne to return to his flat on the evening of 1 August. An *Identikit* image of this man was created from witnesses and circulated.

On 4 August, Thames River Police hauled the naked body of a male out of the water near Wandsworth Bridge; a pile of clothes were found a little further down the riverbank at Putney, a passport identified the man as Italian schoolteacher Guiseppe Perusi. One of the officers believed the corpse to be a good likeness to the suspect for Arne's murder. Forensic evidence placed Perusi in the flat and bloodstains on his clothes were the same group as Peter Arne. The coroner's inquest concluded Arne was unlawfully killed by Perusi and that Perusi had committed suicide; the case was closed.

* * *

Illegal immigrant Victor Castigador arrived in Britain from the Philippines in 1985. He got a job at a Soho amusement arcade, though he and his manager never saw eye to eye; Castigador hatched a plan to rob him of his takings. During the late evening of 2 August 1989, Castigador and several accomplices broke into the arcade and found four members of staff – the manager, cashier and two security guards – counting the day's takings. With guns pointing at their heads, they were doused with petrol, placed into a metal cage and set alight by Castigador who left them to burn alive, locking the door behind him. The two security guards died in the blaze, the manager and cashier survived but with horrendous burns. Castigador was initially given a life term of at least twenty-five years, but this was amended by the home secretary to a whole life tariff, which means this callous evil killer will die in prison.

3rd – Knight to the Tower

Going from British diplomat and Knight of the Realm to a traitor and the indignity of execution, Roger Casement's life was indeed an extraordinary journey. A few lines in this volume cannot hope to encompass fully the story of this man's existence. Casement was British Consul in Portuguese East Africa, Angola, Congo Free State and Brazil. He gained international recognition for exposing the cruelty and exploitation of native labour by white traders in the Congo and the Putumayo River region in Peru resulting in a Knighthood for his efforts. In 1912, he retired due to ill health and returned to his native Ireland. Casement was a fervent supporter of the Irish Nationalist movement and in 1913 helped create the Irish National Volunteers and travelled to New York in 1914 to attain financial backing for his anti-British movement. The First World War provided another opportunity to further advance the nationalist cause. Casement travelled to Germany in an attempt to get support for Irish independence; during his visit, he attempted to arrange a loan from a group of German army officers to fund an uprising. On his return to Irish soil, he was arrested by the British, taken to London and incarcerated in the Tower. The British government decided Casement should stand trial for treason; his trial took place at the Old Bailey in June 1916. He was convicted and sentenced to death and hanged at Pentonville Prison on 3 August 1916.

4th – You Snore!

Irishman Kieran Kelly arrived in Britain during the year 1953; he would go on to kill at least five people. The last of his murders was committed on 4 August 1977 when the victim, William Boyd, was murdered by Kelly in a South London police station cell. Kelly had been arrested for robbery and was sharing the cell with Boyd whose snoring kept him awake; he crushed his skull and garrotted him with his shoelaces. Kelly was sentenced to life imprisonment.

5th – Hammer Time

Mary Anne Madden, a widow with one daughter called Alice from her previous marriage, lived at No. 44 Southampton Street, Holborn. Mary met Herbert Madden, fell in love and Herbert moved in. Mary had two further children with Herbert: Herbert Patrick and Mary Beatrice, aged five and two, respectively. Herbert's character changed starkly over the years; often coming home drunk and on a number of occasions threatened to murder his two young children. On the morning of 5 August 1903, the threat turned into tragic reality. Neighbours witnessed Mary run from her house screaming, 'What have you done, you have killed my two children.' Madden stood at the door shouting, 'Yes I have.' Herbert Patrick and Mary Beatrice were found by police lying on a bed near the kitchen; their heads crushed to a pulp by a hammer that lay nearby. Madden freely confessed that he had murdered his two children because they cost him a lot of money. Later at Kings Cross Police Station when informed by the police that his children were dead, Madden replied, 'I am pleased to hear that.' Pointing to the murder weapon he admitted 'that is the one I did it with … I killed my children deliberately'. Madden was convicted of the murders of Herbert Patrick and Mary Beatrice but declared insane and detained at HM's pleasure in a mental institution.

6th – Devious but Brave

Many Second World War spies were accomplished liars, devious in their conduct but extremely brave – necessary traits of a successful spy. But three spies, who were flown by sea-plane from German occupied Norway on the night of 29/30 September 1940, were at best ill-prepared, at worse incompetent but no less brave than any other. Their plane landed off the coast of Scotland at Gollachy between Buckie and Port Gordon where the spies – two men and one woman – were put into a dingy with three bicycles on which they were to ride south to London. The sea was so rough that the bikes they were relying on got swept overboard. On landing, they split up, Vera Erikson and Karl Drucke stayed together and went to the local railway station, Port Gordon, arriving at 7.30 a.m. The station porter's suspicions were raised immediately when Erikson asked the name of the station they were at. Drucke produced a wallet with a large amount of money inside. Station staff also noticed that Drucke's trousers were soaking wet and Erickson's stockings and shoes were in a similar condition. The local police officer attended and questioned Erickson and Drucke before escorting them to the police station. Erickson and Drucke told officials they were refugees, but when searched found to be in possession of a Mauser pistol, a box of ammunition, a flick knife, wireless equipment, a list of RAF bases, a torch with a makers-mark 'Bohemia', a total of nearly £400 in Bank of England notes and a half-eaten German sausage. Drucke was transferred to London, tried at the Old Bailey in July 1941 and executed at Wandsworth Prison on 6 August. Erikson mysteriously disappeared; the court told simply she would not be appearing and to ask no further questions.

7th – *The Bow Horror Show*

The media love nothing more than a sensational headline that sells newspapers – and The Bow Cinema Murder was an editor's dream. In the early hours of 7 August 1934, Dudley Hoard, the manager of the Eastern Palace cinema Bow Road, East London, was busy counting the Bank Holiday weekend takings amounting to more than £90. Hoard and his wife lived on the premises. He answered a knock on the door and was struck with an axe at least fourteen times. Hoard's wife heard the commotion and came to see what was happening. The young intruder attacked her in a similar manner before stealing the takings. Later that morning, cleaners discovered the murdered Dudley Hoard but his wife, although unconscious with a serious head injury, survived the attack. Mrs Hoard was able to give police a fleeting partial description of her husband's killer from her hospital bed. On searching, the cinema detectives found a blood-covered axe behind the stage and a thumb print in blood on a wall.

Three days after the murder, 10 August, a rather bizarre letter turned up at Lowestoft Police Station signed by a man called John Stockwell admitting to the murder on 7 August. Stockwell had been an employee at the cinema but detectives had eliminated him as a suspect as he was a trusted member of staff and 7 August had been his day off (presumably Mrs Hoard hadn't recognised him on the night due to being struck over the head with an axe). Later on 10 August, a young man fitting Stockwell's description was seen on the beach folding his clothes and leaving a watch, a post office savings book in his name and a suicide note. The sighting was reported to the police; as no body had been recovered, the confession contained in the letter and a description of Stockwell was released to the public via the media. The following day, a man again fitting the description of Stockwell, now wanted for the murder of his manager, booked into an exclusive hotel in Great Yarmouth paying in cash and claiming to be from Luton in Hertfordshire rather than Bedfordshire; the hotel manager reported his suspicions to the police who were waiting when Stockwell returned to the hotel later. John Stockwell pleaded guilty to the murder of Dudley Hoard and was executed at Pentonville Prison on 14 November 1934.

8th – Hung Out to Dry
Pope Saint Pius V's papal bull arrived in London on 24 May 1570 excommunicating Queen Elizabeth I. Catholic John Felton nailed a copy of the papal missive on the front door of the Bishop of London's residence challenging the bishop to declare his allegiance to the Queen or to the Pope. Felton was arrested on 26 May 1570 and sent to the Tower of London where he was tortured, tried and sentenced to be hung, drawn and quartered. This terrible sentence was carried out in St Paul's churchyard on 8 August 1570. This form of execution entailed the condemned being hung until near unconsciousness before being cut down having *his* genitals cut off (women were never hung drawn and quartered *just* burnt at the stake), an incision from throat to pelvis would be made and the intestines drawn from the torso. The head would be then cut off and the torso dissected into four. The head and the quarters were displayed in public as a warning against future disobedience and bad behaviour. John Felton was beatified by Pope Leo XIII in December 1886.

9th – RADA Hopefuls
In the 1960s, homosexual partners Joe Orton and Kenneth Halliwell lived at No. 25 Noel Road, Islington. Both were aspiring

actors who met at the Royal Academy of Dramatic Art (RADA) in the late 1950s. Their acting aspirations never flourished and they turned to literary careers. Orton's career raced ahead of Halliwell's creating friction between the two culminating in murder. On 9 August 1967, a chauffeur arrived at the Noel Road address in order to take Orton to Twickenham Studios. The chauffeur had picked up Orton on previous occasions and was surprised when he didn't answer the door. He looked through the letterbox and saw a bald-headed man lying on the floor in the hallway – the chauffeur immediately knew this was not Orton and so alerted the police, who broke down the door and entered the flat. They found the corpse of Kenneth Halliwell on the floor, naked and covered in blood. In turn, Joe Orton's body, dressed in only a pyjama top, was discovered with fatal head injuries inflicted by a hammer, which lay nearby. A post-mortem concluded that Halliwell had smashed Orton over the head at least nine times before taking his own life by ingesting a cocktail of barbiturates and grapefruit juice.

10th – Keep Out of the Kitchen

A busy restaurant kitchen can be a stressful workplace. Add a couple of volatile Cypriots to the mix and that stress can turn into violence. On 12 May 1933, the Bellometti restaurant in London's busy Soho Square was experiencing a dinnertime rush. Head Chef Boleslar Pankorski instructed his silver service waiter, Varnavas Antorka, to place some plates in the gas oven to be warmed. When his instructions were not complied with, Chef Pankorski shouted at Antorka to do as he was told or he would be sacked. An argument broke out in which Antorka indeed received his marching orders, grabbed his coat and left the restaurant. After the dinner rush had finished, Pankorski left by the back entrance and was immediately confronted by a very unhappy Antorka who exclaimed, 'You gave me the sack you bastard. Take me back or else I will you shoot you.' Suddenly, a shot rang out and the chef fell to the floor dead. At his trial, Antorka would claim that it was all a terrible accident and he only pointed the gun at Pankorski to frighten him into giving him his job back. The prosecution claimed that Antorka had returned home, collected a gun and waited for his victim, which showed premeditation to commit wilful murder.

The jury agreed and Antorka was convicted and executed on 10 August 1933 at Pentonville Prison.

11th – A Kindly Landlady

The degree of violence one human being can inflict on another never ceases to surprise and shock. As we work our way through a year of human brutality, this particular case beggars belief. Eighty-four-year-old Belgian immigrant Madame Eugenie le Maire had lived at No. 15 Perham Road, Hammersmith for nearly fifty years. She occupied the two basement rooms while letting out the upper floors. Due to her age, she had let the property slip into disrepair, but gifted her lodgers with very low rental rates. One such lodger was John O'Connor, who hailed from Londonderry, Northern Ireland. O'Connor would often complain about the accommodation and the meals that his landlady would produce but not to the extent that he would move out. On 11 August 1953, O'Connor went out for a drinking session after work and came home drunk. Eugenie offered to make him a cup of tea, he accepted. For some inexplicable reason, O'Conner grabbed the old woman by the throat and strangled her until unconscious and then raped her. He went up to his room to contemplate his actions and decided the best option would be to return downstairs, arm himself with a knife and stab the old lady several times in the chest before packing his possessions and leaving. It would appear that this most evil of men had a conscience when he walked into a police station two days later to confess to his crime. However, by the time the case reached trial, he had changed his mind and pleaded not guilty, but inexplicably would not allow his defence team to put forward a case of insanity to the jury – his only true chance of avoiding the rope. The jury took just ten minutes to reach a guilty verdict and O'Connor was executed at Pentonville Prison on 2 October 1951.

12th – Shot in the Back

Braybrook Street, East Acton is a quiet residential street near to Wormwood Scrubs and the daunting edifice of the Victorian prison. On 12 August 1966 at 3.15 p.m., an unmarked police vehicle drove into the street on a normal crime prevention patrol when the occupants, DS Christopher Head, DC David Wombwell and PC Geoffrey Fox, who was driving, noticed a suspiciously parked blue estate van with three occupants. Due to the vicinity of the prison, the officers approached the vehicle to ask a few questions. DS Head and DC Wombwell walked towards the van and noticed it had no tax disc displayed. They began to routinely question driver Jack Witney who explained he didn't have an MOT for the car so therefore couldn't obtain the tax disc. DC Wombwell walked around to the passenger side to speak to the front passenger Harry Roberts who produced a Luger pistol and shot DC Wombwell at point-blank range through his left eye; he died immediately. DS Head ran back to the car but was shot through the back of his head by Roberts. The backseat passenger, a man called John Duddy, took a .38 Webley service revolver out of a holdall and ran over to the police car. PC Fox, in an attempt to escape, reversed the car over his colleague DS Head who lay fatally injured on the road. Duddy shot PC Fox three times – all three officers died at the scene.

Witney was the first to be arrested hours after the murders; the van's registration number had been noted by a witness who saw the vehicle being driven at speed away from the incident. Witney admitted being involved and named his two accomplices. Duddy was arrested in Glasgow a few days later but Roberts went into hiding in Epping Forest and evaded capture for three months before being caught. All three were tried at the Old Bailey. Roberts admitted to the murders of DS Head and DC Wombwell, the other two denied all the charges. The jury only took thirty minutes to return guilty verdicts against all for murder and possession of firearms. They were each given life imprisonment with a recommendation they not be eligible for parole for at least thirty years. John Duddy died in Parkhurst Prison in 1981. Witney was released in 1991, five years before the minimum recommended by the trial judge; his life ended the way he lived it – violently, murdered by a flatmate with a hammer. Roberts was released from prison on 11 November 2014 having served forty-eight years inside. In 1988, a memorial was placed at the spot in Braybrook Street where the three officers were slain just for doing their duty.

13th – Blame the Husband

The battered body of three-year-old Marion Ward was discovered dumped in a bomb-damaged derelict house in Langham Court, St John's Wood on 13 August 1949. She was last seen with neighbour Mrs Nora Tierney, who lived next to the Wards in Elsworthy Road, Hampstead. Tierney was arrested on suspicion of Marion's murder. The infant had been hit over the head several times with a hammer. At her trial, the police officer in charge told the jury that Tierney had blamed her husband for the slaughter. She not only claimed she had seen him kill tiny Marion but escorted the officers to the spot where she claimed he had buried the murder weapon. Detectives were not fooled, forensic evidence and sightings of Nora with Marion proved Nora's guilt and she was sentenced to death. An appeal was lodged and the home secretary ordered a psychiatric examination in which Nora was certified insane and sent to Broadmoor mental institution.

14th – Who Killed the Butler?

Frank Edward Rix was a loyal, trusted butler to diplomat Sir George Lloyd, High Commissioner of Egypt. In June 1925, Lloyd decided to spend some time at his country estate leaving Rix to run the London residence at No. 24 Charles Street, Mayfair. On the morning of 7 June 1925, a housemaid knocked on the door of Rix's room in the basement with his normal tea and toast. When she received no reply, she entered to find Rix lay on his bed, his head so severely beaten she could hardly recognise him, and a bloodied hammer lay on the floor beside the bed.

Detectives soon identified a likely suspect, a former seventeen-year-old employee sacked by Rix for incompetence and dishonesty: Arthur Henry Bishop. Bishop was certainly a rough diamond and stole from Rix and another member of the household before leaving. Bishop was tracked down to the village of Shoreham in Kent where he gave himself up to a local policeman. He made a full confession explaining that he had been drinking heavily and come to the conclusion he had been dealt a rough deal by Rix and decided to burgle Sir George's house to gain some financial compensation. He entered via a basement window and went into Rix's bedroom. As he was going through his belongings, Rix stirred; fearing he may wake up, Bishop struck him over the head with the hammer he had armed himself with and continued beating him until he was sure he was dead. He stole a ring with Rix's initials 'F. E. R' engraved into it and a couple of watches. He was tried and convicted; his age would offer no protection as he was sentenced to death and executed at Pentonville Prison on 14 August 1925. Bishop was one of only four eighteen year olds to be executed in the twentieth century.

15th – Fire Starter

Charlotte and Herman Schreiber lived in a small house at No. 165 Boundaries Road, Balham, South London. Charlotte had a five-year-old daughter from a previous relationship, whom she named Miriam. Charlotte and Herman slept on the first floor with their daughter in a nursery on the ground floor. The Schreiber's had a lodger, a furnaceman called John Francis Wilkinson, who liked a drink but rarely caused any problems in the household. In the early hours of 15 August 1953, Charlotte was disturbed by the sound of breaking glass, but she believed it to be cats fighting outside so went back to sleep. A little later Charlotte and Herman were awoken again this time by the smell of smoke, they ran downstairs to find the kitchen on fire. After extinguishing the flames, they checked the nursery and found Miriam motionless under her blankets. When checking they discovered she had been savagely beaten to death.

Detectives soon realised, through a forensic examination of the scene, they were not dealing with an intruder and whoever killed Miriam had been present in the house all along. John Wilkinson was arrested on suspicion of the murder and surprisingly made a full confession. He told them that he had gone down to the nursery with a wooden chair leg and struck Miriam time and time again as she lay under her bedclothes, and when realising that she still wasn't dead he strangled her. A post-mortem examination revealed that Wilkinson had also sexually assaulted Miriam then set light to the kitchen in order to cover his tracks. Wilkinson was executed at Wandsworth on 18 December 1953.

16th – Four Years to Find a Murder Weapon

The female boss of the Adelphi Secretarial Agency in High Holborn was murdered in her own office on 16 August 1949. Daisy Edith

Wallis had been stabbed in the chest with a long-bladed weapon and died where she fell. Thirty-year-old Daisy lived in Cornwall Gardens, Willesden and was a popular figure at work. Police were baffled as to a motive and asked the public for help in tracing anybody that knew her. They discovered she had an extremely busy social life, a member of six clubs and associations: The Vic-Wells Theatrical Association, the Players Theatre Club, the London Film Club, Stratheona Club, Overseas League and the Hanger Hill Country Club. Detectives were hopeful they would catch their man when approached by a chemist who informed them that he had treated a man of 'swarthy appearance' with a deep cut on his arm on the night of the murder but he was never traced.

Nearly six years after the murder of Daisy Wallis, on 23 May 1957, the building in which she formerly worked on High Holborn was being demolished. Workmen found a 4-feet-long sword behind a cabinet in an office adjacent to where the murder took place. The owner of the sword was never identified and the murder remains unsolved.

17th – Don't Flash the Cash

Robbery would seem to be the motive for the murder of forty-six-year-old War Office clerk Leonard Warrens. Warrens had been drinking in a pub in Putney, south-west London on 17 August 1946. During the evening, he was seen in the company of three men, believed to be soldiers. Warrens was in possession of a large quantity of cash, which he had been waving around for all to see. He left the pub later that evening making his way home to Chartfield Avenue when he was shot dead in Westleigh Avenue – the cash and his wristwatch had been taken. Detectives interviewed witnesses from the pub who described the suspects, who departed shortly after the deceased, as having a Canadian accent. Enquiries were made with the Canadian Military Police in the hunt for the killers. A public appeal for two females seen with the three soldiers on the night of the murder was made. London pawnbrokers were alerted to be on the lookout for the victim's distinctive oblong wristwatch being pawned. The search in the nearby River Thames for the murder weapon produced nothing. The three men were never traced and the murder of Leonard Warrens remains unsolved.

18th – Burnt for Defending Herself

In the early eighteenth century, being married to a violent man and subjected to physical abuse was socially acceptable. When a woman *did* react to such violence in self-defence, she was afforded little or no protection from the law. Joyce Hodgkins was a case in point, physically and mentally abused by her bullying husband, shoemaker John Hodgkins. On 18 August 1714, following a violent row, the prosecution alleged Joyce took up a carving knife and fatally stabbed her husband. During her trial, Joyce claimed John had picked up the knife: she had run away, fearing for her life, but when she turned her husband was bleeding; she told neighbours he had inflicted the injuries himself. She was charged with petty treason, a crime deemed more serious than murder as a wife was subordinate to her husband and murdering your husband was an aggravated form of murder. In a last ditch attempt to save her own life she *pleaded her belly,* trying to convince a doctor that she was pregnant. This failed and she was executed in a way reserved for women convicted of petty treason – burnt at the stake.

19th – The Wife's a Drunk

Henry Saunders separated from his wife Francis in December of 1896 due to her drinking habits and adultery. They had a young son, whom Henry was awarded custody of. Henry remained at the address, which they had previously shared, No. 5 Queens Terrace, Leyton. Following a disagreement the following year about maintenance, Francis kidnapped their young son from school and Henry had no idea where she had taken him until he received a visit from the police. He was asked to attend a mortuary in Peckham, South London on Saturday 21 August 1897, where he identified the body of his wife Francis – she had been murdered in a flat at No. 236 Cator Street, Peckham. Police ascertained she shared the lodgings with a man known by neighbours as Vincent. The very same neighbours informed murder squad detectives that the last time they had seen Francis alive was late evening 18 August, but she was heard arguing with Vincent in the early hours of 19 August. She screamed, 'If I could find your irons [burglar's tools] I would put you away before the end of the week.' She continued furiously, 'You hound, I will not work and keep you anymore' (*Belfast News,* 25 August 1897). A little later that morning Vincent asked a neighbour, who had heard the argument, to look after the small child, as his mother had gone away for a while. The neighbour became suspicious and found the body of Francis Saunders; she had suffered terrible head injuries. A doctor gave evidence to the coroner:

> The head was terribly injured a large wound having fractured the skull ... The hatchet [produced to the court] would have caused the injuries. One wound was five inches long and four inches deep across the back of the cheek to the spine. There were four inch wounds to the forehead penetrating the frontal bone and three other wounds on the top of head. She was probably attacked while she was asleep.

Detectives found burglar's tools belonging to the chief suspect in the flat. Vincent's description was circulated: he was now wanted for the murder of Francis Saunders, but there the trail goes cold – Vincent was never found.

***

Commission agent Frederick Henry Thomas, married with two boys, of Poplar, East London was having a passionate love affair with Harriet Ann Eckhardt from Rothbury Terrace, Azof Street, Greenwich. Thomas heard that Eckhardt was also seeing another man. On the night of 19 August 1911, he went to her flat in a rage over her disloyalty (conveniently forgetting his own) and cut her throat. He later admitted that he murdered Harriett out of jealousy. He was executed at Wandsworth Prison on 15 November 1911; before he was hanged, he made a short simple statement: 'For this deed that I have done my darling boys have got to suffer' (*Dundee Courier* 16 November 1911).

20th – Forced to Marry a Violent Man
Naziat Khan married a man chosen for her and with whom she had four children. The marriage was full of abuse and violence inflicted by husband Zafar Iqbal. When she demanded a divorce

and threw her husband out of the house, he decided that this was an attack on his honour and exacted an awful vengeance on his wife and three daughters. Having arranged for his son to go on a trip to Bradford, Zafar Iqbal went to the family home in Streatham, South London on 20 August 2001, and strangled his wife in the presence of his three daughters, telling them they would be next if they told anybody about what they had seen. He then took jewellery from his wife's body, dropped the three girls at a friend's house and fled the country to avoid arrest. His son found his mother's body on his return to London. Detectives believe Zafar Iqbal returned to his village in Pakistan. Britain has no official extradition treaty with Pakistan so efforts to return him to England to face justice have, so far, been frustrated.

21st – 'Any Old Iron'

Henry Hiram Bounds, a forty-five-year-old rag and bone man, murdered his wife Elizabeth, a flower seller, at their home, No. 113, Gloucester Road, Croydon, on 21 August 1942. He claimed he cut her throat because she had nagged him for years. Henry told the jury at the Old Bailey that on the morning of the murder Elizabeth had been nagging him to find a more secure job with a regular income. She picked up a knife and told him she would cut him if he didn't. Henry picked up his razor to defend himself and cut his wife's throat in self-defence. The jury didn't believe his recollection of events and convicted him of murder but with a recommendation for mercy. He was sentenced to death, and an appeal to the Home Secretary also fell on death ears. Henry was executed at Wandsworth Prison on 6 November 1942.

22nd – Having a Dinner Party?

Prolific burglar John Field, alias John Wild, stood trial with four other defendants at the Old Bailey for breaking and entering the home of a Mr Phillip Phillips, a merchant, of Bartholomew Close, King Street on 25 May 1814. An extraordinary amount of property was stolen including 144 knives, 244 pairs of scissors, 144 razors, 754 pocket combs, 46 brooches, 28 purses, 10,000 needles and several banknotes. All five were executed at Newgate Prison on 22 August 1814.

23rd – 'Why Did I Do It'

Most murderers have a motive to kill, it could be one of greed, jealousy, hate or sexually motivated. Stanley Edward Cole, a twenty-three-year-old wood machinist, lived with a young couple of a similar age, Mr and Mrs Girl at No. 77 Hartfield Crescent, Wimbledon. Cole got on well with Doris Eugenie Girl; they would often spend time together at a local pub playing darts. Inexplicably, on the evening of 23 August 1940, without any evidence of a quarrel and no apparent motive, Cole picked up a kitchen knife and stabbed Doris in the back. He then walked into Wimbledon Police Station and informed the police officer on the front desk that 'I have killed a woman at Hartfield Crescent. I stabbed her in the back. Blood rushed out. Why did I do it?' In a later statement, he confessed that 'I picked up a knife from the table and stabbed her in the back. I don't know why I did it. It ran through her like running through butter.' Cole was hanged at Wandsworth Prison on 31 October 1940.

24th – Drank the Profits

Cecil Maltby inherited his father's tailoring business. It was a going concern and making money. However, Cecil was more interested in drinking the profits and placing the remainder on the horses. To bring in some additional funds to finance his lifestyle he let a room in the flat, which he occupied over his business premises at No. 24 Park Road, St John's Wood. His lodger was a lady called Alice Middleton, whose husband was a merchant seaman on a long voyage to the Far East. Mrs Middleton enjoyed the company of the carefree, big-spending Maltby and would often accompany him to race meetings; she was last seen in his company in early August 1922. Towards the end of the year, Mr Middleton returned from his voyage but was unable to track his wife Alice down. He reported her to the police as a missing person. To their credit, the police made enquiries and discovered that Alice had taken a room with Maltby and called on him to ask some questions. He was quite helpful, telling them she had left on 15 August and he had no forwarding address. Officers noticed that the premises smelt dreadfully, Maltby appearing to have no electricity and, although cooperative, was loathed to invite them in. Further enquiries revealed that all the utilities had been cut off, and neighbours informed the officers that Maltby had not come out of the house for months. The police, however, seemed to believe Maltby to be just an eccentric and accepted his explanation regarding the movements of his former tenant.

Eventually the house became a health hazard; following complaints from neighbours, the police entered the premises in January 1923 in order to enforce a local authority health order. The inside was in a terrible state, and as they went up to the first floor, they heard a single gunshot and found Maltby dead. A search of the house revealed a disturbing find: in the bath, wrapped in a sheet under a wooden board, which appeared to have been used for a dinner table, were the decomposed remains of a woman – later identified as Alice Middleton. There was a note pinned to the body of the dead woman that read, 'In memory of darling Pat, who committed suicide on 24 August 1922, 8.30 a.m.' The police also discovered several letters that implied Alice (presumably, Pat was a nickname for Alice) had shot herself, but a post-mortem examination revealed three bullet holes in her back. An inquest recorded a verdict of murder in the case of Alice and Maltby's death as suicide.

25th – To Love and Cherish

Walking the streets of Plaistow as a prostitute since the age of fourteen, Ada Gubb Burrett may have thought her life was on the up when she married her pimp William Burrett. Her husband provided Ada with a roof over her head in Alexandra Street, Plaistow but, unfortunately for Ada, demanded she still earn her living on the streets. Ada found the confidence to challenge her husband on 25 August 1900; she told him to get out and find a job or she would give up 'being on the game'. Burrett reacted badly and stabbed Ada several times with such force he almost disembowelled her. She died later that day in hospital, but not before giving a dying declaration to police. Burrett was charged with her murder and stood trial at the Old Bailey. During the trial, the medical evidence put before the jury was so horrific that the judge advised women in the court to leave. Burrett's defence of provocation was rightly dismissed by the jury. Burrett was hanged at Chelmsford Prison on 3 October 1900.

26th – I Blame It on Mum

John Thomas Rodgers didn't get off to the greatest start in life. His mother, convicted of the manslaughter of his father by cutting his throat, was sentenced to five years imprisonment when John was only four years old. By the time John was twenty-two, he was working in the bar of the Northwood Hotel in Northwood, Middlesex. It was here that he met Lillian Maud Chamberlain, whom he murdered. The prosecution claimed Rodgers went to Chamberlain's flat at No. 47 Green Lane, Northwood on the evening of 26 August 1937 and hit her several times over the head with a flat iron and then strangled her with a nightdress cord. Rodgers admitted that he indeed went to the flat to see if Chamberlain would put him up for the night, but when he arrived Chamberlain was already unconscious on the floor. The jury convicted Rodgers of Chamberlain's murder. He was executed at Pentonville Prison on 18 November 1937 aged twenty-two years.

27th – You Lied to Me

Ex-con John Charles Parr's past caught up with him when his fiancée Sarah Willett discovered he had been to prison for theft and lied about his occupation, telling her he was beliving a French polisher when in fact he was unemployed. Fed up with the lies and knowing she could never trust him, she ended the relationship. On the night of 27 August 1900, Parr followed Willett and two girlfriends to the Foresters music hall in Bethnal Green; he made a nuisance of himself, asking Sarah to take him back but she rebuffed his pathetic apologies, telling him that she wanted an honest, hard-working man not one that robs people. The girls decided to leave but Parr followed them out, and as they approached Bethnal Green Police Station he drew a revolver out of his pocket and shot Sarah Willets at point-blank range in the head. A police officer ran out of the station on hearing the gunshot and was confronted by Parr, still with the revolver in his hand, shouting out 'I have done it'. As he was arrested, he told the officer, 'It's all her own fault, she deserves it.' Sarah was helped into the police station but died soon after. At his trial, Parr's defence team attempted to hoodwink the jury, claiming the existence of insanity in the Parr family and that Parr himself had received a blow to his head a few years before in a gymnasium. The defence barrister referred to the revolver as nothing more than a toy (conveniently forgetting that this 'toy' had actually killed somebody) that had gone off accidently. The jury convicted Parr of murder, and he was executed at Newgate on 2 October 1900.

28th – Pentonville's First

Costermonger John McDonald was living on the edge, sleeping in a Salvation Army shelter in Middlesex Street, situated between Aldgate and Bishopsgate (better known as Petticoat Lane). It hit him hard when what little money he had was stolen from him while asleep. He suspected Irishman Henry Groves to be the thief and confronted him with the allegation, but Groves denied it. McDonald's suspicions heightened when Groves went missing the following night. On 28 August 1902, McDonald caught up with Groves going into a shop in Old Castle Street; he followed him in and an argument started that spilt out onto the street. Groves attempted to defuse the situation by walking into nearby Wentworth Street but he was followed by his accuser. The men became embroiled in a fistfight until McDonald pulled a knife from his pocket and plunged the blade into Groves' neck, severing an artery and his windpipe. McDonald was detained by witnesses to the murder until the arrival of police. John McDonald was tried for the killing but pleaded that he was so drunk he couldn't remember anything about the incident. Witnesses gave evidence that they heard McDonald making threats to kill Groves when he caught up with him. McDonald was executed at Pentonville Prison – the first man to be so following the closure of Newgate.

29th – Bravest of the Brave

A call from an alert member of the public resulted in the discovery of a suspicious package in a shop doorway situated in Kensington Church Street on 29 August 1975. The package contained a bomb fitted with an anti-handling device planted by the PIRA. The area was cordoned off and the scene attended by Captain Roger Phillip Goad, the senior bomb disposal expert on duty. As Goad attempted to defuse the bomb, it exploded killing him instantly. Captain Goad had received the British Empire Medal in 1958 for his courageous actions while serving as a member of the Royal Army Ordnance

Corps in Cyprus, where he disarmed many terrorist bombs. When he retired, he joined the Metropolitan Police as a civilian explosives officer. Captain Goad was posthumously awarded the George Cross.

30th – The Show Must Go On
Another bomb attack occurred on 30 August 1970 but without the tragic consequences previously alluded to. The Angry Brigade, a British anti-capitalist terrorist group, were targeting British politicians, banks and a number of embassies in London. The group planted a bomb in a BBC outside broadcast vehicle near the Albert Hall that was covering the imminent Miss World Contest due to take place later that day. The device was small and ineffective, causing damage to the vehicle but resulting in no loss of life.

31st – Enticed With a Bag of Sweets
The last sighting of four-year-old Edwina Taylor alive was on the afternoon of 31 August 1957; her parents, fraught with worry, contacted the police to report her missing. A search of the local area in Croydon where she lived commenced. Police enquiries revealed a thirty-one-year-old man with a conviction for indecent assault lived a few doors away from the Taylor's at No. 14 St Aubyn's Road: his name was Derrick Edwardson. When detectives went to speak to Edwardson he had disappeared. Tragically, a search of Edwardson's ground-floor flat found the body of young Edwina – she had been badly beaten and sexually assaulted. When the detectives caught up with Edwardson, he admitted that he enticed the young girl into the flat with the offer of sweets, hit Edwina over the head with an axe and *accidently* strangled his victim as he attempted to resuscitate her. He was sentenced to life imprisonment on 25 October 1957 at the Old Bailey.

9

SEPTEMBER

1st – *There Was No Money*

At the same time police were hunting for missing Edwina Taylor in Croydon, across London on a construction site in Digby Road, Hackney, the body of night-watchman Charles Cutler was found in a small security hut on the morning of 1 September 1957. He had been bound and gagged with a piece of cloth forced into his mouth and died from asphyxiation. The hut had been ransacked and the telephone line cut. Misinformation had been spread around the local criminal community that Cutler was guarding large sums of money for the workmen who employed him; this turned out not to be the case and the killer(s) gained little from killing this harmless man. Nobody was ever arrested or charged with the murder.

2nd – *A Holiday Hideaway*

Married man Patrick Herbert Mahon promised his mistress, typist Emily Beilby Kaye, trips abroad, plus a love nest on a tranquil part of the Sussex coastline between Eastbourne and Pevensey Bay known as the Crumbles. By 12 April 1924, Mahon's passion and interest for thirty-seven-year-old Kaye had diminished. He purchased a knife and a saw before travelling down to Eastbourne; shortly after he arrived, he callously murdered her. Mahon would later claim the death was accidental, that they had argued and Emily fell, hitting her head on a coal bucket.

On his return home, Mahon's wife became suspicious of her husband's whereabouts for the previous few days when he gave vague answers to her questions. Suspecting he was having an affair, she searched through the pockets of the suit he had worn while away, and found a left luggage ticket for Waterloo Station. Mrs Mahon, now on a mission to uncover her husband's deceit, presented the ticket at the station left luggage and was handed a Gladstone bag, in which she discovered bloodstained female clothing. Frightened by what she had found she alerted the police, who replaced the bag and lay in wait for Mahon to retrieve it and then arrested him. Mahon told detectives the blood was from dog meat he had previously carried but his story was easily discredited when the blood was found to be human. When detectives visited the bungalow in Sussex, they were horrified to find the dismembered body of Emily Kaye. Mahon had attempted to cover up his crime by destroying the evidence: boiled human remains were found in a saucepan, lumps of flesh in a hat box, luggage trunk and a biscuit tin, and charred bone fragments in a fireplace; Emily's head was never recovered. Pathologist Sir Bernard Spilsbury pieced together what was left of the dismembered body: he discovered that Emily had been two months pregnant. Mahon was tried at Lewes Assizes in July 1924, found guilty and sentenced to death. He appealed but failed to overturn the conviction and sentence, with the presiding judge describing the crime as a 'most cruel, repulsive and carefully planned murder'. Mahon was executed at Wandsworth Prison on 2 September 1924.

3rd – 'I Have Rendered Europe a Great Service'

German socialist Hermann Francis Jung befriended a young Frenchman called Marcel Fougeron. On 3 September 1901, Fougeron visited Jung at his home at No. 4 Lower Charles Street, Clerkenwell. Jung spoke to him about his political views and how he thought Joseph Chamberlain, Secretary of State for the Colonies, who had overseen the Second Boer War, should die. Fougeron recounted the conversation during his evidence for the murder of Hermann Jung:

He [Jung] said, 'Don't you think all the misery of that war is due to Chamberlain and that he deserves to be stabbed just to make him feel a little of the misery he has inflicted on others ... I am not rich myself but I will undertake myself, through intermediaries, to guarantee a fortune to the man who will do that deed.'

Fougeron explained to the jury that he rejected the suggestion by Jung that he should be the assassin, which so annoyed Jung that he attacked Fougeron with a flat iron. Fougeron in turn defended himself with a knife he drew from his pocket and stabbed Jung in the neck. Fougeron protested that, although he had not intended to kill Jung and was acting in self-defence, he in fact had rendered Europe and Great Britain in particular a great service. The jury did not agree – Fougeron was executed at Newgate on 19 November 1911.

4th – Italian Tony

In the autumn of 1974, a gangland slaying took place in the Golden Goose amusement arcade, situated at No. 36 Old Compton Street in London's Soho district. A frequent visitor to the arcade was gangster Alfredo Zomparelli, who came to blows with a man named David Knight. Zomparelli, also known as 'Italian Tony', stabbed David Knight to death. Knight was the brother of Ronnie Knight, who attained celebrity status when he married actress Barbara Windsor. A contract was taken out on Zomparelli. On 4 September 1974, Zomparelli was playing a machine in the Golden Goose when another gangster called Nicky Gerard allegedly approached 'Italian Tony' and shot him in the back. Both Ronnie Knight and Gerard stood trial for conspiracy to murder but both were acquitted. Eight years later, Nicky Gerard was gunned down outside his Canning Town home after upsetting an East London gangland boss.

5th – A Lover's Snare

Lovers William Yeldham and Elsie McKenzie were desperate for money to fund a future together. Living on the breadline in an outhouse in Ilford, in May 1922, Elsie met her golden goose – George Grimshaw, a fifty-four-year-old businessman who owned his own decorating company based in Walthamstow. It seems Grimshaw became infatuated with twenty-two-year-old

Elsie and would pay to have sex with her. On the night of 17 May 1922, Yeldham and Elsie hatched a plan to murder the affluent Grimshaw. Elsie met up with Grimshaw at their regular rendezvous, Highams Park on the edge of Epping Forest, and while they had sex Yeldham, who had followed Elsie to the rendezvous as planned, struck Grimshaw over the head several times with a large plumber's spanner. As Grimshaw lay on the floor unconscious, the malevolent pair robbed him of cash and his watch. Grimshaw was found – still alive – an hour later and taken to Whipps Cross Hospital but died of his injuries. Yeldham and McKenzie caught a train to Braintree in Essex and got married three days after the murder. But detectives learnt from associates close to the deceased about the 'special arrangement' between McKenzie and Grimshaw. At their trial, both were convicted of the killing and sentenced to death. McKenzie was given a reprieve and served nine years in prison; Yeldham was executed at Pentonville Prison on 5 September 1922.

6th – A Baby-Faced Killer

Prostitute Ellen Carlin arrived home at her flat in Lillington Street, Pimlico just before midnight on 5 September 1954 in the company of a man whom the detective in charge of the investigation, Superintendent Judge, later described as a white male, 6 feet to 6 feet 2 inches tall, of proportionate build, aged twenty-two to twenty-four years, with flaxen hair, clean shaven, possessing blue eyes with a 'baby face'. Ellen was murdered by her guest in the early hours of 6 September 1954, repeatedly struck around the head and then strangled with one of her own silk stockings. The suspect was believed to be a United States serviceman, and police enquiries led to the US airbase in Ruislip, Middlesex where two airmen were detained on suspicion of murder and transferred to Chelsea Police station in order to assist with the police's investigation; they were accompanied by a member of the American Special Investigation Branch. Due to lack of any evidence, the men were later released without charge. The murder of Ellen Carlin remains officially unsolved, although Scottish serial killer Peter Manuel confessed to several murders, including that of Carlin, just before he was executed in 1958.

7th – The Sting of Death

Bulgarian novelist and playwright Georgi Markov defected from his homeland in 1969. Offered sanctuary in the United Kingdom, he signed his own death warrant when he began broadcasting thinly veiled anti-communist rhetoric on the BBC World Service.

On 7 September 1978, forty-nine year-old Markov was due to broadcast on the BBC World Service from Bush House, Aldwych. He parked his car on the south side of Waterloo Bridge and proceeded to cross the bridge on foot. As he passed a busy bus stop he felt a sharp sting to the back of his right thigh. He looked behind him and saw a man with an umbrella, who apologised in a thick foreign accent. Markov continued his journey and on arrival at Bush House discovered an inflammation on his leg. During the course of the afternoon, Markov began to feel unwell; later that evening his condition had deteriorated to such a degree he was admitted to St James' Hospital, Balham. Doctors were initially baffled by his symptoms and diagnosed and treated him for septicaemia. Georgi Markov died two days later. A post-mortem examination discovered a tiny capsule the size of a pinhead containing the lethal toxin ricin embedded in the wound inflicted on Waterloo Bridge. The capsule, only 1.5 mm in diameter, was fired from an ingeniously designed gun concealed in a cleverly adapted umbrella. The assassination (revealed many years later) was ordered by the then Bulgarian President Todor Zhivkhov.

8th – The Last of 135

Double murderer Henryk Niemasz became the last man to be executed at Wandsworth Prison in 1961. Niemasz befriended Alice Bateman and pleaded with her to leave partner Hubert Buxton, but she refused. On 12 May 1961, Niemasz went to the Buxton's home at Pantile Bungalow, Frith Road, Aldington, Kent, armed with a shotgun. He shot Hubert at close range in the scullery before beating Alice to death. The beating was so severe he broke the shotgun stock, with which he beat her, in two. When the bodies were found, the police discovered half a broken shotgun together with love letters from Niemasz. It didn't take too long to track down Henryk, but the investigation was complicated by wife Grypa giving her husband an alibi for the time of the murder. When police searched Niemasz's house, they found the stock of the shotgun that matched the broken barrel from the crime scene. He was tried and convicted of the murders and sentenced to death. His execution took place on 8 September 1961 and became the last of one-hundred and thirty-five executions carried out at Wandsworth Prison between 1878 and 1961. The gallows were kept in working order up until 1993 and tested every six months. When they were dismantled in 1994, the gallows' trap door and lever were sent to the Prison Service Museum in Rugby. The room in which the deaths of so many men took place is now a prison officer's tea room.

9th – Happy Slapping

Homeless forty-three-year-old Gary Mark Turner was soundly asleep in The Grove, Stratford during the early hours of 9 September 2006 when he became a victim of a violent and motiveless crime. Turner took such a beating to the head and abdomen from three men, who had earlier attacked two other men at a bus stop, that he died at the scene. Turner's future was looking bright and secure: although sleeping rough on the night of his death, he was about to move into his own flat in the area. Enquiries by murder detectives revealed Turner had initially been attacked a few hours earlier by the same men when he was punched in what was described as a 'happy slapping', an internet craze where the offenders would assault their victim while filming the attack on a mobile phone before posting it on social media. The same attackers returned to their earlier victim and punched and kicked Turner to death while again recording their sick attack. Three men were arrested in connection with the killing: Thomas Slater, aged 22, and David Selby, aged 23, were convicted of the murder and given life sentences, while a third man who filmed the incident, Muyazzim Rohman, aged 22, was convicted of manslaughter and jailed for ten years.

10th – French Passion

Mary Anne Snow cohabited with common-law husband, Frenchman Louis Bourdier, a currier by trade. They had three children and lived at No. 3 Milstead Terrace, Old Kent Road. Mary had decided it was time to move on and told Louis that she was leaving him. The Frenchman decided he could not live without her. On 10 September 1867, he slit her throat, inflicting a deep 6-inch wound from which she died. Bourdier was found guilty of his lover's murder and executed at Horsemonger Lane Gaol (just south of Tower Bridge, Horsemonger Lane still exists) by infamous public executioner William Calcraft.

* * *

Thirty years later on 10 September 1897, James Harris murdered his wife Annie and attempted to kill his two children. Harris was a platelayer, working on the London Midland Railway. He lived with his wife and two children in a single room on the second of three floors at No. 30 Palmerston Road, Kilburn. This was a poor working-class area and five other families shared the accommodation. These terrible conditions would not have been conducive to a happy family life, and Harris often took his frustrations out on his wife and children, to a point that regular complaints were filed with the landlord, who had in turn given the Harris family notice to leave. Harris accused his wife of being unfaithful to him and took an axe to her in an attack of such violence that he virtually decapitated Annie, before turning his attention to his children, who managed to get out of the room with superficial injuries. Harris was found with deep cuts to his own throat but survived his efforts to kill himself. This brutal man was tried and sentenced to death but reprieved a week later and incarcerated in a mental asylum.

11th – A Cop with Attitude

A little less than twenty-four hours after the butchering of Annie Harris, a second murder took place less than two miles away. Friends Frederick John Smith, a coal porter, and Archibald Farrant a packer, were walking along Cardington Street, near Euston Station, just before 11 p.m. Although they had been out for an enjoyable evening neither of the friends had been drinking. They were passed on the pavement by a man called Henry Samuel Kimber, a former police inspector in the Metropolitan Police, now employed, as reported in the *London Evening Standard*

(28 September 1897), as an unredeemed pledge dealer of Robert Street, Hampstead Road. Farrant later claimed he and Smith had simply walked past the former cop with no contact; Kimber made counter-claims that Smith and Farrant had bumped into him. A pointless macho confrontation began with an exchange of boorish comments, the sort which often precede violence; Kimber stopped and turned around and exclaimed in a rather dictatorial manner, 'What are you doing here?' Farrant said they turned around to face him answering, 'What has that got to do with you?' Kimber replied, 'Get on with your business and stop following me.' Smith walked towards Kimber and a confrontation took place resulting in Kimber appearing to punch Smith in the stomach – no weapon was seen by Farrant. Smith walked about six yards back to his friend and collapsed, holding his stomach that was bleeding badly from a stab wound. Farrant followed Kimber to the junction with Hampstead Road on which stood a PC; Kimber was arrested on suspicion of inflicting serious injury. In the meantime, the ailing Smith was taken to the nearby London Temperance Hospital where he died of a single stab wound to the stomach that had penetrated as far as the spinal cord. Kimber was tried at the Old Bailey and pleaded self-defence but was convicted of the murder and sentenced to death.

12th – The Perfect Marriage

Most murders are committed by a partner in a relationship or a killer known by the victim. The aftermath of murder by one spouse on another will often take friends, family or neighbours by surprise; that they were the 'perfect couple' or 'devoted to each other' is often banded around the media. Ernest and Alice Elmes seemed to have had that perfect marriage. They lived in Tottenham and he worked at a local factory as a boiler maintenance man responsible for the working and cleaning of the equipment. On 12 September 1953, a neighbour heard the shrill screams of a woman coming from the Elmes household, but not wishing to get involved in domestic matters she ignored them.

Two days later Ernest Elmes walked into Tottenham Police Station to report that his wife had gone missing and believed she had run off with a policeman; this story changed when he told another witness that she had in fact run off with a sailor. The police were suspicious from the start as Elmes was very nervous and seemed to be suffering some mental distress – behaviour that could be related to the shock of his wife leaving him, but there seemed to be more to the case. In the meantime, Elmes had returned to work and was instructed by his foreman to clean the boilers as a penance for his absence. Elmes happily agreed. Following interviews with witnesses, the police decided to search Elmes' home. They found a bloodstained hammer with which Elmes had beaten his wife to death, and a number of saws and knives used to dismember his dearly beloved's body into several pieces before burning the remains in the factory boilers. A forensic examination revealed large bloodstains on carpets and blood splattering on some walls. A search of the ashes in the boiler unearthed several of Alice's bones, some displaying saw marks matching tools found in the house. The 'perfect marriage' had come apart when Alice Elmes met an ambulance driver on a first aid course. Before he could be arrested, Elmes committed suicide and escaped the hangman's noose.

13th – A Colourful Duo

Marilyn Anne Bain and her lesbian lover Jean McVitie were neighbours from hell. Bain had served as army nurse in the Far East before being discharged in 1959 and coupling up with McVitie. They moved into a small ground-floor flat at No. 60 Redcliffe Square. The pair were a colourful duo, often prostituting themselves with men and women in order to pay the rent. They were often drunk, which could, at times, turn into violent arguments and even physical violence. In the early hours of 13 September 1962, the pair were drunk and very loud while playing a game of cards. An argument developed about who should tidy up the cards, when they fell to the floor resulting in Bain punching her partner, knocking her unconscious. Bain claimed that she went to the toilet to be sick; on her return she found McVitie with a fatal stab wound to her chest. At her trial, a small knife was produced by the prosecution: the court accepted the defence argument that McVitie had fallen on the weapon when she fell to the floor. Bain pleaded guilty to manslaughter, which was accepted, and the murder charge was not proceeded with. Bain was given a three-year prison sentence.

14th – They Were on Our Side, You Know

Only four months had elapsed since the end of the Second World War in Europe when two British soldiers attacked a Canadian army officer on the streets of central London. Reginald Douglas Johnson and another soldier called Connolly were in Bouchier Street, Soho on 14 September 1945 when they attacked Captain John Alexander Ritchie with a brick before rifling his pockets. Johnson was caught as he tried to escape, but Connolly was never identified. Captain Ritchie died of his injuries. Twenty-four-year-old Johnson, who had served with distinction and survived the war, was sentenced to a most dishonourable death at the end of the hangman's noose, a sentence that was carried out on 29 December 1945 at Wandsworth Prison.

15th – Another Bad Cop

People kill for the most senseless of motives. Former PC Daniel Harnett had been a tenant of Edith Binks for over eight years when a dispute about an increase in rent led to the tenant murdering his landlady. The murder took place on 15 September 1920 at No. 46 Victoria Road, Stoke Newington. Harnett appeared to have hit some bad times and his rental payments were becoming increasingly irregular. Edith Binks stopped cooking and cleaning for him and increased his rent from 3s 6d a week to 4s. Harnett stormed out of the house in order to purchase some fish for his dinner. On his return the two exchanged some harsh words, during which (according to Harnett) Binks picked up an iron and threatened him with it. In retaliation Harnett took hold of a hammer and struck her over the head. Police officers found the body of Edith Binks in her kitchen with a rather large hole in her skull. It appeared Harnett had thought about covering his tracks, detectives finding a mattress soaked in paraffin on the upper level with three used matches discarded nearby. Harnett gave himself up to police later the same day; he was charged with murder but found to be unfit to plead to the charge and detained at HM's pleasure in a secure mental institution.

16th – Euston Road Murder

Elizabeth Wilmott, who lived at No. 17 Argyll Street, Kings Cross, was having a relationship with engraver Henry Victor from

Camden. On 16 September 1896, Henry Victor shot Elizabeth on Euston Road outside St Pancras Railway Station in what was believed to be a crime of passion before turning the gun on himself. Elizabeth and Henry were taken to the Royal Free Hospital in Hampstead – Elizabeth was dead on arrival, Henry died soon after. During the subsequent coroner's inquest, the expected verdicts of murder and suicide were recorded.

17th – A Clairvoyant Detective
Seventy-one-year-old Margaret Marshall opened the front door of her house at No. 10 Pell Grove, Old Ford Road, Bethnal Green to an unknown male late in the evening of 17 September 1897. The intruder subjected her to a horrific attack, smashing her face with a hammer and then stabbing her repeatedly before making good his escape. The police investigation drew a blank. Detectives were desperate for information from any member of the public who was in the area at the time – help came from an unexpected source. At the inquest a few days later, the coroner was handed a letter purporting to be from a clairvoyant. The letter provided a description of a suspect, a detailed, accurate account of the sequence of events leading up to the murder, explained that the suspect had watched the house for a number of nights, and listed specific details of the violent act itself. The letter was passed onto detectives at Scotland Yard for investigation – was this really a clairvoyant or maybe a witness not prepared to speak to the police regarding their observations, or indeed the killer himself? We will never know: the case remains unsolved.

* * *

Uruguayan national Augusto Alfredo Roggen arrived on the shores of Great Britain in May 1915. He travelled from the south up to Edinburgh where he registered with the police, as all foreign nationals were required to do, purporting to be a farmer. He sent a number of postcards to an address in Amsterdam, Holland that was known to British intelligence services as a German intelligence drop. He was arrested on 9 June 1915 in his room at the Tarbet Hotel. The intelligence services found a Browning automatic weapon with ammunition, invisible ink, several maps of the local area including Loch Long in Argyll and Bute and a list of German contacts. Security Services believed Roggen intended to spy on the Arrochar Torpedo range opened three years earlier. Roggen was tried at Middlesex Guildhall and convicted under the Defence of the Realm Act. He was executed by firing squad at the Tower of London on 17 September 1915.

18th – A Truly Dreadful Case

Richard Kwakye poured petrol through the letterbox of a family home in Camberwell on 18 September 2010 to avenge a firearms incident and a custody battle over a child. The resulting fire killed a young girl of just eighteen months. Kwakye was convicted of murder and his half-brother Dimitri John-Lewis, who supplied the petrol, convicted of manslaughter. The prosecuting counsel commented that the incident was a 'horrifying arson attack' and a 'truly dreadful case'.

19th – Hero Gives Chase

Hard-working motor mechanic and father of six children Alec de Antiquis ran a repair garage in Colliers Wood. On 29 April 1947, he made a rare venture up to central London on his motorbike for a business meeting, arriving at his destination, Charlotte Street, in the early afternoon. He passed Jay's Jewellers, located at Nos 73–75 Charlotte Street, and heard shots being fired from inside the premises. Three men ran from the shop, at least one armed with a gun. Realising the situation, he bravely gave chase on his bike, catching the robbers at the junction with Tottenham Street. As de Antiquis attempted to cut them off, he was shot cold-bloodedly through the head and died while being transported to hospital. Charlotte Street is a busy West End thoroughfare, and many witnesses came forward to assist the police. A taxi-driver recalled seeing two of the masked men entering a building on Tottenham Court Road in which detectives found a raincoat and a folded scarf used as a mask. The raincoat was traced to twenty-three-year-old Charles Henry Jenkins, a career criminal who had a number of criminal associates. Two of these associates were arrested in connection with the robbery and subsequent murder, Christopher

James Geraghty and Terence Peter Rolt. All three were members of the 'Elephant Boys' gang from South London. The suspects were charged with murder and robbery and stood trial at the Old Bailey in July 1947. The jury took just fifteen minutes to convict them; Jenkins and Geraghty were sentenced to death, while Rolt – only seventeen years of age and therefore too young to be hanged – was detained at HM's pleasure. Both Jenkins (who fired the fatal shot) and Geraghty were executed on 19 September 1947 at Pentonville Prison. Rolt served nine years before being released on licence in 1956.

20th – Why Frank?

'A murder without a motive' was how defence counsel for killer Frank Joseph Freiyer described the murder of Freiyer's girlfriend Joyce Brierley, strangled on 20 September 1946 in a public shelter in Maryon Park, Woolwich. Freiyer, a twenty-six-year-old telephone engineer, was executed at Wandsworth Prison on 13 November 1946.

21st – A Right Old Ear-Bashing

On 21 September 1998, Kathleen Pennington was murdered by her husband Brian, who suffocated her at their home in Feltham, Middlesex. At his trial, Brian Pennington claimed his wife used to 'nag' him a lot. He was sentenced to life imprisonment in April 1999.

22nd – Bad Customer Service

French soldier Henry Plunket was wanted for murder in his native France; he fled to the shores of England and made his way to London in the early part of the eighteenth century. Plunket settled in the parish of Soho. In August 1714, he went to a wig-maker called Thomas Brown and ordered a bespoke wig, which a few days later he returned to collect. Brown charged Plunket £7; Plunket, aghast at the cost, bartered Brown down to £4, but was so enraged by the exorbitant price originally charged that he pulled Brown's head back sharply and cut his throat with a razor. Brown lived long enough to describe and name his murderer; a sword and gloves left behind by the killer in his haste to escape sealed his fate. He was executed at Tyburn on 22 September 1714.

23rd – Murder in the Lord Nelson

Preston and Jane Starkey were landlord and landlady of a small intimate public house called the Lord Nelson on Whitechapel Road. Jane's sister Mary Hardwick helped out behind the bar on a regular basis; unfortunately for her, she had attracted the attentions of a rough, uneducated man called Charles Jeremiah Slowe. Slowe would often try his luck with the attractive barmaid but his advances were always rejected. On one such occasion, Slowe was heard to say, 'I'll put her light out one of these days.' On 23 September 1903, frustrated by her latest rejection, Slowe entered the pub and punched Mary Hardwick in the face and stabbed her with a knife before running from the scene. Mary died almost immediately; her killer was arrested nearby and charged with murder. Slowe's defence barrister attempted to convince the jury that he should be found guilty of manslaughter not murder as he had shown no premeditation. The jury rightly came to the conclusion that a man carrying a knife and publically stating that one day he was going to 'put her light out' was sufficient premeditation to convict of murder. Slowe was executed at Pentonville Prison on 10 November 1903.

24th – Intent on Robbery

On 4 June 1722, three armed men roamed the main carriageway heading west from central London to Kensington in the vicinity of Hyde Park intent on robbery. Robert Wilkinson, James Lincoln and Thomas Milksop shot Fleetwood Clark through the thigh before stealing his sword and 10s. The men walked triumphantly back toward Piccadilly when they identified a second opportunity and robbed elderly Chelsea pensioner Peter Martin, stealing his pistol. Martin shouted out 'thieves' but was punched to the floor and stabbed several times in the back with the sword they had just stolen from Fleetwood Clark. Many other offences were attributed to these three malevolent men, including numerous robberies and the rape of some of the victims. They were sentenced to death and executed at Tyburn on 24 September 1722.

25th – A Court Order

Ernest Alfred Sly married nineteen-year-old Beatrice Finney on 14 August 1895; they lodged at No. 250 Essex Road, Islington.

By the August bank holiday weekend a year later it had all gone wrong and Beatrice was back home living with her parents at No. 17 Little Cross Street, Islington. The couple tried to repair the damage to their marriage but it proved difficult, and Beatrice applied for a maintenance summons from her estranged husband, which increased the friction between them. On the night of 24 September 1896, Beatrice met husband Ernest outside the Little Cross Street address and went for a walk to try and sort out their differences. They returned to the house in the early hours of the 25th and went to Beatrice's room. Beatrice's father could hear heated exchanges, and finally a number of gunshots rang out. Beatrice was found on the floor with Ernest standing over her with a revolver in his hand. 'What have I done?' he exclaimed. The police arrived and Ernest was taken into custody; Beatrice was still alive and taken to St Bartholomew's Hospital. Charles Collette, a police inspector, realising that Beatrice's prognosis was not good summoned Ernest to the hospital where he took a dying declaration off Beatrice in the presence of her husband, which Beatrice signed. Beatrice died of her injuries on 29 September. At Ernest's trial Dr William Clarke, the house surgeon at St Bartholomew's Hospital on the night of the shooting, gave evidence of Beatrice's injuries, identified five bullet holes, three entry wounds and two exit wounds, the fatal shot passing through her abdomen. The jury took into consideration Ernest's action after the incident – he ran to the local doctors to summon help – and the extreme stress he was under due to the breakdown of his marriage, as well as the remorse he exhibited for his actions, and found him guilty of the lesser charge of manslaughter. He was sentenced to three years imprisonment.

26th – Death of 'Ginger Raye'
Prostitute Rachel Annie Fennick, also known as 'Ginger Raye', had well over eighty convictions for theft, prostitution and brothel keeping; she lived in a flat in Soho's Broadwick Street. On 26 September 1948 she was stabbed in her bedroom with a long-bladed knife. The obvious suspect would have been her last client but he was never traced. Her murder remains unsolved.

27th – One-Eyed Boxer

West Indian stoker and former boxer James Phillip Smartt was a man of violence, having lost an eye during a previous bout. He married twice: his first wife died of natural causes, but the second survived being shot by Smartt following his discovery of her infidelity. Towards the end of 1952, Smartt was unemployed and in need of extra cash, so he allowed a fellow West Indian, Arthur Nicols, and his Irish girlfriend, twenty-three-year-old Eleanor McCombs, to lodge at his flat, No. 63 Charlotte Street. On the morning of 27 September 1952, Arthur cooked all three breakfast and then went off to work. When he returned home that evening, McCombs was nowhere to be seen. Smartt told his lodger that his girlfriend had upped and left him. Smartt lent Nicols a pair of his trousers and shoes in order to search for McCombs in Irish pubs and clubs in the West End but they were unsuccessful. On returning to the flat Smartt seemed very keen on Nicols moving out immediately, which aroused Nicols' suspicion. He went to the police and reported his girlfriend missing and told them of his suspicions. Nicols became a suspect when detectives noticed blood on the trousers and shoes he was wearing; he explained that in fact both items had been lent to him by Smartt. The police went to the flat and searched the premises: they found the battered and strangled body of Eleanor McCombs under a pile of dirty laundry. Smartt was tried at the Old Bailey in November of 1952 and found guilty of murder but insane. He was sent to Broadmoor mental institution.

28th – A Control Freak

Accomplished pianist and music hall performer Flo Dudley enjoyed the height of her success in the early 1900s. She had been married and widowed at a young age before meeting tobacco manufacturer James Kelly. They had a relationship that lasted between the summer of 1911 and April 1912. Following the break-up of this relationship, she met a man called Edward Hopwood, who professed to be a successful managing director of his own company and unmarried. A few weeks into their relationship, Hopwood began to shower Flo with gifts and numerous marriage proposals until Flo finally agreed to marry him. It was at this point that Hopwood began to control Flo's life, convincing her to give up her stage career, getting her agent to cancel all her contracts and taking over the running of her financial affairs. Flo moved in with her sister in Ilford; Hopwood became paranoid about Dudley's movements and the people she would meet, accusing her of being unfaithful. At one stage, he even paid British Rail employees at Liverpool Street Station to report back to him when she travelled between Ilford and London. Flo eventually discovered the truth that Hopwood was, in fact, married with three children and in dire financial straits; she immediately finished the relationship and contacted her former agent in an attempt to resurrect her career.

Hopwood stalked her everywhere she went but she refused to speak to him. On 25 September 1912, Hopwood booked into a hotel in Brighton under the name of Flo's former lover James Kelly and purchased a revolver. He sent a telegram to Flo, in his assumed name, asking her to meet him for dinner in London, to which Flo agreed. The following day, 28 September 1912, Flo went to the restaurant and to her complete surprise was confronted by Hopwood. To avoid a scene, she had dinner with him and he escorted her, in a taxi, towards Fenchurch Street Station to catch a train back to Ilford. As the cab was driving along Fenchurch Street, the cabbie heard a number of loud bangs – assuming his tyres had blown he stopped the cab. On discovering his tyres were okay he opened the passenger door to check on the occupants: Flo Dudley fell into his arms bleeding from gunshot wounds to her head and chest. A police officer patrolling nearby heard the shots and ran to the taxi. Flo was near to death, and Hopwood had attempted to shoot himself but the bullet had only grazed his forehead. Flo Dudley died a few minutes after arriving at Guy's Hospital. Hopwood was charged with Miss Dudley's murder. He was tried at the Old Bailey and convicted; following an unsuccessful appeal he was executed at Pentonville Prison on 29 January 1913.

29th – Yardie Killing
Jamaican community worker Junior George Collins was shot outside a Rastafarian temple in Kennington, South London on

29 September 1999 in what was believed to be a 'Yardie'-style killing. Two men stood trial for his murder; both were convicted of firearms offences but acquitted of the more serious charge. The motive for the killing was believed to be drug related.

30th – Strength in Numbers

PC 204 'R' William Aldridge was patrolling the dangerous streets of Deptford in the early hours of 30 September 1839. A mob of five to six hundred men had formed the previous evening and remained in the area until the early hours when they became very rowdy. PC Aldridge attended the area to assist other officers and attempted to make an arrest of a man called John Pine, a woodcutter, for disorderly behaviour. The mob turned on Aldridge, throwing stones and bricks at the unarmed officer until he fell, mortally wounded, and died in a nearby house soon after. The Metropolitan Police had only been established for ten years and were generally hated, seen as agents of the government of the day. A number of rioters were arrested including John Pine, his brother William and a man called Joseph Pickering. The prosecution struggled to prove the intent to murder and only William Pine was convicted of the manslaughter of the officer.

IO

OCTOBER

1st – No Lucky Horseshoe Here

Hutton Sargent Philp, a thirty-two-year-old blacksmith who lived in Wynch Place, Walworth, was married to Rose and they had several children. Philp decided that he could no longer financially support his wife and children; this led to Rose and the children moving to her sister's address in Mawbey Place, Old Kent Road and her filing for an order of separation through the courts. Philp turned up at the sister's address on the evening of 26 July 1912 and demanded to see his estranged wife, stating that due to her actions he hadn't eaten in three days. Philp caused such a disturbance that Rose ran out of the house to escape him, but only got a short distance when her husband caught her and slit her throat with a shoemaker's knife. Philp was arrested soon after his wife's murder, and simply told the police that he was guilty and that 'she deserved it'. He was tried and convicted. During his trial, evidence was given that Philp said he would 'rather swing than pay her any money'. He received his wish on 1 October 1912 when he did indeed swing at Wandsworth Prison.

2nd – He'll Grow Out of It

The sexual behaviour of fifteen-year-old Sidney Goulter was both unnatural and a constant worry for his parents. His father was a retired police inspector who would often discuss his son's worrying behaviour with former colleagues. Sidney had taken to openly masturbating in the family home, following his mother around the house and showing a sexual interest in his younger sister to the point that their father would drive her to and from school and tell her to lock her bedroom door at night. However, as Sidney matured, his outlook towards the fairer sex seemed to mature. He qualified as an engineer and left home, and he even got himself a girlfriend, a lovely young lady called Constance Oliver, a twenty-one-year-old typist. Oliver introduced his new girlfriend to his parents, who were impressed with the new young woman in their son's life. On the evening of 2 October 1927, Constance told her parents that she was going out to meet Sidney – she never returned. A few days later after a frantic search for Constance, a body of a young woman was found in a remote copse in Richmond Park near to the Goulter's home. Constance had been found strangled and partially burnt. Sidney Goulter became an obvious suspect and was arrested shortly after the discovery. He was charged with Constance's murder and admitted that he had strangled her but was in fact insane. The medical evidence proved otherwise and Goulter was executed at Wandsworth on 6 January 1928.

3rd – Three's a Crowd

In 1909, Edith Graydon met Percy Thompson. They married in 1916 following a long engagement and moved into a house at No. 41 Kensington Gardens, Ilford. After four years of marriage, the pair became acquainted with a young merchant navy seaman, eighteen-year-old Freddy Bywaters. The three got on so well that Percy naively invited Bywaters to lodge with them between voyages. Edith formed a deep affection for Freddy, whom she found very attractive, enthralled by his tales from around the world in comparison to the rather dull life her husband led. It was inevitable that an affair between Freddy and Edith would develop. Percy found out about the affair and threw Freddy out of the house and had a violent altercation with his wife. Freddy went back to sea, though during this period he and Edith would write to each other. When he returned a year later, they conducted a clandestine love affair. On the evening of 3 October 1922, Percy and Edith attended a show at the Criterion Theatre in London's Piccadilly Circus. As they walked from Ilford Station towards their home in Kensington Gardens, Percy was attacked by a man who jumped out from behind a bush. Edith was struck and fell to the ground while Percy was stabbed during the violent struggle and mortally injured. When police arrived at the scene in Kensington Gardens, Edith volunteered almost immediately that she believed the attacker to be Freddy Bywaters. Bywaters was arrested and found to be in possession of dozens of love letters from Edith; both were charged with conspiracy to murder.

The trial of Edith and Freddy took place at the Old Bailey in December 1922. Bywaters, who confessed to the police following his arrest and led them to the murder weapon, which he discarded after the killing, was adamant that Edith had no knowledge of what he had planned. However, the letters proved to be Edith's downfall, describing in detail how she tried to poison Percy on at least two occasions and how she urged Freddy to 'do something desperate'. Edith seemed to enjoy the notoriety the trial brought her and confidently entered the witness box (although advised not to by her barrister). Her testimony was a disaster, as she lied to the court, alienating the judge and the jury. Both Freddy Bywaters and Edith were found guilty of the murder on the basis of sharing a common purpose and sentenced to death. They were executed simultaneously at 9 a.m. on 9 January 1923 – Thompson in Holloway Prison, Bywaters in Pentonville.

4th – Lunchtime Murder
Washerwoman Elizabeth Buchanan lived in a small cottage at Millfield Farm, Millfield Lane, Highgate with common-law husband of twenty years James Dobbins, a turncock for the Hampstead Water Work Company. On 4 October 1814, Dobbins left Elizabeth at lunchtime and went about his work. That afternoon Dobbins partnered up with employee William Clark; when Clark became thirsty, Dobbins invited him to go to his house and get some water. Clark returned and told Dobbins that he couldn't get through the door and he could hear moaning from the other side. Dobbins returned to find Elizabeth laying on the kitchen floor with a serious head injury, bleeding profusely; a bloodied poker lay nearby. Fifteen minutes later Elizabeth died of her injuries without regaining consciousness. A murder hunt started and several witnesses came forward having seen a man, later identified as Thomas Sharp, in the

vicinity of the house at the material time. Sharp was arrested nearby in possession of property (some items of clothing) from Dobbins' house. He was charged with the murder and tried at the Old Bailey. Sharp pleaded not guilty and told the court he had bought the clothing from a gypsy. Sharp was convicted and executed on 31 October 1814 at Newgate Prison.

5th – They Got Away with This One

The Turner Steam Bread and Biscuit Factory was located at No. 151 Borough High Street in 1875. Jane Soper was housekeeper to the factory's owner Mr Turner. On Sunday 22 September 1875, Turner had gone to his country residence and all other staff had a day off except Jane Soper, who was preparing the factory for the working week ahead. Two men broke into the premises; surprised to see anybody inside, they sneaked up and quickly dispatched Jane Soper by striking her over the head. Although the assault was extremely violent, Jane Soper seemed to recover from the ordeal, giving police as much assistance as she could. But a few days later Jane had a relapse and died on 5 October 1875. Suspicion for what was now a murder fell on a man named Sherman Fletcher Morley after his brother-in-law admitted to a friend that Sherman was the one who had struck what turned out to be the fatal blow. Morley and his brother-in-law went underground; police were determined to catch the offenders and kept observations for many weeks on the home address of Morley, until their patience and tenacity were rewarded with their return in February 1876. Sadly, the police had insufficient evidence other than whispers and innuendo and the two were released without charge. The murder remains officially unsolved although detectives were convinced they had the right men.

6th – The Girl in Green

Britain had been at war for three years by 1942, and many of London's children faced separation from their families and evacuation to the countryside. Eleven-year-old Sheila Margaret Wilson was one such child, sent to Wiltshire but returned home to the family address, No. 67 Leahurst Road, Lewisham in May 1942. On 15 July of the same year, Sheila was playing outside the house with her younger brother when she disappeared. Many volunteers, organised by the police, searched local bombsites for Sheila. Her disappearance warranted a considerable press interest, with the papers naming it the 'Girl in Green' case as Sheila was wearing a green dress when she vanished. Police conducted house-to-house enquiries, convinced the answer lay with local people. Five days later, on 20 July, detectives visited No. 19 Leahurst Road, a small lodging house, the home of a man named by locals as Patrick William Kingston, who had left his lodgings soon after Sheila disappeared. The house was searched by police and the remains of Sheila were found under some floorboards; she had been strangled and sexually assaulted. The former ARP man had a distinctive limp and had part of his left index finger missing – blown off during an explosion. On 23 July, Kingston inexplicably returned to Leahurst Road and was arrested by a local constable. Kingston told the officer that 'I strangled her and then got scared and ran away'. His appearance and sentence at the Old Bailey was one of the shortest recorded in the annals of this historic hub of British justice – a guilty plea and a death sentence passed in five minutes. He was executed on 6 October 1942.

7th – Shot to Impress

American soldier Private Karl Gustav Hulten had gone AWOL from his Newbury barracks and travelled to London. On the night of 7 October 1944, Hulten hit it off with an exotic dancer from the Blue Lagoon Club in Carnaby Street, who used the stage name Georgina Grayson. They left the club and hailed a taxi; as they travelled through Chiswick, Karl Hulten shot the cab driver, George Heath – it seems in order to impress Grayson. Heath's body was found in Staines. Murder detectives traced the stolen taxi to Lurgan Avenue, Fulham and waited for somebody to return to it. A few hours later, Hulten came out of a nearby address. As he got into the car he was arrested on suspicion of murder and found in possession of a Remington automatic pistol and ammunition. At first he gave his name as Second Lieutenant Richard Allen. He was interviewed at length by the American Army Criminal Investigation Department at Hammersmith Police Station. After several hours of interrogation, he broke down and revealed his real name, claiming he had found the car near his Newbury barracks and that Georgina Grayson would provide an alibi for his movements on the night of the murder. Grayson was brought in and at first confirmed the alibi but later retracted it and told the police that she was with Hulten when he shot Heath. The American Government granted the British judicial system jurisdiction to deal with Hulten; he and Georgina, whose real name was Elizabeth Jones, were tried and found guilty of the murder. The Bonnie and Clyde wannabes were both sentenced to death. Two days before the execution date Jones was reprieved and her sentence commuted to life imprisonment – she was released in 1954. Hulten was hanged at Pentonville on 8 March 1945.

8th – Killer Headmaster

Reverend John Selby Watson had both a distinguished career in the church and in education. In 1839, he was ordained deacon to the Bishop of Ely but it was a poorly paid position. Due to his penury, his intended marriage to fiancée Ann Armstrong was delayed until January 1845, following their move to London the year before when Watson secured the position of headmaster at Stockwell Grammar School in South London. He held this position for many years, until redundancy without a pension in 1870. The couple lived at No. 28 St Martins Road, Stockwell. Following his fall from grace Ann Watson, who was much younger than her husband, started to chastise him for his inability to provide an income and to please her in the bedroom. On the morning of 8 October 1871, both Mr and Mrs Watson left for church, returning home in the early afternoon. The housekeeper, Mrs Eleanor Payne, made them some lunch before leaving for her afternoon off. When she returned at 9 p.m., John Watson told her that her mistress had gone out of town and wouldn't be back until the following day. As the housekeeper retired to bed, she observed Watson come out of the library. He indicated to a dark red patch on the library floor, explaining to Payne, 'This stain on the floor is port wine your mistress has spilt, in case you might wonder what it is – I have told you.' The following day, Watson informed Payne that his wife would not be home for a further couple of days. On Tuesday night, 10 October, Watson commented to Payne that should she find anything wrong with him the next morning to contact Dr Rugg. Payne asked if he was ill. Watson replied, 'I may require medicine in the morning.' The following morning, 11 October, Payne made breakfast for Watson. He then went out, returning at 11 a.m. and going up to his bedroom. The housekeeper went to his bedroom to offer him tea and heard him groaning in some pain. Bearing in mind his instructions the night before, she entered the room and found Watson on his bed unconscious. Placed on the bedside table were two letters and a phial. One of the letters was addressed to Payne containing a £5 note and in Watson's handwriting the words, 'For the Servant Ellen Payne, exclusive of her wages. Let no suspicion fall on the servant, whom I believe to be a good girl.' The other letter was addressed to Dr Rugg who Payne fetched immediately. Rugg attended to his patient first before reading the letter addressed to him:

> I have killed my wife in a fit of rage to which she provoked me; often, often has she provoked me before, but I never lost restraint over myself with her till the present occasion when I allowed fury to carry me away. Her body will be found in the room adjoining the library, the key of which I leave with the paper. I trust she will be buried with the attention due to a lady of good birth.

Dr Rugg found Annie Watson in the room described – she had been dead for several days, suffering fatal head injuries inflicted by the butt of a horse-pistol.

Watson stood trial at the Old Bailey in January 1872. Instead of pleading provocation he choose to plead insanity, which the judge dismissed following medical evidence of his fitness to stand trial. He was convicted and sentenced to death. However, following the trial many affidavits were submitted from several doctors stating Watson was indeed insane at the time of the murders. The case was referred to the Home Secretary and the sentence commuted to life imprisonment. Watson died in Parkhurst Prison, aged eighty, following a fall from his hammock.

9th – The Best of Mates

London street traders and great friends Peter Cyril Johnson and Charles Mead were almost inseparable, spending much of their spare time in each other's company. On the evening of Saturday 28 June 1952, Johnson, a West Indian from Brixton, crossed the

Thames to meet up with Mead at his local pub in Bethnal Green in London's East End. The friends got involved in a game of cards, and following a rare disagreement both men went outside the pub to settle the quarrel. This escalated into a full-blown fight from which Johnson emerged victorious. Both men went to a friend's house nearby to clean themselves and hoping to patch up their friendship. Following a truce, they then made their way to Mead's house in nearby Minerva Street, Bethnal Green. During the short walk, they started to argue again, leading to more violence and Johnson inflicting injuries so severe on his friend that they proved fatal. The prosecution would allege that Johnson picked up a piece of concrete and battered Mead to death; Johnson claimed that it was Mead who had first attacked him with the concrete and he had killed Mead in self-defence. The jury convicted Peter Johnson of murder and he was executed at Pentonville on 9 October 1952.

10th – Dear Len

Victoria Villas were located on Victoria Road, Kilburn. No. 13 was the home of Mary Alice Maud Moncrieff, otherwise known as Fullick, aged sixty, and her daughter Beatrice Maud Fullick, a shop assistant. Beatrice had been having an on/off relationship with a wood machinist named Leonard George Hucker over a period of two years. Around 11 August 1939, the couple had an argument resulting in Beatrice telling Leonard she no longer wanted to see him – she broke the news by sending him a postcard on which she wrote, 'Dear Len – shall not be seeing you again as I have made other arrangements', signed 'Trix'. The 'other arrangements' seemed to be a new man in her life called Reg. Leonard went around to the house on 16 August to clear the air and attempt a reconciliation. However, he ran into Beatrice's mother, Mary. A confrontation was inevitable and as Mary walked towards the coal shed in the basement, Leonard stabbed her in the chest with a knife. Hucker then walked to a local police station and informed the desk officer that 'I have murdered a woman today at Victoria Villas. She is Mrs Fullick my girl's mother. I stabbed her. Here is the key.' Hucker was arrested and the body discovered. During his trial, Leonard stated that both he and the deceased got very angry with each other on the day of the incident. He took a knife from his pocket, which he had previously purchased to kill himself but had lacked the courage, to frighten her as she approached him, and the knife became embedded in her chest. Hucker was found guilty of the crime and executed on 10 October 1939 at Wandsworth Prison.

* * *

Daniel Raven was a man of little wealth and no great career prospects; he had served in the Royal Air Force with distinction during the Second World War and gained employment as an advertising agent. When he proposed to his girlfriend Marie Goodman, her parents, wealthy businessman Leopold and wife Esther, were not overly enamoured with their future son-in-law, but their daughter loved him so they tried to get on. They were married in 1948 and Leopold purchased a house for them in Edgwarebury Lane near to their own house at No. 8 Ashcombe Gardens, Edgware. The only legitimate complaint Daniel seemed to have is that his mother-in-law would continuously nag and belittle his efforts to properly support their daughter. He may well have gone some way to placate his mother-in-law when the couple announced they were expecting their first child. On 6 October 1949, Marie delivered the Goodman's first grandchild. They visited the nursing home in Muswell Hill four days later on 10 October and were delighted, congratulating Daniel before leaving to travel home by car. Daniel followed them home in his own car and then drove onto Edgwarebury Lane a short distance away.

Just before 10 p.m. that night, Leopold's brother-in-law and business partner visited the Goodman's house. As he entered the premises he was deeply shocked to discover Leopold and Esther had been murdered, both severely beaten around their heads. Detectives ruled out burglary as a motive as there had been no forced entry and nothing seemed to have been stolen. Daniel Raven turned up at the house seemingly shocked at the murder of his in-laws and telling the police how they had recently been concerned about burglaries in the area, but when he left them earlier in the evening they were in perfectly good health. The police became suspicious of Raven's over-acted emotions and, as he appeared to be the last person to see the Goodman's alive, they decided to search Daniel's house, and found a bloodstained suit stuffed into a boiler and recently cleaned shoes. He was arrested on suspicion of the killings and eventually charged with the murder. At his trial in November 1949 at the Old Bailey, the prosecution case was a strong one. The forensic evidence was compelling: the blood on the suit, which he had tried to burn, was the same group as both the Goodman's. The likely murder weapon – the weighty base of a television aerial – was found in the kitchen of his house, and a large amount of cash present in the room in which they were murdered was untouched (so unlikely to be a burglar). An intelligent defence was put to the jury in order to try and introduce the slightest degree of reasonable doubt in order to secure an acquittal. Daniel claimed he returned to the address because he was, as he explained to the police, concerned about burglars. When he found the bodies he got blood over his suit and shoes, and fearing he may become a suspect went home and tried to destroy the evidence. The jury were not to be deflected from the strong prosecution case and he was convicted following fifty minutes of deliberation. An appeal failed, as did a petition of many thousands of signatures; he was executed on 6 January 1950 at Pentonville.

11th – Starved to Death

The distasteful practice of 'baby farming' often led to negligence and cruelty of children in the *care* of these heartless women, and at worst resulted in infanticide. One of the first women to be executed for this practice was Margaret Waters, who was hanged on 11 October 1870. Waters, from Brixton in South London, would trick or force children in her care to take appetite-suppressing drugs and watch them starve to death; she was believed to be responsible for the murder of at least nineteen children. Waters was tried on a specimen charge for the murder of infant John Walter Cowen and executed at Horsemonger Lane Prison.

12th – Burglary Gone Wrong

Commercial Road, Stepney in 1904 was a dangerous place but still home to sixty-five-year-old Matilda Emily Farmer, who ran a small tobacco and newsagents business from No. 478. At 6.30 a.m. on 12 October 1904, Charles Gillingham was delivering papers to the shop and was surprised to see the door of the premises insecure.

Concerned for the safety of Matilda Farmer, he entered the premises and found her body on the bed face down; she had been bound and gagged and died of asphyxiation. A local man informed police he had seen two men come out of the premises earlier that morning, one of whom he recognised and provided the name and address to detectives. Two local men, Conrad Donovan, a thirty-four-year-old sailor, and his half-brother, twenty-two-year-old Charles Wade, were arrested. Both were charged with Miss Farmer's murder and burglary and tried for their crimes in November 1904. The jury convicted both following a three-day trial, and the brothers were executed at Pentonville on 13 December 1904.

* * *

At 1.13 p.m. on 12 October 1992, a telephone call was made to a radio station stating that PIRA had planted a bomb in the 'Leicester Square area'. The call was accompanied by a recognised authenticated code word, but police were up against huge odds to discover the exact location and evacuate in time. The bomb went off just seventeen minutes later at 1.30 p.m. in the gentlemen's toilets of the Sussex Arms pub in Long Acre (200 m from Leicester Square). A number of people were injured by a bomb designed to target the lunchtime trade.

13th – Judgement Day
Fashion student Phiona Davis murdered her boyfriend Keith Fernandez on 13 October 2003 by stabbing him fifty-eight times, before murdering her great-grandmother, whom she stabbed one-hundred and thirty times. Davis, who lived in Green Lanes, Palmers Green, North London, was found not guilty of murder due to diminished responsibility at the Old Bailey in 2004. She stated to doctors that she thought Fernandez was a robot and her great-grandmother the devil and she attacked them as she believed 'Judgment Day' had arrived. Davis was given a hospital order under the Mental Health Act and sent to Broadmoor Hospital.

14th – Conman to Murderer
Career criminal Harold Dorian Trevor was a confidence trickster who had been in and out of prison most of his life. Sitting in his

cell, days before his release from his latest prison term, he planned his next crime. On the morning of 14 October 1941, he made his way to No. 71A Elsham Road, Kensington, where a room had been advertised for rent. He introduced himself to the owner, Mrs Theodora Jessie Greenhill, as Doctor Trevor. Harold intended to look around the house, pocketing a few valuables as he did so. They came to an agreement for the rent and Mrs Greenhill issued a receipt in the name of Dr H. D. Trevor. Mrs Greenhill was a little more astute than Harold gave her credit for, witnessing him pocket a silver cigarette box. She went to telephone the police but was knocked to the floor by the callous criminal and strangled.

The reason for Trevor's frequent prison stints during most of his adult life was his unprofessionalism and incompetence, often leaving his fingerprints at the scene of his crimes. He had now escalated the level of his criminality by committing murder, a crime that would prove to be his last as detectives discovered the receipt he had left behind together with his fingerprints. Trevor, now wanted for murder, left London for Wales and evaded capture until early 1942 when arrested in Rhyl. He was returned to London to stand trial at the Old Bailey and convicted on the basis of overwhelming evidence, including an eyewitness who had seen him leave the address. He was executed at Wandsworth Prison on 11 March 1942.

15th – She Saw the Light

Liverpudlian Agnes Oates came down to London for work and found employment in the Crown Tavern, Salmon Lane, Limehouse. She met lighterman John Wiggins and their relationship developed into a marriage proposal; Agnes soon moved in with Wiggins. The couple both possessed explosive temperaments and could often be heard quarrelling, usually about money. On 31 August 1867, following another argument, John Wiggins cut Agnes' throat. At his trial, Wiggins stated that Agnes had been the one to pick up a knife and attack him – he had several knife wounds to his own throat when arrested – and then she cut her own throat. The sequence of events and the delivery of the fatal wound appeared to prove otherwise, and the jury convicted Wiggins of the murder. He was executed at Newgate on 15 October 1867.

16th – Just Plain Daft

Killers often used bizarre excuses to save themselves from the rope. Some can be inventive, even convincing; who really knows how many killers have talked their way out of a murder charge or conviction. But some are just plain daft. Lee Kun was a twenty-seven-year-old Chinese national, who earned his living at sea. He lived with an English woman called Clara Thomas in Pennyfields, Poplar, East London. Kun was not happy when Clara announced that their relationship was over and she moved in with friend Harriet Wheaton a few doors away. On 16 October 1915, Kun turned up at Harriet's house demanding to see Clara. Clara took Kun out into the backyard and a few minutes later Harriet heard screams. She went to investigate and saw Kun standing over her friend, stabbing her with a large kitchen knife. Kun then turned his attention to Harriet, undoubtedly with the intention of killing the only witness to the crime. Harriet fought off her attacker with a broom handle as she screamed for help; Clara died of her injuries. Kun was arrested at the scene and placed on trial, offering the defence that he had come around to the house to collect some money he had lent Clara; she started to get hysterical, produced a knife and set about stabbing herself, inflicting the injuries to which she succumbed. The jury dismissed the implausible defence and convicted Kun. He was executed on New Year's Day 1916.

17th – Who Killed Miss Smith?

A young Polish Jew called Esther Prac was murdered in her own bed on 17 October 1908. Miss Prac had used the name of Smith to book the room in the lodging house just off Bernard Street near to Russell Square. The following morning the landlady of the boarding house noticed that 'Miss Smith' hadn't come down from her room. When this was still the case by mid-afternoon she started to worry and knocked on her door but got no reply. She summoned her son who again knocked before entering the room; the door was unlocked. At first they could find no sign of Esther, until they pulled the sheets of the bed back revealing the corpse of the unfortunate girl; a towel had been tied tightly around her neck. Scotland Yard attended the scene: mysteriously they found two lengths of copper wiring in the room, one tied around the bedstead, another entwined in the towel that had been used to strangle her. The killer was never discovered and the case remains unsolved.

18th – The Butcher of England

John Tiptoft was an English nobleman whose fearsome reputation led him to be known as 'The Butcher of England'. Tiptoft enjoyed a successful political and military career, bestowed with the earldom of Worcester in 1449, followed by Lord High Treasurer and Lord Deputy of Ireland. He received the Order of the Garter from King Edward IV and became Constable of the Tower in 1463. As Lord High Constable, he presided over the trials and executions of Lancastrians during the War of the Roses and implemented his regime with extreme cruelty, often having them beheaded, quartered and impaled. As Chancellor of Ireland, again his cruelty knew no bounds, executing Thomas FitzGerald for treason. His past caught up with him on the Readeption of Henry VI in October 1470. Tiptoft failed to escape with Edward IV and his supporters and was captured by the Lancastrians. He was executed by beheading at the Tower of London on 18 October 1470 with the honour he wickedly denied others. He asked his executioner to behead him with three blows of the sword for the sake of the Holy Trinity.

19th – The Business of Spying

Fernando Buschman was born in Paris of Brazilian parents. Before the First World War Buschman started up a successful import/export food business mainly between Brazil, Germany and England, so was a frequent visitor to Britain. The commencement of war obviously created a great deal of anti-German feeling in Britain, and Buschman went to Hamburg to run the business from there. He was still a frequent visitor to these shores and in April 1915 stayed in London at the Piccadilly Hotel on business. During this stay, he visited major south-coast ports on the pretext of business but was in fact spying for Germany. British secret services watched closely, intercepting incriminating telegrams, and eventually Buschman was arrested and put on trial at the Middlesex Guildhall and sentenced to death by firing squad. Buschman asked permission to keep his beloved violin with him in his cell at the Tower of London the night before his execution. He was granted this last request and played for most of the night. At 7 a.m. on 19 October 1915, as he was led from his cell he laid the violin down and said, 'Goodbye I shall not want you anymore.' He was led to his death in just a shirt, which he pulled open and refused a blindfold; he faced death with a smile on his face.

20th – Serial Poisoner

The last woman to be hanged in public in England was nurse Catherine Wilson. Wilson attempted to murder Sarah Carnell, a woman whom she was caring for, in February 1862. She was charged with the attempt, but while waiting for the trial detectives started to look at other deaths that had occurred during her nursing career. One in particular stood out, the death of Mrs Maria Soames in a nursing home in Alfred Street, Bloomsbury, who died on 17 October 1856, poisoned with large doses of colchicum. Wilson was acquitted on the charge of attempted murder of Sarah Carnell but immediately arrested and charged with the murder of Maria Soames. Detectives believed Wilson had in fact poisoned several other women in her care, all for financial gain, but she never confessed. She was executed in public outside at Horsemonger Lane on 20 October 1862.

* * *

William Danso worked as a doorman and security guard at the Brixton Academy nightclub on Stockwell Road, Brixton. The thirty-one-year-old had a confrontation with Gary Nelson, a man later described by police as one of the most 'violent and dangerous men to walk the streets of Britain' (*The Telegraph*, 18 February 2006). Danso had refused Nelson entry into the Brixton Academy; a further incident occurred a few weeks later when Danso – working on this occasion as a security guard at a mobile phone shop – broke up a fight in which Nelson was involved. Nelson accused Danso of 'disrespecting' him. On 20 October 1993, Nelson went to Danso's home address in Cato Road, Clapham with two other men and 'executed' Danso in the hallway of his house. At the time of the murder a uniformed police officer Patrick Dunne was attending an unconnected domestic dispute in Cato Road opposite Danso's house and heard the gunshots, but as he ran to investigate he was shot in the chest and died of his injuries. The killers walked away from the scene laughing and firing a triumphant shot in the air. Nelson was the main suspect and was arrested, but the Crown Prosecution Service (CPS) decided that there was insufficient evidence to proceed. In the meantime, Nelson was jailed for possession of firearms in relation to another incident. The CPS, with the introduction of further evidence, charged Nelson with the murders in 2004 and he was convicted. He was sentenced to a minimum of thirty-five years imprisonment. A memorial stands in Cato Road on the spot PC Dunne lost his life while performing his duty.

21st – Close Call for Londoners
The year 1992 was one of PIRA's most prolific years for attacks on mainland Britain. Earlier this year, huge bombs had exploded in St Mary Axe and Staples Corner. On 21 October, three small bombs exploded. The first at Silver Street Railway Station was placed on the track and detonated as a train was passing; two people were treated for minor injuries. The second device slightly injured three at the Princess Louise TA barracks in Hammersmith Road W6. The third, finally, exploded in Harrow Road, where there were no reported casualties. Before these explosions, the police had received sixty-one reports of devices that day alone: all proved to be hoaxes.

22nd – Close Call for Prime Minister
A 2.5 kg bomb exploded in Brooks Club in St James' Street Mayfair on this day in 1974. The bomb exploded near to the dining room in which Conservative Party Leader Edward Heath was dining. Three waiters were slightly injured and extensive damage was caused to the ceiling of the room. Although no direct evidence was found nor claims made that Heath was indeed the target – the club was used by retired military personnel – he did become the direct target of assassination later that year when a bomb was placed at his home just before Christmas.

23rd – Sugar of Lead
Following the death in 1882 of her husband, who was a great deal older than her, Louisa Jane Taylor received a small pension that she could barely live off. She contacted a close friend of her husband's, former customs officer William Tregellis, who was well into his 80s

and lived with his sickly wife Mary Anne, who was eighty-two. Louisa suggested that she move into their home in Plumstead, south-east London, and help take care of Mary Ann. The Tregellises agreed and decided it best that she sleep in the same bed as Mary Ann, William moving to the front room. William begun to notice some of their possessions were going missing, and the obvious suspect was Louisa. At the same time, Mary Ann's health was deteriorating fast, suffering fits and violent bouts of vomiting. The family doctor was summoned, who asked Louisa to retain a sample of Mary Anne's vomit for analysis – a request Louisa failed to follow. Around the same period, Dr Smith had been prescribing Louisa with lead acetate, more commonly known as 'sugar of lead' to aid her complexion. William called in the police when his pension disappeared. Louisa had been seen leaving the house in possession of the cash. Dr Smith was again at the house when the police turned up and arrested Louisa for theft. The penny seems to have dropped when he realised that the lead acetate he had been subscribing Louisa had probably been used to poison Mary Ann and that he had inadvertently been supplying it. Examining Mary Ann, armed with his suspicions, he noticed telltale signs of such poisoning, in particular a dark blue line at the edge of her gums. Mary Ann accused Louisa, in the presence of the doctor and the police, of poisoning her. The unfortunate victim died a few days later on 23 October 1882.

Louisa was tried at the Old Bailey in December 1882. Evidence was heard from William about the thefts and the deterioration in his wife's condition and her agonising death. Medical evidence was produced detailing the amount of lead found in the deceased's major organs. Louisa was found guilty of murder after just twenty minutes but with a recommendation for mercy, which was dismissed by the judge; whilst sentencing Louisa to death he told her that the murder was 'cruel, treacherous and hypocritical'. She was hanged at Maidstone Prison on 2 January 1883.

24th – Business is Business

Jewish antique dealer Isaac Marks fell in love with Caroline Barnard in the early part of 1874. Following their courtship, Isaac asked Frederick Barnard, Caroline's father, for his permission to marry his daughter. Frederick was a fellow Jew and an umbrella maker of Newington Butts. He checked out his future son-in-law's business credentials and prospects and agreed to the marriage. Shortly before the marriage was to take place, in 1876, Isaac's house was burnt down, Marks turning to his future father-in-law Frederick for help in claiming the insurance to rebuild the house in which the couple were to live. Frederick did indeed help but presented Isaac with a very large bill for his services. Isaac reacted very angrily and broke off the engagement to Caroline. On the evening of 24 October 1876, Isaac purchased a gun from a local gunsmith and waited outside a shop in Penton Place, Southwark, when Frederick Barnard appeared he shot him three times, threw the gun down in the street and walked to Kennington Lane Police Station and surrendered himself into police custody. At his trial, Marks' barrister offered insanity as a defence as both the defendant's parents had died in lunatic asylums. This was rejected by the jury who convicted him of murder; he was executed at Horsemonger Lane prison on 2 January 1877.

* * *

Metropolitan Police officer Nina Mackay attended Arthingworth Street, Stratford on 24 October 1997 in order to make a routine arrest of a male who had broken his bail conditions. Mackay and fellow officers forced entry into the premises occupied by the wanted man Magdi Elgizouli, an unemployed paranoid schizophrenic. Mackay was confronted by Elgizouli in the hallway of the premises armed with a large kitchen knife, which he thrust into the officer's chest. Nina Mackay was rushed to hospital but died of her injuries two hours later. She was aged just twenty-five and had been in the police service five years. Elgizouli was charged with her murder and, in October 1998, found guilty of manslaughter due to diminished responsibility and ordered to be detained indefinitely in a secure mental hospital; he was released back into society just ten years later. This brave officer – killed in the execution of her duty – will never be forgotten, not least by members of her family and colleagues but also by the residents of Stratford where a memorial, unveiled by Prime Minister Tony Blair, stands near to where she fell. A small close just off Arthingworth Street has been named after the officer as well as a River Thames vessel of the Metropolitan Police's Marine Policing Unit.

25th – Too Neat for a Doctor

Drug addict Josun Soan walked into a Boots chemist located on Lower Marsh, Waterloo on 25 October 1980 and attempted to obtain drugs using a forged prescription. An astute chemist thought the writing on the document too neat for a doctor and kept Soan waiting while a colleague called the police. Within minutes, PCs Frank O'Neill and Angela Seeds arrived. Soan realising the game was up struck out with a knife, stabbing PC O'Neill in the stomach. Both he and Angela Seeds chased Soan but Frank O'Neill collapsed and later died of his injuries. Angela Seeds, displaying extreme courage, continued to chase the killer as far as Lambeth North tube station where she detained him. Soan was tried at the Old Bailey in May 1981 for PC O'Neill's murder. He claimed in court that when the officer approached him he had been hallucinating and thought him to be a 'big brown bear', which he slashed out at. Soan was found guilty and sentenced to life imprisonment. O'Neill – a father of four – was posthumously awarded the Queen's Gallantry Medal and a Metropolitan Police building on Clapham Road in south London is named in his honour.

26th – Bravest of the Brave

There can be few braver men and women than those who place their lives on the line to defuse IEDs, whether in the theatre of war or on the streets of Great Britain. Many have died protecting their colleagues and the ordinary citizen. Kenneth Howarth, a civilian explosives officer, was employed by the Metropolitan Police. Mr Howarth had a distinguished military career, serving twenty-three years with the Royal Army Ordnance Corps in many parts of the world; he retired at the rank of Warrant Officer Class 1. He joined the Metropolitan Police in 1973, at a time when the PIRA was at its most dangerous, and routinely faced life-threatening situations. On 26 October 1981, police received an authenticated warning from PIRA that a number of bombs had been placed in various retail premises on London's busiest shopping area – Oxford Street. A booby-trapped device was discovered in the basement toilet of a Wimpey restaurant; while Mr Howarth was attempting to defuse the device, it exploded and he was killed instantly. Mr Howarth, who was married and had two children, was posthumously awarded the George Medal. Two terrorists were eventually convicted of this and several other attacks, receiving prison sentences with a recommended minimum of thirty-five years. They were released in 1999 under the Good Friday Agreement having served only fourteen years.

27th – A Shake of Hands

Another German spy to be shot at the Tower of London was American-born Irving Guy Ries. Ries travelled to London via New York and Liverpool in July 1915 booking into the Cecil Hotel on London's Strand. This hotel was popular with Americans at the time and Ries claimed he was a sales representative for two New York based companies. On 9 July, the British Security Services intercepted a telegram destined for Ries at the Cecil Hotel originating from an address in Amsterdam, Holland transferring £40. The address was known to the British as a German intelligence drop; from this point on, he was placed under surveillance. The telegram was delivered to Ries who cashed the £40 in a post office in Southampton Street, Holborn. Ries booked out of the hotel and travelled to Liverpool, Newcastle, Glasgow and Edinburgh before returning via Liverpool to the Cecil Hotel in London – arriving back on 28 July 1915. He received a further telegram authorising a second money transfer, which he again cashed at the same post office. On 9 August, he attended the American Embassy to apply for a visa to travel to Rotterdam, Holland. A sharp-eyed member of embassy staff spotted that the passport was a forgery and contacted the police at Scotland Yard. The following day, Ries was arrested at the Cecil Hotel. He admitted that the passport was a forgery but denied spying for the Germans and insisted that the payments were genuine business transactions. He was tried at Middlesex Guildhall: the prosecution had no evidence that Ries had actually passed any information to the Germans but his travel patterns and intention to return to Holland to probably pass on such information verbally was enough to convict him of spying. He was executed at 7 a.m. on 27 October 1915, having shaken hands with the firing squad.

28th – Met His Match

German Jew Noah Woolf had lived in Britain since 1871. The Victorians spent a great deal of time and effort promoting the Christian religion among Hebrews, Woolf and his wife among those to convert to Christianity. Woolf managed to secure accommodation in the Home for Aged Hebrew Christians at No. 43 St John's Villas, Upper Holloway. However, he was not popular among his peers due to his bad language and propensity to smoke and drink whiskey (which he would often smuggle in), behaviour deemed unfitting for a respectable Hebrew Christian. Mrs Woolf died in March 1909; Woolf managed to cling onto his residency even though he made no effort to moderate his behaviour. In February 1910, Woolf met his nemesis, an argumentative, dislikeable man called Aaron Simon, who took up residence at the home. Simon quickly became a conduit between the residents who kept their opinions to themselves and the management. He would often verbally attack Woolf in the presence of the others accusing him of being a foul-mouthed drunk who had no place in such an establishment. By July 1910, Simon had achieved his aim and forced the house superintendent to expel Woolf, who left on 4 July moving into lodgings at No. 68 Myddleton Street in Clerkenwell. He survived for a while by returning to his former trade of bookbinding; this work soon dried up and he found himself destitute and in squalid lodgings in Canonbury Road, a stones-throw from St John's Villas. He appealed to be let back in but was refused.

Woolf decided on revenge as a focus for his anger. Arming himself with a knife, he returned to the home on the evening of 27 October 1910, and attempted to gain entry but was turned away by a new member of staff who informed him that Simon was asleep in his room. Woolf returned the next day, 28 October, and this time was successful. He asked Simon to withdraw his allegations, which formed the basis of his expulsion, but Simon refused. Woolf drew the knife from his pocket and stabbed Simon in the neck and chest before making himself scarce. Although only in his late fifties Woolf realised that he had no future on the run and gave himself up at a local police station, admitting fully to the killing of Aaron Simon. He was tried at the Old Bailey but had little defence and was convicted, but supported by a plea of mercy from the jury. The plea fell on deaf ears and he was executed at Pentonville on 21 December 1910.

29th – 'My Young Lady'

John Ernest Smith, a twenty-one-year-old labourer, was in love with his girlfriend Christina Dicksee and planned to marry her as soon as he could. Smith lived at his mother and stepfather's house on Old Kent Road, Southwark, and Christina with her parents on the Downham Estate in Kent. When Smith told Christina's parents of their plans they, although not against the marriage, asked them to wait for a while. Smith seems to have taken this as a rejection, becoming paranoid that her parents were intent on separating them. The pair were together in Smith's room late at night on 29 October 1941 when Smith's stepfather heard screams coming from the room. When he investigated he found the blood-soaked body of Christina – she had been stabbed thirty-four times. Smith was arrested and told the police that 'I have stabbed my young lady'. During a later statement he admitted, 'I was determined that they [Christina's parents] were not going to part us. My intention was to have a last talk with her and kill her.' (*Derby Daily Telegraph*, 14 November 1941). During the trial, evidence was introduced by the defence of the couples adoration and love for each other, once exchanging thirteen love letters in one day. But the ferocity of the attack left little manoeuvre for any successful appeal and Smith was executed at Wandsworth on 3 December 1941.

30th – Baby Clegg

Joan Clegg became pregnant during the last few months of the Second World War following a brief fling with an unknown soldier; she attempted to keep the pregnancy a secret from her parents. Seven months into the pregnancy, her astute father noticed his daughter's changing body shape and confronted her. Adoption was discussed and decided upon. As Arthur Clegg attempted to make arrangements to have his daughter's child adopted at birth, Joan was taken into St Bart's Hospital where she gave birth to a healthy baby girl, whom she named Jill. Joan was released from hospital after a few days, leaving her daughter in the care of hospital staff until the adoption was finalised. On 30 October 1945, with all efforts to find adoptive parents for Jill exhausted, Arthur Clegg attended the hospital and collected his eleven-day-old granddaughter. When he arrived home a couple of hours later he was alone. The body of an infant was washed up on the bank of the River Thames in Richmond days later. A hospital tag attached to the tiny wrist simply read 'baby Clegg'. Police traced the birth tag back to St Bart's and in turn to the Clegg's home. As Arthur Clegg opened the door he reportedly said to the police, 'Ah, well I have been expecting this.' He tried to convince the police and eventually a jury that he *had* found an adoptive parent called Mrs Clark, to whom he had handed over his granddaughter. No trace was ever found of Mrs Clark. Clegg was found guilty of murdering his granddaughter and executed at Wandsworth Prison on 19 March 1946, aged forty-two.

31st – Blodie Belgiam

Regent Square in 1917 was, as it is today, a quiet residential square located between Euston Road and the popular district of Bloomsbury. A bloody discovery in the confines of the square sparked an investigation that shook Edwardian London to the bone. On 2 November 1917, a road-sweeper made a gruesome discovery. A large parcel, wrapped in a sack, had been left by the railings bordering the central gardens. Inquisitive as to its contents, he opened it up to reveal the headless corpse of a woman, still dressed in fine lace lingerie, wrapped in a blood-soaked linen sheet. A scribbled out note accompanied the grisly find that read simply 'Blodie Belgiam'. Shocked by his discovery the road-sweeper looked around him for any further clues and spied another package, this time wrapped in brown paper, in which he uncovered a pair of severed legs; the killer(s) had, it seemed, disposed of the head and hands more thoroughly to avoid the victim's identification. The eminent pathologist Sir Bernard Spilsbury conducted a post-mortem on the remains concluding the victim had been killed in the previous forty-eight hours and the dissection was carried out by a skilled man. Detectives had one major clue – an embroidered laundry mark sewn into the sheet in which the torso had been wrapped that read 'II H'. The investigation team tracked down the mark to a laundry, and subsequently a house, in Munster Square, over a mile from Regent Square. No. 50 was the home of separated Frenchwoman

Emilienne Gerard. Detectives had good reasons to believe they had traced their victim, as Gerard had not been seen since 31 October. Inside the house was an IOU addressed to Emilienne Gerard for the sum of £50 signed by a man called Louis Voisin.

Detectives traced Voisin to No. 101 Charlotte Street; he was not alone but in the company of a woman called Berthe Roche. When questioned about his movements and his relationship with Emilienne Gerard they discovered that he was a butcher by trade, information sufficient for him to be taken into custody for further interview. Detectives established through questioning that Voisin had been involved in a relationship with Emilienne Gerard for eighteen months and had last seen her on the night of 31 October 1917, when she told him she was leaving London to return to France to visit her estranged husband. Police were sure they had their murderer but had no conclusive evidence to charge him, or even that the dismembered remains were that of Gerard. Detectives had an ace up their sleeves – the misspelt note found with the body parts. The prisoner was asked to write out the words 'Bloody Belgium' several times, which he did. Voisin was an uneducated, semi-literate man; he attempted to disguise his handwriting but still misspelt the phrase in the same manner as the note found with the torso. Detectives believed that the note was left to try and suggest the murder had been politically motivated. This spurred the officers on, who returned to No. 101 Charlotte Street to conduct an in-depth search. Human blood was found in the kitchen, an earring later identified as belonging to Gerard was found in a towel and, most damning of all, Madame Gerard's head and hands were discovered in a cask of the crystalline compound Alum.

Voisin claimed later at his trial that he discovered the dismembered remains of Madame Gerard at her Munster Square residence and panicked, fearing he would be accused of her slaughter. The evidence of the note coupled with basic forensic evidence rebutted this defence comprehensively, and Voisin was convicted of the murder of Madame Emilienne Gerard and executed at Pentonville Prison on 2 March 1918. Berthe Roche was charged and tried as an accessory to murder; she was convicted and sentenced to seven years imprisonment but subsequently found to be insane and detained in a mental institution, dying in May 1919.

NOVEMBER

1st – *Irish Rose Didn't Want to Die*

The human body can be very resilient to violence and trauma; murder is not always the easiest of tasks to perform. George Brain was a driver for a boot suppliers based in the St Pancras area. Brain was allowed to take his vehicle home to Paradise Road, Richmond, where he lived with his parents. Late on 13 July 1938, a prostitute – Rose Muriel Atkins, more commonly known as 'Irish Rose' – was last seen alive getting into a green van. Her body was found the following morning in Somerset Road, Wimbledon. She had been stabbed with a cobbler's knife, beaten over the head with an engine-starting handle and then ran over by the driver in the van. The police had limited clues: the sighting of Rose getting into the green van and the clear tyre marks found on her body identified as coming from specific car models manufactured by Austin or Morris. Two days later Brain's employers reported to police that their driver had disappeared with £30 and the company vehicle, a green Morris Eight van. Detectives investigating the murder of Atkins made the link with their investigation and traced the van to a garage owned by one of George Brain's workmates. They found blood and a knife inside the cab; these items were forensically linked to the victim Atkins. The fugitive's photograph was circulated and he was arrested in Sheerness on the Isle of Sheppey, Kent. Brain claimed in his defence that 'Irish Rose' had tried to blackmail him after they had had sex in his van and he lost his temper and struck out, not intending to kill her. This defence was rejected by the jury, who took only fifteen minutes to return a verdict of guilty. George Brain was executed at Wandsworth Prison on 1 November 1938.

2nd – 'Let Him Have It Chris'

A burglary on a commercial warehouse belonging to the Barlow and Parker confectionary company at 27–29 Tamworth Road, Croydon, on 2 November 1952 would lead to one of British justice's most contentious trials and executions. Derek Bentley, aged nineteen, and his sixteen-year-old companion Christopher Craig were spotted climbing up a drainpipe in an attempt to gain entry into the building and police were alerted. Both men were armed: Bentley with a sheath knife and a knuckle duster, Craig with a Colt revolver, which had a shortened barrel. When police responded to the call, Bentley and Craig hid behind the lift housing. Detective Sergeant Frederick Fairfax spotted the would-be burglars and climbed the drainpipe, managing to grab hold of Bentley. Fairfax gave evidence that he asked Craig to hand over the gun and that Bentley then uttered one of the most infamous phrases in British judicial history: 'Let him have it Chris.' Bentley always maintained, firstly, that he had never said those words; his defence barrister argued even if he did he was asking Craig to hand over his weapon. Of course, the prosecution claimed he was in fact telling Craig to shoot Fairfax. Craig fired at Fairfax, injuring his shoulder. Other police arrived on the scene and were directed to the roof. The next to reach the incident was PC Sidney Miles, who was shot through the head by Craig. He continued to discharge the firearm until he exhausted his supply of ammunition and then jumped thirty feet onto a greenhouse, fracturing his spine and wrist.

Both men were charged with murder as a 'joint enterprise' and appeared at the Old Bailey in December 1952. Evidence given by ballistic experts apprised the jury that the modification made to the gun barrel made it highly unlikely Craig had aimed and fired the gun while specifically targeting PC Sidney Miles, as the gun was only accurate within 6 feet. The jury considered the evidence for only seventy-five minutes before returning a guilty verdict against both for the murder of PC Miles. Bentley was sentenced to death while Craig, being under the age of eighteen, would be detained at HM's pleasure. Following a failed appeal Bentley was executed at Wandsworth Prison on 28 January 1953. Craig was released after ten years and became a plumber.

Bentley was granted a royal pardon in 1993 in respect of the death sentence and his conviction was quashed by the Court of Appeal in 1998. Sidney Miles was posthumously awarded the George Cross.

3rd – A Walk on the Marshes

Early morning on 3 November 1864, two Germans went for a walk on the Plaistow Marshes. One of them would not return. Ferdinand Edward Karl Kohl, a butcher by trade, had been resident in England for several years and married an English girl. Earlier in 1864, Kohl travelled home to Germany for a visit and on his return trip, by steamship, made the acquaintance of fellow German John Fuhrop. Kohl introduced Fuhrop to a landlady with whom he had previously lodged; Fuhrop stayed for a while before moving in with Kohl and his wife. Fuhrop was very open with Kohl about his favourable financial circumstances, and it would appear that Kohl formed a plan that would allow him to escape the life of poverty he had endured.

On 8 November 1864, shipwright's apprentice Richard Harvey was wildfowling on the marshes. He went into the reeds to disturb and direct the wildfowl towards his shooting companions when he came across the gruesome remains of a headless, rotting corpse. The police were alerted and PC Bridgeland attended the scene and found the corpse partially clothed in dark trousers, Wellington boots and remnants of a white shirt. He also cleverly deduced from the crime scene that an indentation in the mud had been where the head had rested before decapitation, as small fragments of bone and brain matter were still present. Plaistow surgeon Edward Morris believed the body had been in situ for several days, as the muscles around the shoulders, neck and hands had been gnawed by rats; the marks on the neck indicated that the head had been cut off with the use of a knife and axe. The police did have one clue to focus on: a handwritten note in German found in a trouser pocket. The media focused on the fact that the body was unidentified, resulting in many local people coming to view the remains in an attempt to assist with its identification. This seems pretty ghoulish but paid dividends when German shoemaker Heinrich Zuelch recognised the boots as those he had recently repaired: they belonged to a man whom he knew as 'German John', who he informed the police was lodging with Ferdinand Kohl and his English wife at No. 4 Hoy Street, Canning Town. When questioned by detectives Kohl confirmed that Fuhrop had been lodging with him and that on the morning of 3 November they had left together in order to go to the Commercial Road, some five miles away, to look for work and that he [Kohl] had gone into a sugar factory, and when he came out Fuhrop had disappeared and had not seen him since.

The detective investigating, Superintendent Daniel Howie, was not convinced and brought Ferdinand and his wife to Plaistow Police Station for further questioning while their house was searched. Officers found several pawnbroker tickets relating to the dead man's clothes. Further examination of the scene revealed that Fuhrop had been killed several yards from where his body had been found. Two pairs of footprints were found with blood smears several feet from the final resting place, together with a circular bloodstain where detectives believed the head had been placed, following decapitation, while the body was moved. The head of the victim was found buried in a field a short distance from the torso the following day, 9 November, from which the cause of death was identified as two blows to the back of the skull. Ferdinand Kohl was charged with the murder. At his trial evidence was given that both the prisoner and the deceased were seen in each other's company walking towards the marshes on 3 November. Detectives discovered that Kohl had borrowed an axe from a neighbour that morning, which he returned the same day. The axe's blade matched the injuries inflicted post-mortem during the decapitation. Kohl was convicted of the murder and sentenced to death; he was the last person to be executed at Springfield Prison, Chelmsford, on 26 January 1865.

4th – The End of French Fifi

Yet another murder of a prostitute in Soho on 4 November 1935, the killing taking place in a flat in Archer Street. The prostitute was forty-one-year-old Josephine Martin, better known by the colourful street name of 'French Fifi'. Martin was suspected by the police to play hostess for foreign prostitutes smuggled into the capital by infamous crook 'Red Max'. She was found strangled with one of her own stockings. Her murderer has never identified.

5th – Public to the Rescue

Westminster University psychology lecturer Steven Reid was a thirty-four-year-old loner who suffered from depression. On 5 November 1999, he battered Cambridge University graduate and researcher Elizabeth Stacey to death with a rolling pin in a research laboratory on the Regents Street campus, leaving her to die. She wasn't discovered until the following day. Reid went missing and became the prime suspect for detectives hunting the killer. A public appeal was launched on the BBC's *Crimewatch UK* appealing for information regarding Reid's whereabouts. He was arrested twelve days after the attack. Medical evidence was submitted to the court at his trial claiming Reid had been suffering from an untreatable personality disorder combined with a state of depression, which led him to kill. Reid was sentenced to life imprisonment in July 2000, having been found guilty of manslaughter.

6th – Weapon of Choice – A Brick

Murder of a stranger is extremely rare: most victims of homicide know their attacker through work, a physical relationship or a member of their own family. Any investigation where no such association exists between killer and victim can be the most challenging for police to detect. One such murder occurred on the night of 6 November 1946. Olive Nixon, a fifty-seven-year-old widow, had left an evening meeting in order to walk home. She was later found dead in a narrow alleyway one-hundred yards from her house in Park Village East, Regents Park. She had been beaten around the head with a brick, but no motive was apparent. Police enquiries failed to unearth any witnesses to the attack or any reason why this ordinary woman should be the subject of such a brutal act. Another similar attack took place in Torquay eighteen months after the murder of Olive Nixon. Although geographically miles apart, the *modus operandi* was very similar – a lone woman attacked in a secluded location by a man armed with a brick. The woman survived her injuries and assisted police in identifying her assailant as Adam Ogilvie, who was charged with a serious assault and sentenced to three years imprisonment.

The attack was never linked to the murder of Olive Nixon. Nixon's murder would have remained undetected if it were not for the killer, troubled by his past and frightened that he may kill again, giving himself up at a police station on 10 August 1956 – ten years after committing the original offence and confessing to the murder of Olive Nixon. Adam Ogilvie's confession outlined an irrefutable knowledge of the murder, including facts only known to the police and the killer. He was charged with the murder and appeared at the Old Bailey. He seems to have had a change of heart as he faced the prospect of the hangman's noose. He withdrew the confession, stating that it was false and he had been informed of the facts of the case by another man whom he refused to identify. He told the court, 'I made it up to prove my innocence to my wife – to get her back. I pretended to her that I did the killings and told her I would murder her too, if she didn't stop quarrelling with me. I thought if I were acquitted she would come back.' The claims were rejected by the jury who believed the original confession and convicted Ogilvie of the ten-year-old murder. He was sentenced to death, the sentence commuted to life imprisonment as a debate raged in the public and parliamentary arenas regarding the abolition of capital punishment.

7th – Tied and Left for Dead

Argyle Square and Argyle Street, Kings Cross have been synonymous with the small hotel trade for many years. One such hotel was kept by octogenarian proprietor Esther Bowen; it was common local knowledge that she kept a large amount of money on the premises. In the early hours of 7 November 1918, Esther was murdered. She was discovered in her room, her wrists roughly tied to the bedstead above her head, a handkerchief stuffed into her mouth secured by a towel tied around her head, which resulted in asphyxiation. A witness gave evidence to the coroner's inquest that she had heard two men, whom she named as George William Bray and a man with a surname of Miles, talking about breaking into the hotel and stealing from Esther Bowen, and that later she saw them splitting the spoils of their crime. The men were arrested on suspicion of the murder but insufficient evidence meant they were never charged with the offence. Esther Bowen's murder remains unsolved.

8th – Undeserving of Children

A sickening tale of domestic violence and the murder of a young innocent child make this case one of the most horrific to be featured in this volume. Albert and Ada Williams married in 1913 and settled in Battersea, a home they shared with their two children and a bastard son, born to Ada before she met Albert; his name was John Patrick Dunn, aged four. Albert was a labourer and a man of great strength and Ada a barmaid not averse to stealing from her employees. Albert would often verbally taunt Ada about her illegitimate son John; this would escalate to violence when he had a few drinks. Towards the end of 1918, Ada had had enough of being a punchbag and left the marital home with son John, moving to No. 21 Comyn Road, Battersea. But after missing Albert, she came to a decision that she wanted her husband more than her son so, on 8 November 1918, she strangled young John to death. She dismembered his corpse and burnt his body parts in the fireplace of her temporary home. The enormity of her actions must have at some point overcome her and she gave herself up to the police and confessed her crime, showing them to the murder scene and the remains of her son. The media latched on to Ada's story as she awaited her trial, showing her and the situation that led to her killing her son in a very sympathetic light, turning her from evil child-killer to celebrity. She gained the support of a pro-feminist brigade and a number of clergymen including the Bishop of Manchester. Several newspapers, in particular the *John Bull*, started a petition for her release. The *Daily Mirror* took the decision to publish Ada's photograph on its front page. Ada's defence barrister attempted to have the charge of murder reduced to manslaughter, claiming her actions were influenced by poverty, despair and domestic misery. The judge rejected the appeal and Ada stood trial for a murder she had confessed to. She was found guilty and sentenced to death, but claimed that she could not be executed as she was pregnant. A 'Jury of Matrons' was convened (the last time this would ever take place in British judicial history) and concluded that indeed Ada was pregnant. She was spared from the rope, giving birth in Holloway Prison in March 1914, and was released subject to licence in 1921. The one person forgotten during this circus was the murdered child John, whose miserable life ended in such a violent manner. Sadly today, prominent members of society including politicians and the clergy are still prepared to jump on the bandwagon of human rights to endorse injustice, often forgetting about the suffering of the offender's victim and family.

9th – Grim Reading

Mary Ann Kelly was the last victim of the infamous Victorian serial killer 'Jack the Ripper'. She had been murdered in the early hours of 9 November 1888. Her badly mutilated body was discovered on her bed by an ex-soldier called Thomas Bowyer who had been sent to Mary's rented accommodation to collect her unpaid rent. She lived at No. 13 Miller's Court, Dorset Street, Whitechapel. Detectives were alerted and a post-mortem examination carried out by Dr Thomas Bond, which makes grim reading:

> The body was lying naked in the middle of the bed, the shoulders flat but the axis of the body inclined to the left side of the bed. The head was turned on the left cheek. The left arm was close to the body with the forearm flexed at a right angle and lying across the abdomen. The right arm was slightly abducted from the body and rested on the mattress. The elbow was bent, the forearm supine with the fingers clenched. The legs were wide apart, the left thigh at right angles to the trunk and the right forming an obtuse angle with the pubis.
>
> The whole of the surface of the abdomen and thighs was removed and the abdominal cavity emptied of its viscera. The breasts were cut off, the arms mutilated by several jagged wounds and the face hacked beyond recognition of the features. The tissues of the neck were severed all round down to the bone.
>
> The viscera were found in various parts viz: the uterus and kidneys with one breast under the head, the other breast by the right foot, the liver between the feet, the intestines by the

right side and the spleen by the left side of the body. The flaps removed from the abdomen and thighs were on a table.

The bed clothing at the right corner was saturated with blood, and on the floor beneath was a pool of blood covering about two feet square. The wall by the right side of the bed and in a line with the neck was marked by blood which had struck it in several places.

The face was gashed in all directions, the nose, cheeks, eyebrows, and ears being partly removed. The lips were blanched and cut by several incisions running obliquely down to the chin. There were also numerous cuts extending irregularly across all the features.

The neck was cut through the skin and other tissues right down to the vertebrae, the fifth and sixth being deeply notched. The skin cuts in the front of the neck showed distinct ecchymosis. The air passage was cut at the lower part of the larynx through the cricoid cartilage.

Both breasts were more or less removed by circular incisions, the muscle down to the ribs being attached to the breasts. The intercostals between the fourth, fifth, and sixth ribs were cut through and the contents of the thorax visible through the openings.

The skin and tissues of the abdomen from the costal arch to the pubes were removed in three large flaps. The right thigh was denuded in front to the bone, the flap of skin, including the external organs of generation, and part of the right buttock. The left thigh was stripped of skin fascia, and muscles as far as the knee.

The left calf showed a long gash through skin and tissues to the deep muscles and reaching from the knee to five inches above the ankle. Both arms and forearms had extensive jagged wounds.

The right thumb showed a small superficial incision about one inch long, with extravasation of blood in the skin, and there were several abrasions on the back of the hand moreover showing the same condition.

On opening the thorax it was found that the right lung was minimally adherent by old firm adhesions. The lower part of the lung was broken and torn away. The left lung was intact. It was adherent at the apex and there were a few adhesions over the side. In the substances of the lung there were several nodules of consolidation.

The pericardium was open below and the heart absent. In the abdominal cavity there was some partly digested food of fish and potatoes, and similar food was found in the remains of the stomach attached to the intestines.

Mary Jane Kelly was the most severely mutilated of the Ripper's victims, as the killer had more time and opportunity to carry out his disturbing work in the confines of a private dwelling.

10th – Love is Blind

Milliner's assistant Kitty Byron was deeply in love with a man who treated her despicably. Arthur Reginald Baker, often addressed as Reggie, was a heavy-drinking stockbroker who worked in the City's Square Mile. Baker wasn't averse to using his fists on Kitty and would often take most of her paltry weekly wage leaving her with little to survive on – but she still loved him. The couple lived in lodgings in Duke Street, south of Oxford Street, and could often be heard arguing by other tenants. Following a major bust up, the landlady asked both Reggie and Kitty to vacate their lodgings. Baker approached the landlady behind Kitty's back and asked if he could stay on if he got Kitty to leave; this was reported back to Kitty, who was furious, telling the landlady she would 'kill him before the day is out'. On 10 November 1902, Kitty purchased a knife, which she secreted in her clothing. She sent Reggie a message to meet her urgently at Lombard Street Post Office in the City of London close to his workplace. Reggie arrived at the post office and a loud verbal argument ensued that spilled out onto the street, where Kitty produced the knife and stabbed Reggie in the stomach twice, who fell to the floor dead. Kitty was tried at the Old Bailey – she was represented by Charles Dickens' son Henry Dickens, whose mitigation on behalf of his client was so powerfully dramatic it could have come from the pages of one of his father's novels. However, the jury still convicted Kitty for the killing of her lover but with a recommendation for mercy. Kitty received a sentence of life imprisonment, reduced to ten years in 1907 and released after serving six.

* * *

Following a heavy drinking session on 25 June 1960, Francis 'Flossie' Forsyth, a road-worker, Norman 'Flash' Harris, an unemployed driver, Christopher Darby and Terence Lutt, an unemployed labourer, decided they would rob the next passer-by. They concealed themselves on a footpath at the bottom of James Street, Hounslow and set upon twenty-year-old Alan Jee, who had just said goodnight to his girlfriend and was walking home. They kicked the innocent victim unconscious before leaving empty-handed. Jee died of his injuries two days later at West Middlesex Hospital in Isleworth. A witness to the assault gave police a good description of the four offenders that led to their arrests. A trace of the victim's blood was detected on the winkle-picker shoes and trousers of Forsyth. The evidence at the trial indicated that Lutt had been the one to administer the first blow but the fatal injuries were delivered by the feet of Forsyth and Harris. The victim received at least five kicks to his head. Forsyth, Harris and Lutt were found guilty of murder under the newly introduced Homicide Act 1957. Forsyth and Harris were executed on 10 November 1960 – Forsyth at Wandsworth Prison, Harris at Pentonville. Forsyth was the last eighteen-year-old to be executed in England. Lutt was detained at HM's pleasure due to his age, serving ten years, and Darby was given life imprisonment for non-capital murder as he was deemed not to have inflicted any physical injury on the victim.

11th – For the Love of My Daughter

Fulham boot-maker Henry Williams was a loving, hardworking family man who was devoted to his common-law wife Ellen Andrews and their young daughter Margaret. Henry, a reservist in the 14th Surrey Militia, was called up for active service during the Second Boer War and served his country between 1900 and 1902 before returning home. War has a habit of changing a man beyond recognition – Henry was profoundly affected by what he witnessed in the service of his country. On arriving back in London, he discovered that his wife Ellen had been openly unfaithful to him with a sailor named Baker and had badly neglected their daughter Margaret, now five years of age, who appeared underweight, dirty and dressed in clothing that had seen better days. The couple, however, seemed determined to make a go of their marriage for Margaret's sake and Henry moved back into the family home – two rented rooms on the upper floor of No. 40 Waterford Road, Fulham. Although he gained employment with a local boot-maker, George Cohen, Henry's problems started to surface, changing him from a happy-go-lucky family man to a violent drunk unable to come to terms with his battlefield experiences, his wife's infidelity and neglect of their daughter. Events took a turn for the worse when Cohen informed Williams that his wife was still seeing Baker, who was 'pimping' her out to several other men while grooming the young Margaret into prostitution.

The thought of his beautiful daughter unknowingly being led into a world of prostitution ripped the soul out of Henry; he went to Waterford Road and took his daughter up to her bed and slit her throat with a razor. Henry went into a neighbour's house and confessed his crime before walking to the Lord Palmerston pub on King's Road. PC Lewis was called by the neighbours and gained entry into No. 40 Waterford Road, finding the murdered girl before going to the Lord Palmerston and arresting the distraught father. Williams was later interviewed by Detective Inspector Walter Dew and confessed:

> I did kill my lovely daughter to save her from becoming a prostitute. It is not many men who would have had the heart to do it, but I bleeding well did it, and now I shall hang for it. I did it to save my old woman from putting her in bed with other men. God blind me she was my child, and I loved her, and I will walk like a man to the scaffold.

The jury at the Old Bailey trial found Williams guilty of the murder of his daughter but due to the extenuating circumstances recommended mercy to be shown. Alas, Williams was sentenced to death and executed on 11 November 1902. Williams did indeed walk to the gallows with his head held high; executioner Henry Pierrepoint described Henry Williams as the bravest man he had ever hanged.

12th – Burying the Rubbish

The listed Art Deco Hoover Building stands back from the Western Avenue in Perivale, West London. Built in 1933 for the Hoover Company, it manufactured upright domestic hoovers. During the Second World War, the factory was used for the manufacture of aircraft parts for the RAF and the building was camouflaged to avoid German bombers. In 1940, married father of four Lionel Watson, who worked at the factory in a protected occupation, thus avoiding inscription, met Phyllis Croker, who had an eighteen-month-old daughter called Eileen. They soon started a relationship. When Phyllis left the company in late 1940, Watson moved into her flat at No. 9 Goring Way, Greenford. Watson tried to divorce his wife but understandably she refused, so Watson married Phyllis bigamously in January 1941.

Watson was a serial womaniser and it wasn't long before he started another relationship with a seventeen-year-old girl at the factory and decided that he needed Phyllis and Eileen out of the way. He stole a quantity of sodium cyanide from his workplace and poisoned both Phyllis and young Eileen, burying their bodies in the communal garden of Phyllis' flat. A nosey neighbour, Mrs Bounds, who had taken an instant dislike to Watson, saw him digging and asked him if he was 'digging for victory'. Watson replied that he was just burying some cabbage leaves and other rubbish. Mrs Bounds enquired of the whereabouts of Phyllis and young Eileen; Watson told her that they had gone to Scotland for a holiday. As May turned into June, the neighbours started to notice a noxious smell coming from the garden. Watson claimed it was just the drains but was seen pouring a strong disinfectant over the patch of garden he had previously dug. The smell got worse and suspicious neighbours started to investigate by digging up the area from which the smell emanated: they found rotting human flesh.

Watson was arrested for murder later, claiming he had returned home on 20 May 1941 to find that Phyllis had murdered Eileen and committed suicide. He panicked and decided to bury the bodies in the garden. He was found guilty of the killings and sentenced to death. Watson was executed at Pentonville Prison on 12 November 1941.

13th – Domineering Ways

On 13 November 1906, a jealous, possessive twenty-two-year-old Frederick Reynolds was executed at Wandsworth Prison for the vicious murder of his former girlfriend, eighteen-year-old Sophia Lovell. The couple had been seeing each other for about eighteen months when Sophia ended the relationship, tired of Reynolds' domineering behaviour. Reynolds' never recovered from the brush off and swore revenge on her, often making threats to Sophia and anybody in her company. In September 1906, Sophia met another man, a baker called Edward Limbourne. He gave evidence of meeting Sophia in the Prince and Princess of Wales pub in Kingslake Street, Bermondsey. On the night of 10 September 1906, Sophia and Limbourne met at the same pub, leaving about 9 p.m. in the company of Sophia's cousin Annie Bristow. Limbourne gave a harrowing account of the killing when giving evidence for the prosecution at the Old Bailey trial:

> On September 10 I met her at the same public-house about eight o'clock; she was with her cousin, Annie Bristow. The three of us left together. As we were walking along prisoner came up and asked Sophy who she was looking at; she said she was not looking at him. Then he started rowing with her, and after a time he walked away. I went walking with Sophy to see her home. We had got over the Greyhound Bridge, about 60 yards down Willow Walk; this was about 9.30. We were walking arm-in-arm. Prisoner came up behind and struck Sophy once upon the neck and twice on the face. She fell down with her head against the wall. Prisoner knelt down by her side and did something. I went to catch hold of him, but as I did I saw the blood coming from Sophy's neck. I could not see how it was caused. Prisoner said, 'I swore to do it, and I'm doing it.' When I saw the blood I did not know what I was doing. I staggered into the road and called for help. I said, 'Come quick, he is cutting her throat.' Two men came along and picked her up, and prisoner was arrested.
>
> (*Old Bailey Online*)

The injuries inflicted were appalling and outlined to the jury by Doctor Reginald Marshall:

> The last part of her left index finger had been severed as she tried to defend herself; the most severe injury was the deep 4" cut along the throat from right to left extending into the gullet above the windpipe. Sophia suffered nine smaller wounds she died of blood loss and shock.

14th – A Race Across the Atlantic

A North London Railway train arrived at Hackney Station from Fenchurch Street just after 10 p.m. on Saturday 9 July 1864. Two bank clerks boarded one of its empty first class carriages. They were shocked to find the seats and windows covered in blood. The train guard was summoned: on examining the interior he found a hat, walking stick and a black leather bag. The carriage was sealed and the police called. In the meantime, two railway track workers happened upon a smartly dressed man badly injured lying on the track between Hackney and Hackney Wick stations. He was carried to a nearby public house and a doctor called, the man dying of severe trauma to his head twenty-seven hours later. The victim was identified as Thomas Briggs, a chief clerk at a bank in Lombard Street, City of London. He had caught the Fenchurch Street train in order to travel to Hackney, a short walk from his home in Clapton Square. Detectives worked on a motive of robbery as Briggs' gold-rimmed glasses and gold watch and chain were missing. It was established that the property in the carriage belonged to the deceased apart from the hat, which they deduced to be the killers' who, it seemed, had picked up the wrong hat after the attack. The hat was traced to a hat-maker in Crawford Street, Marylebone and the missing gold chain to a jeweller in Cheapside. The incident received great media attention as it was believed to be the first murder on a moving train on Britain's railways. A cabman, who lived at No. 16 Park Terrace, Old Ford Road near Victoria Park, Hackney, responded to the request for information stating that he had a lodger called Franz Muller, who was German. The cabman identified the hat found in the carriage as belonging to Muller and a photograph of Muller was shown to the jeweller who positively identified the image as the man who sold the gold chain to him. Police enquiries revealed that Muller had boarded the *Victoria* sailing ship bound for New York. Detectives boarded a faster steamship, the *City of Manchester,* arriving in New York ahead of the *Victoria* and arrested Muller for the murder of Mr Briggs. Muller was wearing Mr Briggs' hat as he disembarked and the victim's watch was in Muller's luggage. He was returned to England and stood trial at the Old Bailey in October 1864; he was found guilty and executed outside Newgate on 14 November 1864.

15th – The Lambeth Poisoner

Another high profile execution outside Newgate took place on 15 November 1892. The condemned man was infamous poisoner Dr Neill Cream. Cream was born in Glasgow but emigrated with his family at a young age to Canada. Cream studied medicine, and following graduation he travelled to London and enrolled as a postgraduate at St Thomas' Hospital. He returned to Canada and set up a lucrative business as an abortionist. Following the deaths of two patients, he fled to America and set up a similar business in Chicago. Following the death of another patient he was charged with murder, but the case collapsed due to lack of evidence. He stayed in Chicago and was charged with murder again in 1881 when he poisoned a male patient. This time his luck run out and he was convicted of second-degree murder. The sentence was reduced from life imprisonment to seventeen years on appeal, and with good behaviour Dr Cream served only ten years. On his release in 1891, he travelled to England, settled in the sleazy district of Lambeth, south London, taking lodgings at No. 103 Lambeth Palace Road. From his base he unleashed a murderous rampage that would take the lives of four female victims – poisoning them with strychnine. When arrested, seven bottles of the poison were found at his lodgings. He was dubbed by the press of the day as the 'Lambeth Poisoner'.

16th – Hacked to Death

On 16 November 2009, young mother of two Geeta Aulakh was returning to her Greenford home after working at a local community radio station as a receptionist when she was viciously attacked with a machete. During the assault, she received appalling injuries including a severed right hand. She was found metres from the home of her son's childminder by a passer-by who called an ambulance, but Geeta died of her injuries at London's Charing Cross Hospital. Geeta's estranged husband Harpreet Aulakh was arrested for conspiracy to murder. Police discovered CCTV of Harpreet purchasing the machete used during the attack. He had arranged for two young men to illegally enter the UK specifically to carry out the murder while providing himself with an alibi by visiting a local pub at the time murder took place. Detectives pieced together a picture of a man who abused his wife and following their separation followed her, threatened other staff members of the radio station where she worked and hacked into her Facebook and email accounts. Following a six-week trial at the Old Bailey, Harpreet was convicted of the murder of his wife and given life imprisonment to serve a minimum of twenty-eight years. Nineteen-year-old Sher Singh, who actually carried out the attack, and the lookout Jaswant Singh Dhillon were imprisoned for a minimum of twenty-two years each.

17th – Not in Front of the Children

Frank Hollington was courting eighteen-year-old live-in housemaid Annie Hatton. On the evening of 17 November 1928, Annie's employers, Mr and Mrs Markovitch, went to the theatre leaving Annie in charge of their two young children at No. 17 Loddiges Road, Hackney. On their return one of the children was crying, but they received no answer when they called out for Annie. A search of the house revealed the lifeless body of Annie on the kitchen floor; she had been bound, gagged and battered around her head. The Markovitch's informed detectives that Annie had been seeing a man called John Dennis (an alias used by Hollington) and that he had a history of violence towards her. A few nights earlier Hollington had seen Annie with another man and come around to Loddiges Road that night to confront her, lost his temper and beat her to death – one can only hope the children were not witness to the brutality that took place.

At first Annie's death appeared to be a burglary gone wrong: money and other items had been stolen. But listening to the relationship history, detectives concentrated on Hollington who was now the No. 1 suspect. The fact that Annie had been bound and gagged was an attempt, detectives believed, by Hollington to cover his tracks. Hollington wasn't traced until 29 November when tracked down to his father's address in Warner Place, Bethnal Green. Hollington didn't offer any resistance to his arrest just asking the police not to 'make a noise, I don't want my father to hear. I know what you have come about, it is the girl.' He was arrested for the murder of Annie Hatton. He admitted to the police that he had lost his temper and struck her several times, then attempted to conceal his involvement by making it look like a burglary gone wrong. He was tried at the Old Bailey. His defence team put forward a case for manslaughter, but this was rejected by the judge and Hollington was found guilty with no plea for mercy. He was executed at Pentonville on 20 February 1929.

* * *

Considered among the top ten most beautiful women in New York, socialite Barbara Daly Baekeland had the world at her feet when she married Brooks Baekeland, the grandson of Bakelite plastic inventor Leo Baekeland. Their marriage produced a son called Anthony, but they divorced in the late 1960s. Anthony was diagnosed with mental health problems and arrested for the attempted murder of his mother in July 1972 when he attempted to throw her under oncoming traffic in Cadogan Square, where they shared a penthouse. Barbara didn't press charges against her son but arranged psychiatric help for Anthony at home. At some point, the psychiatrist became extremely concerned about Anthony's mental state, even warning Barbara that her son was capable of murder. On 17 November 1972, this concern turned into tragic reality when he murdered his mother with a kitchen knife. Anthony was sent to Broadmoor Hospital, where he remained until July 1980 when he was unbelievably released back into society. Immediately after his release, now aged thirty-three, he flew to New York and stayed with his paternal grandmother, Nina Daly. Within six days of his arrival, Anthony stabbed his grandmother with a kitchen knife eight times and with such force he broke several bones.

He was arrested and charged with murder; during his remand in custody at Rikers Island Prison awaiting his trial Anthony was found dead in his cell – suffocated by a plastic bag over his head.

18th – Bloody Mary

Catholic Queen, Mary I, the only child produced from Henry VIII's marriage to Catherine of Aragon, restored Catholicism to England following the short period of Protestant reign under her half-brother Edward VI. During her five-year reign (1553–58) she ordered two-hundred and eighty Protestants to be burnt at the stake, earning the posthumous sobriquet 'Bloody Mary'. One of these was Richard Gibson, described in contemporary records as a 'gentleman' burnt at the stake at Smithfield on 18 November 1557.

19th – The Brain Recorder

Great Britain had been at war for four years, and it was a familiar sight to see soldiers, sailors and airmen enjoying precious leave from the horrors of war in the pubs and clubs of the capital. One such serviceman was twenty-two-year-old Terence Casey, a member of the Royal Army Medical Corps. He met Bridget Milton, a woman twice his age in a Putney pub on the night of 13 July 1943; he later admitted consuming twelve pints of beer. Shortly after closing time two air-raid wardens found Bridget in the front garden of No. 8 Gwendolyn Street, Putney, only a few yards from her house in Cambalt Road; she lay face down and had been strangled. Casey was arrested in the vicinity following identification by witnesses from the pub. He was charged with murder. Casey was tried at the Old Bailey, and his defence team produced medical evidence that at the time of the murder Casey could well have been suffering from some mental disorder brought on by the amount of alcohol he had consumed. Eminent neurologist Doctor Denis Hill gave evidence to the court of tests he had conducted on the accused using an electro-encephalograph or 'brain recorder'. Hill told the court that he had simulated Casey's intake of liquid by getting him to drink four pints of water every hour for three hours to equal the consumption of alcohol he had drunk on the night of the murder. He concluded that Casey's brain readings indicated that after one hour, the brain appeared to be unstable and after three, the readings showed signs of apparent mental instability. Dr Hill also added that impulses from Casey's brain during the experiment suggested he was telling the truth when he denied the murder. The medical evidence that Casey could have been suffering from some sort of epileptic episode following the consumption of such a quantity of alcohol seemed too far-fetched for the jury and he was found guilty of the murder of Bridget Milton and executed on 19 November 1943 at Wandsworth Prison.

20th – Love Triangle

William Charles Benson and Sydney Harbor were work colleagues and friends. When car-body worker Benson fell on bad times, his pal Harbor invited him to move in with his wife and children in their small two bedroom lodgings in Kentish Town. The children slept in the smaller bedroom while the three adults slept in the larger room. Benson eventually lost his job and at the same time was accused by Harbor of having an affair with wife Charlotte. Benson was thrown out of the lodgings onto the street. But alas, this was not the end of the affair as Charlotte wanted to continue her relationship with Benson. They rented a small flat in Littlehampton where they could spend time with each other before Charlotte would return home to her husband Sydney. On 6 September 1928, Charlotte and her youngest child met up with Benson in Coulsdon, Surrey, and broke the news that she wanted to end the affair and try to repair her marriage with Sydney. Benson took the news badly, stabbing the young mother to death in front of her young child. Later the same day, the killer approached a local beat officer and confessed to him that he had murdered his girlfriend. He escorted the officer to land near Coulsdon Golf Club where he showed the officer the corpse. Charlotte had been stabbed several times; the child was found unharmed next to her. Benson, who claimed he had murdered Charlotte to keep her from her husband, pleaded insanity at his trial, which was dismissed at a subsequent appeal. He was executed at Wandsworth Prison on 20 November 1928.

21st – Lucky Yank

An argument between two Americans, Denis Francis Doherty and Michael Graham, ended in fatal circumstances. The incident occurred at Graham's London lodgings at No. 47 Woburn Place, Bloomsbury on 21 November 1887. During the disagreement, Doherty pulled a revolver on his friend and shot him dead. At his trial, Doherty's defence team put forward a case of accidental death – he hadn't intended to kill his friend, claiming the gun had discharged accidently. The jury returned a verdict of not guilty to murder but guilty of manslaughter. Doherty was sentenced to twenty years penal servitude. The trial judge commented strongly on the odious practice of carrying revolvers.

22nd – Shards of Glass
Fourteen-year-old Gary Wilson was dumped, partially naked, behind a shop in Comet Road, Deptford, south-east London on 22 November 1978. The young victim had been beaten, raped and stabbed with what the pathologist believed to be shards of glass before being strangled. A local man was arrested – a man who was known to fantasise, often making-up stories to impress his peers. He confessed to the killing rather than admit he had lied to the police, and was convicted on the basis of that confession with little or no other corroborating evidence. He was cleared of the crime after serving sixteen years in prison. Nobody has since been arrested and charged with this evil murder; the case remains unsolved.

23rd – Criminal History in the Making
On 23 November 1910, an infamous killer was hanged at Pentonville Prison. Dr Hawley Harvey Crippen's crime was no more vicious or cruel than many crimes in this volume; in fact, we have discussed crimes that make Crippen's seem fairly mundane – if murder could ever be described as such. What made this case of such interest to the public and media are the circumstances of Crippen's evasion of the law and his eventual capture, circumstances that would make criminal history.

Dr Crippen was an American who married a music hall artist called Cora, who used the exotic stage name Belle Elmore. Crippen and Cora moved to London in 1897. After living at various London addresses, they moved into No. 3 Hilldrop Crescent, Kentish Town, in 1905. Cora was an attractive woman and often had affairs, berating her husband for his inability to provide the lifestyle she thought she deserved. Crippen had met a young secretary called Ethel Le Neve in 1903; she became Crippen's mistress in 1908. After a party at Hilldrop Crescent on 31 January 1910, Cora Crippen disappeared. On 31 March, Louise Smythson walked into the foyer of Scotland Yard and reported that Cora Crippen had not been seen by any of her friends for exactly two months. Mrs Smythson told police that a letter had been received by the committee of the Music Hall Ladies Guild, of which Cora was honorary treasurer, on 2 February 1910. The letter set forth that Cora had gone home to America because of an illness in her family and that she was resigning her position; she had left no forwarding address and left with such haste that her husband had handwritten the letter on her behalf. Just over a month later, Hawley Crippen announced to Cora's friends that she had been taken gravely ill and died; Crippen placed a respectful obituary notice in *ERA*, the theatrical newspaper. Chief Inspector Dew of Scotland Yard was approached about the disappearance and the strange circumstances surrounding it. Eventually he visited Crippen at Hilldrop Crescent and spoke to Ethel Le Neve, who had now moved in with Crippen and was indeed wearing both Cora's clothes and jewellery on the day of his visit. Dew took a statement from Crippen at his place of work in New Oxford Street. He informed the detective that he had lied about the family illness and that Cora had in fact left him for another man and returned to America to be with him, and he had been too embarrassed to tell anybody the truth. Dew instructed two officers to return with Crippen to his house and make a cursory search, which revealed nothing suspicious. Dew suggested that Crippen try and contact his wife in America to clear up the matter.

A few days later, on 9 July 1910, Dew went to Hilldrop Crescent to tie up a few ambiguities in the statement but found that Crippen and Le Neve had disappeared. Eventually the remains of Cora were found buried in a tiny coal cellar near the kitchen; Crippen and Le Neve were circulated as murder suspects. Detectives discovered they had travelled to Antwerp and boarded the SS *Montrose* bound for Canada, when the ship's Captain, Henry Kendall, recognised Crippen and the fact that his companion dressed as a boy was in fact a female. Kendall instructed that a wireless telegram be sent to the British authorities – the first time in British Criminal history that such a method would lead to the capture of a fugitive. Dew caught a fast steamship and arrested Crippen and Le Neve when they arrived in Quebec. Crippen was convicted of murder and executed, Le Neve acquitted. The Crippen murder was later featured in a popular song of the day:

> Dr. Crippen killed Belle Elmore
> Ran away with Miss le Neve
> Right across the ocean blue
> Followed by Inspector Dew
> Ship's ahoy, naughty boy!

24th – Tax Dodging Killer

Former serviceman Frederick Keeling returned to his pre-war trade as a plumber and plasterer. He had previously been married but separated for several years. Keeling also supplemented his income by running a boarding house at No. 34 St Georges Road, Tottenham, where he lived with a woman called Ada Haines as man and wife. Keeling continued to claim married tax allowances with regard to his estranged wife. He treated Ada badly, often beating her, and she left him. Keeling then met Emily Agnes Dewberry, and she and her eighteen-year-old niece Maud moved in paying a monthly rent. On 11 November 1921, Ada Haines was released from Holloway Prison where she had served a short term for alcohol-related offences. Keeling and Haines met up again on the night of her release at a pub they both often frequented. The next day Emily Dewberry and her niece were moved upstairs and Ada moved back in. Emily was very angry with her treatment, and when a tax office official visited the address to check on the pension status of Keeling, Emily let it be known that Keeling was in fact claiming for a wife he no longer had. Keeling was arrested a few days later and charged with fraud – Emily was to be a material witness for the prosecution. Late on 24 November 1921, Keeling badly beat Ada Haines to within an inch of her life and then went upstairs and murdered Emily, beating her around the head with a hammer. Keeling disappeared for ten days; he was eventually captured by police when information, as a result of a reward being offered, reached them of Keeling's whereabouts. Keeling was tried and convicted of murder and executed at Pentonville Prison on 11 April 1922.

25th – A Mad Jack

On 25 November 1894, a twenty-one-year-old Irishman Reginald Saunderson disappeared from his supervised boarding house in Hampton Wick. The young man was seen later that evening in the Haymarket area of London's West End. He next turned up in leafy Holland Park Avenue at 11.30 p.m., attacking a lady called Augusta Dawes. He at first tried to strangle her – following a gallant struggle for her life, he cut her throat. Saunderson ran from the scene and disposed of the murder weapon. Police enquiries and witness statements revealed the suspect was the same as the absconder from Hampton Wick, one Reginald Saunderson. The murder weapon was found close to the murder scene, jammed into a scaffolding pole erected on a building site. Detectives initiated a nationwide search for Saunderson who had disappeared. Bizarrely, on the morning of 28 November 1894, a letter with a Dublin postmark arrived at Kensington Police Station purporting to have been written by Saunderson. The letter read:

> Dear Sir – the murder that was committed – I did it just to the right of a door of a gentleman. I got her by the throat and tried to choke her. I cut her knife [presumably meant throat] with a knife it was a very good cut. When I cut her there was someone coming up and I flew for my life. My knife was thrown away in a back lane in a back street. I thought the knife was in the door but I believe it remained on the roof. I did the murder. So goodbye. On the job.
>
> Jack the Ripper

Urgent liaison was made between the Metropolitan Police and Irish police; Saunderson was traced, arrested and brought back to England to face a murder charge. His claims to be 'Jack the Ripper' were dismissed due to his age and mental state. Saunderson appeared before a judge at the Old Bailey and declared insane. He was ordered to be detained in an asylum at HM's pleasure and incarcerated in Broadmoor.

26th – A Tragic Case of Mistaken Identity

The Sussex Stores pub (now called The Sussex) is located on the junction of Long Acre and Upper St Martins Lane, Covent Garden. In 1916, it was popular with servicemen on leave from the conflict in Europe. On the evening of 26 November 1916, two local men, William James Robinson, a former soldier but now a messenger, and John Henry Gray, a newspaper packer, got into an argument with Canadian soldier Alfred Williams, who was having a quiet drink with his girlfriend Margaret Harding. As Williams got up to leave the pub, the argument continued resulting in Williams receiving a fatal stab wound to the neck. Harding told police that Gray had pushed Williams but it was Robinson that had struck the fatal blow with a broken glass. Robinson, who gave his address as No. 26 Museum Street, Holborn, and John Gray were charged with the murder. Both stated that it was a case of mistaken identity, but Harding and other patrons of the pub had identified the pair. Robinson was convicted of Williams' murder, Gray his manslaughter. Robinson wrote a letter from his cell admitting the killing and that the punishment he was to face was correct: the motive had not been for gain but the fact he had had a disagreement the previous night with a man whom he mistook for Williams. Robinson was executed at Pentonville Prison on 17 April 1917; Gray was sentenced to three years imprisonment but his conviction was quashed on appeal.

27th – An Important Visitor

On 27 November 1835, James Pratt and John Smith became the last men in England to be executed for the offence of sodomy. Both men were caught having sex in the rented room of William Bonill, aged sixty-eight, in Blackfriars Road, London. Bonill's landlord suspected that such activities were taking place as he had witnessed Bonill inviting men to his room on previous occasions; this time he had peered through the window and then the keyhole to witness the events. The landlord called a police officer and all three (Pratt, Smith and Bonill) were taken into custody. The trio were tried at the Old Bailey, and Pratt and Smith were convicted under relatively new legislation: the Offences against the Person Act 1828, which had replaced the Buggery Act of 1533, and sentenced to death.

Bonill was charged as an accessory and sentenced to fourteen years penal transportation. The men received some support from the committing magistrate Hensleigh Wedgwood, who asked for the sentences to be commuted to life imprisonment, but both men were publicly executed outside Newgate. Charles Dickens visited the men before their deaths and described his observations in *Sketches by Boz,* titled 'A Visit to Newgate':

> The other two men were at the upper end of the room. One of them, who was imperfectly seen in the dim light, had his back towards us, and was stooping over the fire, with his right arm on the mantel-piece, and his head sunk upon it. The other was leaning on the sill of the farthest window. The light fell full upon him, and communicated to his pale, haggard face, and disordered hair, an appearance which, at that distance, was ghastly. His cheek rested upon his hand; and, with his face a little raised, and his eyes wildly staring before him, he seemed to be unconsciously intent on counting the chinks in the opposite wall.

28th – Ahoy Captain

The *Speranza*, a working Thames sailing barge, was moored on the river at North Woolwich Causeway on 28 November 1931. On board were fifty-seven-year-old Captain Charles William Lambert from Grays, Essex and his barge hand, twenty-five-year-old William Harold Goddard of Kemp Street, Ipswich. Mid-afternoon the men were securing the vessel on the deck when Goddard asked Lambert if he had received any letters. Lambert replied that he had two and one was from his fiancée, whom he referred in a derisory fashion, enraging Goddard. The barge hand struck Lambert on the jaw with his fist sending him backwards down the stairs into the cabin. Goddard went below to see if he was okay but was greeted by an irate captain with a coke hammer in his hand. Goddard ducked the impending blow but was caught on the back of his neck. A fight ensued during which Goddard took hold of the hammer and hit Lambert on the head. He left the barge and returned at 5 p.m. to find the captain dead. Goddard relieved the corpse of its watch and chain in order to indicate robbery, placed a rope around the neck to dispose of the body over the side but lacked the required strength to drag him up the stairs to deck-level. Goddard left Lambert where he lay and went to the Barge Pub and borrowed 15*s* against the stolen watch and chain. The next day he returned home to Ipswich and surrendered himself to the local police station, informing the police that he had killed his captain and where he could be found.

Goddard was charged with the murder and stood trial at the Old Bailey, claiming provocation as his defence; the defence was rejected by the jury, who found him guilty and sent him to his execution at Pentonville Prison on 23 February 1932.

29th – Cop Hater

Cop-hater Nicholas Vernage was released from prison in November 1991 and went on a four-week burglary spree, which culminated in murder. During this period, Vernage killed his girlfriend Lorna Bogle, whom he stabbed twenty-one times. While committing a burglary in Higham Hill Road, Walthamstow on 29 November 1991, Vernage was disturbed by the homeowner, Javiad Iqbal, a part-time minicab driver who Vernage stabbed to death. As Vernage left the flat with proceeds of the burglary, he was spotted by Police Sergeant Alan King. King, without fear for his own safety, confronted the wanted man. Vernage stabbed Sergeant King repeatedly in the chest, head and neck. King fought gallantly for his life but sadly died of his injuries in hospital. This was not to be the end of Vernage's violence. He was spotted sleeping in a car by two PCs, John Jenkinson and Simon Castrey; Vernage stabbed PC Jenkinson in the neck and PC Castrey five times in the neck and face before finally being cornered in a garden shed and detained. Vernage was given five life sentences for offences of murder and attempted murder. Sergeant King, aged just forty-one, was posthumously awarded the Queen's Commendation for Brave Conduct. A memorial stands at the spot he fell, unveiled in 1993.

30th – On Medical Advice

PC Henry Dyer was approached on the streets of Soho on 30 November 1883 by a very excited man who seemed incapable of standing still. 'The doctor told me to do this' he excitedly exclaimed to the bemused officer whose first thoughts were probably to find this man a place of safety. PC Dyer ascertained his name was William Crees and that he lived at No. 55 Greek Street. PC Dyer marched Crees to his first-floor flat, concerned about his mental state. He found Mrs Crees lying on her back, having been stabbed and beaten to death; a knife and poker lay nearby. Crees was found criminally insane and spent the rest of his life in a secure mental hospital. He died in Broadmoor aged 85 in 1932.

* * *

Lewis Henry Salmon was found murdered on 30 November 1917 in his shop at No. 4A Bishops Road (now Bishops Bridge Road). Salmon dealt in antiques and second-hand uniforms. His murderer was never identified.

* * *

A dog-walker discovered the battered and almost decapitated body of a woman, later identified as thirty-nine-year-old Jacqueline Queen, in an East Finchley Park on 30 November 2005. She had been struck with a claw hammer and her neck hacked with a knife. Police identified her killer as boyfriend James Seaton, an unemployed bricklayer who lived at Gainsborough House, Thorpedale Road, Finsbury Park. Seaton claimed Queen had revealed to him that she was a lesbian and wanted to end their relationship. Seaton claimed diminished responsibility in relation to mental health issues suffered at the time and therefore not responsible for his actions. The jury rejected the defence and Seaton was imprisoned for life on 13 October 2006.

12

DECEMBER

1st – *She Had to Die*

Sadly, we begin December as we finished November with a man lacking in sufficient character and self-confidence to move on after a brush off from the fairer sex. Patricia Wood lived with her mother at No. 91 Godolphin Road, Shepherds Bush. Wood was employed at the BBC studios in Lime Grove as a canteen assistant, a short walk from her home. Wood was engaged to Christopher Owden, a twenty-three-year-old salesman, who lodged in the same road. Wood, a year younger than her fiancée, had become concerned about Owden's strange behaviour over a period of a month leading up towards the end of November 1954, so much so she decided to end their engagement and returned his engagement ring. Owden's anguish turned to rage, who made angry threats to Patricia that if she did not marry him he would kill her. Owden was serious – this was no idle threat. He purchased a knife and returned to Wood's flat to intimidate her by showing her the weapon. But Patricia was made of sterner stuff. They argued before Owden left frustrated; Wood was still adamant the relationship was over. In a later interview with detectives, Owden admitted he had decided that night he would kill her.

The next morning, 1 December 1954, Patricia went to work as normal but received a disturbing telephone call purporting to be from the police at Askew Road Police Station. In fact it was Owden disguising his voice. She was told that her boyfriend had committed suicide by throwing himself into the Thames; his body had been recovered by the River Police. Wood went to the police station concerned and in deep shock, but the police officer she spoke to denied any knowledge of the telephone call or Christopher Owden committing suicide. She returned home in a very distressed state trying to understand the morning's events, her distress turning to anger when Owden turned up at her front door. Owden describes what happened in a statement made to police:

> She answered the door and told me she had been to the police station and asked me if I thought it funny what I had done. We carried on talking at the door then I pushed her into the hall and took out the knife and stabbed her. There was a struggle and I picked up a bottle of milk and I hit her on the head with it and then stabbed her two or three times more.

In fact, Owden stabbed Wood twenty-five times before running from the premises. Wood was found by a neighbour but she died on the way to hospital. Detectives linked Owden's telephone call, Wood's visit to the police station and the subsequent murderous attack. He was eventually arrested in Richmond Old Deer Park a few days later. Owden was tried at the Old Bailey in January 1955; during his trial his antecedents revealed a history of mental illness and attempted suicide, and he was found guilty but insane and incarcerated in Broadmoor Hospital.

2nd – Off to the Tower

British Security Services intercepted a letter in 1915 bound for a Dutch address they knew to be a German intelligence cell. The letter contained a long message in invisible ink, which opened with the paragraph:

> I hope that you have received my first letter. I have been to Chatham. The Royal Dockyard is closed entirely, but I got in in spite of all. There are a few cruisers there and a lot of guns as well as destroyers, for instance, Duncan, 2nd class, 14,000 tons, Lowestoft, 3rd class, Boadicea, Lance, Pembroke, Wilder and Actaeon etc. The mouth of the Thames

is guarded by steel like the Humber, but even more so. The ships pass at night and this is indicated from a watch boat through three vertically arranged red lanterns.

The letter had been sent by Dutch-born Albert Meyer, who arrived in England in 1914 and worked as a cook and waiter in London and Blackpool. He was granted permission to leave the UK in 1915 to travel to Copenhagen via Germany and then returned to London in May 1915, moving into accommodation in Soho. He married English girl Catherine Rebecca Godleman shortly after. The Security Services monitored Meyer and his wife and intercepted a second letter, at which point Meyer and his wife were arrested. Catherine was released soon afterwards but Albert was charged and faced a court-martial at the Middlesex Guildhall in November 1915; he was found guilty and sentenced to death by firing squad. The sentence was carried out at the Tower of London on 2 December 1915. Meyer was the penultimate German spy to be executed at the Tower – and, aged just twenty-two, one of the youngest.

3rd – Addiction That Led to Murder

American-born doctor George Henry Lamson came to England to study medicine. He had a distinguished early career and was decorated for his work as a volunteer surgeon in Serbia and Romania. He settled down in a Bournemouth practice but became addicted to morphine. His addiction led to personal and financial difficulties, which lent themselves to drastic measures. On 1 December 1881 Lamson sent a letter to his brother-in-law Percy Malcolm John, a student at Blenheim House School, Wimbledon, who was paralysed in the lower limbs and unable to walk. Lamson wrote that he was about to go to the Continent and wished to visit him before his departure. Lamson visited Percy at 7 p.m. on 3 December 1881. During his brief stay he poisoned Percy, administering a dose of aconitine, a plant-based poison, which led to an excruciating death. The motive was pure greed to secure a larger share of the family inheritance. Lamson believed that aconitine was untraceable, but forensic science and knowledge had progressed greatly since his medical school days and his lack of up-to-date knowledge was his downfall. Lamson was hanged at Wandsworth Prison on 28 April 1882.

4th – Robbed of a Father

Music producer Olu Olagbaju was enjoying a night out with friends celebrating his twenty-sixth birthday at Shadans nightclub in the City of London. The young father had a bright future and was expecting his second child. In the early hours of 4 December 2006, Olagbaju was confronted by a group of men; a disturbance followed, during which Dashem Tesfamichael, twenty-three and from Camden, stabbed Olagbaju in the chest with a broken bottle. The bottle pierced his heart and he died in hospital soon after. Tesfamichael, also in the music industry, fled to Italy then Miami before being extradited back to the United Kingdom to stand trial with four other men. Eritrean-born Tesfamichael was convicted of murder and received life imprisonment, to serve a minimum of thirteen years. The other men received much shorter sentences for offences including violent disorder. Olagbaju's girlfriend gave birth to a son in July 2007.

5th – She Loved Life

Glasgow-born widower Annie Doohan, a happy-go-lucky figure, had given birth to several children and had ten grandchildren. In 1960 she moved to Fulham, West London and shared a flat at No. 86C, Lillie Road with daughter Helen, who was due to get married. Annie was well known in the area: she worked part-time at Fulham swimming baths and had a reputation for enjoying herself. On 5 December 1965 she went to the Old Oak pub on North End Road for a night out and to say farewell to friends as she would be moving away from the area after her daughter's marriage. She left the pub late evening – it was the last time Annie was seen alive. The alarm was raised by daughter Helen, and the following morning Annie's naked body was found in the basement of a disused church on North End Road, a short distance from the Old Oak pub; she had been severely beaten. Detectives initially dismissed a sexual motive or robbery as her possessions were nearby. A local unemployed man whom Annie had spent some time with on the night of her death was arrested: Morgan Williams, a man of no fixed abode. Williams told police that he had drunk excessively on the night of the murder and admitted entering the basement with Annie in the hope of sex. He claimed not to remember what happened next but conveniently recalls standing over her battered body. Further enquiries revealed that Annie's watch *had* been taken and pawned by Williams. Articles of clothing worn by Williams on the night of the murder were sprayed with Annie's blood and found at a Church Army hostel in Star Street where he had stayed following the murder. Williams was found guilty by an Old Bailey jury and sentenced to life imprisonment in March 1966.

6th – Murder at the Café Royal

The murder of night porter Marius Martin in one of London's most exclusive restaurants has never been solved. Martin was employed at the Café Royal, Regent Street, *the* place to be seen in the 1890s, with a clientele that included Oscar Wilde, Aleister Crowley and Virginia Woolf, to name but a few. Martin was on night duty in the early hours of 6 December 1894 when he was shot at point-blank range just inside the Glasshouse Street rear entrance. Martin was an impressive figure, well over six feet tall and muscular, a well-known figure in the nearby seedy, crime-ridden streets of Soho. When Martin was found later that morning, mortally wounded but still breathing, a local doctor was under the impression that he may have suffered some sort of stroke! He was sent straight to hospital with little or no examination; on arrival, medical staff discovered two bullet holes: one above the right ear, the other entering through the left side of his face – this was now a murder investigation. Police searched the hotel to try and establish a motive. The safe containing the previous night's takings had not been touched. Martin still had the door keys on him when found and there was no forced entry, so it seems likely that Martin knew his killer. Detectives concluded the motive was revenge, the killer having a grudge against the big man who had initiated the sacking of several staff members over the years. The case still remains a mystery and is unlikely to ever be solved.

7th – London's Most Dangerous Road

The Highway is a section of road that runs for approximately one mile just east of Tower Bridge through to the Limehouse basin. It was formerly known as Ratcliff Highway, a route that dates from Roman times and infamous in the eighteenth and nineteenth centuries as an area of vice and highway robbery. Two incidents resulting in seven murders occurred during December 1811. The first murderous attack took place late on 7 December 1811 at a draper's shop located at No. 29 Ratcliff Highway where the Marr family both worked and lived. The family consisted of Timothy Marr, his wife Celia and their young fourteen-week-old son Timothy junior. Apprentice James Gowan and servant girl Margaret Jewell also lived at the address. Margaret Jewell had been sent out to buy oysters for her mistress, and when she returned she found the front door locked but could hear noises inside – now scared, she knocked much louder, attracting the attention of several neighbours. James Murray, the Marr's next-door neighbour, entered the back of the premises and was faced with what can only be described as absolute bloody carnage. James Gowan was lying on the floor, his face smashed to a pulp; blood and brain matter were sprayed across the wall. Celia and husband Timothy were found in a similar state. Murray rushed upstairs to discover a sight that would live with him for the rest of his days: young Timothy had one side of his face crushed, and the killer had then taken a knife to his throat with such force the head had been virtually severed from his body.

Twelve days after the murder of the Marr family, a second, similar attack occurred at the King's Arms, New Gravel Lane (now Garnett Street). Publican John Williamson, his wife Elizabeth and their servant Bridget Harrington were murdered in similar circumstances. The public were now demanding the arrest and execution of the offender(s). A prime suspect emerged from the investigation: John Williams (aka John Murphy), a seaman who lodged in the area, was arrested, as he matched the description of a man seen in the vicinity of the King's Arms murders. Williams was charged on the basis of circumstantial evidence, which – to be frank – could have fitted many local people in relation to opportunity and motive. He never stood trial, committing suicide in his cell. Of course, this was an answer to the prayers of those responsible for law and order; the Home Secretary assured the public the man responsible for these despicable crimes was now dead. His suicide was seen as a confirmation of his guilt, and the public were safe. On New Year's Eve following Williams' execution, his body was paraded along the Ratcliff Highway to assure the local community that the alleged murderer was dead. Nobody can definitively say Williams was responsible for the Ratcliff Highway murders or it was a fact that he was indeed guilty and couldn't handle the stigma of being accused of such butchery, but no similar killings occurred in the region after his death – well not until 1888, of course.

8th – He Will Never Be Forgotten

The slaying of school headmaster Philip Lawrence outside St George's Roman Catholic School, Maida Vale sent a shock around the nation. The extremely experienced and popular Mr Lawrence went to the aid of a school student who was being attacked by a gang of boys outside the gates of the school on 8 December 1995. Mr Lawrence – only concerned about the safety of the student – attempted to stop the attack. One of the gang, Learco Chindamo, punched Lawrence and then stabbed him in the chest; he died of his injuries in hospital that evening. Chindamo was convicted of murder at the Old Bailey in October 1996 and jailed with a recommendation that he serve a minimum of only twelve years. Philip Lawrence was posthumously awarded the Queen's Gallantry Medal in June 1997. The Philip Lawrence Awards honouring outstanding achievement by young people are a fitting tribute to Mr Lawrence's work and a huge positive to emerge from such a traumatic and tragic waste of life. Frances Lawrence, whose incredible tolerance and self-control was an example to us all, was awarded the MBE for her services to charity in the setting up of the award.

9th – She Found a Younger Man

A pitiful story emerged at the Old Bailey in November 1902. The man standing forlornly in the dock was forty-nine-year-old Thomas Fairclough Barrow, a London dockworker, accused of the murder of Emily Barrow, his common-law wife. Emily, aged thirty-two, was significantly younger than Thomas, and many indeed believed Emily to be his daughter, but it emerged during Thomas' evidence that they had been together for many years living as man and wife. Emily worked as a tin solderer and met a much younger man called Harry Lorimer. Thomas saw the couple talking to each other outside her place of work and dragged Emily away and back to their Bermondsey home. Thomas Barrow made a very candid entry in a notebook shortly after the incident in which he recorded,

> I was coming from the People's Place and found my darling Emily who has been my wife for fifteen years and the mother of my child, talking to a strange man. I don't know his name she called him Harry. As I dragged her away she called out to him, but he was too frightened to interfere. I have long been a martyr to Emily's deceit. I have never denied her anything, and brought home all my earnings to her. She has left me a lonely, stranded man. What I am going to do God only knows. I have not the strength of mind to how to act; but I will have my revenge.

On 18 October 1902, Barrow could contain his fury no longer and followed Emily to her work in Glamis Road, Shadwell and stabbed her five times in front of witnesses, including Harry Lorimer. Barrow stood trial at the Old Bailey and a defence of insanity was put forward but dismissed by the jury who convicted him of murder. Thomas was executed on 9 December 1902 at Pentonville Prison.

10th – Should Have Ditched the Evidence
On 20 July 1946, Mona Vanderstay, a forty-six-year-old mother of five children who lived in Camden with husband Robert, was reported missing after she failed to return home from the cinema on Holloway Road the night before. Police searched Holloway Road and found Mona's body in the grounds of St Luke's Church; she had been strangled, some clothing had been removed and there were signs of sexual assault. Property including clothing coupons, a chequebook in her husband's name and her ID card were stolen from her handbag. Detectives interviewed several people known to be in the vicinity of Holloway Road that night including a man arrested and in custody for being drunk and disorderly; his name was John Mathieson, a sailor on leave from his ship HMS *Victory*. Presumably, Mathieson had only undergone a cursory safety search the night before as a more thorough search revealed the stolen clothing coupons, the ID card and the chequebook in the name of Robert Vanderstay. Mathieson told police he had

no recollection of the incident and claimed he was suffering from a form of somnambulism (sleepwalking) when the murder was committed. A forensic examination revealed blood on Mathieson's coat matched the victim's blood group. Mathieson was convicted and executed at Pentonville on 10 December 1946.

11th – Killed with a Hat Rack
Rachel Samuel, a seventy-year-old widow, was brutally murdered in her own home at No. 4 Burton Crescent, Bloomsbury on 11 December 1878. Her injuries were extensive and probably inflicted with a hat rack found near the body. The prime suspect was Samuel's live-in maid, forty-year-old Mary Donovan, who failed to return home that night. She was traced, arrested and put before stipendiary magistrate Flowers at Bow Street Magistrates Court. The evidence produced by detectives included human bloodstaining on Mary Donovan's clothes and boots, but Mr Flowers decided the prosecution had not proved a *prima facie* case against Donovan and released her – she was never seen again.

Another twist to this murder emerged two years later in January 1880 when a man named James Phillips, alias Wells, then incarcerated for an offence of theft, claimed to have murdered Rachel Samuel during a burglary with another man. Phillips appeared at Bow Street Magistrate's Court again in front of Mr Flowers, who had previously released the most likely suspect. The prosecution and the police seemed unhappy with the confession and asked for a remand to investigate further. It was proved that Phillips would have been logistically unable to have murdered Samuel as he was in prison at the time. Flowers asked him why he had confessed to a murder he couldn't have committed. Phillips explained that he had been treated so badly in the prison in which he had been incarcerated he decided that by confessing to this murder he would probably be moved to another establishment. The murder of Rachel Samuel has never been solved.

12th – The Balcombe Street Siege
The eighteen-month period between mid-1974 through 1975 saw an intense campaign of bombings and assassinations by the PIRA on mainland Britain: forty bomb explosions, thirty-five killed and

many more injured. On 6 December 1975, an Active Service Unit (ASU) returned to Scott's restaurant in Mount Street, Mayfair, a previous attack site where they had killed one person and injured fifteen others in a bomb attack the month before. This time the ASU sprayed the restaurant with semi-automatic gunfire as they passed in a stolen Ford Cortina. A car containing armed police officers was positioned at the end of Mount Street; they gave chase through the streets of London until cornering the occupants in Balcombe Street, Marylebone. The four terrorists fled into a council block and took refuge in a tiny flat, No. 22b Balcombe Street, occupied by Mr and Mrs Matthews.

The four men, Martin O'Connell, Edward Butler, Harry Duggan and Hugh Doherty, negotiated with police, demanding a plane to take them and their hostages to the Republic of Ireland. It has always been the stance of the British Government that no negotiations would take place with any terrorist group; this refusal to negotiate triggered a siege that lasted for six days and became commonly known as 'The Balcombe Street Siege'. The siege ended on 12 December 1975 when the terrorists gave themselves up to police. The four men were convicted of several offences including multiple murders, causing explosions and the false imprisonment of Mr and Mrs Matthews, who survived the ordeal unharmed. O'Connell, Butler and Duggan received twelve life sentences and Doherty eleven. After serving twenty-four years in prison, the men were released under the Good Friday Agreement in 1999.

13th – Never Off Duty

Detective Constable Jim Morrison was walking through Covent Garden on the evening of 13 December 1991 having completed his day's duty at Bow Street Police Station. The alert detective spotted a bag thief operating near to the London Transport Museum. Morrison challenged the man who pulled a knife and threatened him before running off. DC Morrison bravely gave chase and cornered the thief in the secluded Montrose Place near the Indian Embassy, Aldwych. The thief struck out as the unarmed officer tried to detain him; DC Morrison received a fatal injury and was pronounced dead on his arrival at hospital. The killer, who was believed to be of North African origin, has never been found or the murder weapon traced.

14th – Look Aunty I Can Swim

The murder of ten-year-old Vera Page on 14 December 1931 shocked the residents of Notting Hill. Young Vera failed to return home from the short trip to her auntie's house to show off her swimming certificates. Her distraught parents, who lived in Blenheim Crescent, reported her missing and a search for the child commenced. Two days later Vera's body was discovered by a milkman, concealed under shrubbery outside No. 89 Addison Road, three-quarters of a mile from her home; she had been strangled and sexually assaulted. Percy Orlando Rush became the police's prime suspect. The evidence against him was circumstantial but convincing: he knew Vera Page and her him; a piece of lint smelling of ammonia with a trace of fingernail was found on Vera's body – Rush had a similar injury at the time and been seen wearing a similar dressing before Vera's disappearance. A witness came forward to say that she had seen a man of similar description to Rush pushing a wheelbarrow towards the area the body was found on 16 December; the barrow contained a bundle covered by a red tablecloth. The police searched Rush's flat and found such a tablecloth, but the witness failed to pick Rush out on an identification parade. Rush was never charged with this horrendous murder and it remains unsolved. Today the advances in forensic science, in particular DNA profiling, would have proved Rush's guilt or indeed his innocence.

15th – 'I Didn't Want to Leave the Child Without a Mum'

Royal Air Force aircraftsman Charles Koopman and his wife Gladys Patricia from Hanwell, West London were on the run following Koopman's desertion from the services. They kept their heads down at a former girlfriend's flat in Grove Place, Ealing. Her name was Gladys Levina Brewer, married to a sailor who *was* serving his country. Brewer had a young daughter, two-year-old Shirley.

On 8 September 1943, Koopman became agitated at Gladys Brewer's questions about his future and the concern she had about her husband eventually returning home on leave to find a former boyfriend camped in their living room. Koopman snapped and in the presence of his own wife struck Gladys over the head several times with a coal hammer. He then took young Shirley into an adjacent room and battered her to death. He would tell police later he didn't want to leave the child without a mother. Koopman helped himself to money and jewellery before leaving his victims to rot. Neighbours discovered the scene of carnage days later and alerted the police.

It was soon established who had been staying at the flat and both the Koopman's were traced, arrested and charged with murder. By the time the case had reached the Old Bailey, charges had been dropped against Gladys Koopman and Charles stood in the dock on his own. He claimed that he suffered an epileptic fit prior to the murders due to one of three reasons: the vaccinations he had received from the RAF, his excessive drinking, or carrying the burden of guilt he felt by deserting his country. Doctors gave evidence at his trial that they had found no evidence of insanity or any subsequent epileptic episodes. Koopman was executed on 15 December 1943 at Pentonville Prison.

16th – A Failed Actor

The London theatre was a thriving industry in the 1890s; one of its stars was actor-manager William Terriss, who specialised in light comedy thrillers and was often seen treading the boards of many London West End theatres. Terriss knew what a hard, cut-throat business the theatre could be. When he became acquainted with a young Scottish actor named Richard Archer Prince, he went out of his way to find him work and guide his career path, and lent him money to support himself knowing full well he was unlikely to be repaid. But Prince had underlying character flaws, was often moody and petulant and caused his benefactor many moments of profound embarrassment when he lost his temper in public, to the point the generous Terriss cut him loose. Prince struggled to make headway in his chosen career, often blaming Terriss for purposely obstructing his advancement. On 13 December 1897, Prince arrived at the Vaudeville Theatre adjacent to the Adelphi where Terriss regularly performed and managed. Prince tried to use his past relationship with Terriss to gain entry but was refused a complimentary ticket and left the Vaudeville in a foul temper, blaming Terriss for his latest rejection. Three days later, on 16 December 1897, Prince concealed himself in a small alcove next to London's oldest restaurant, Rules in Maiden Lane, observing the Adelphi's stage door until

Terriss appeared and was about to enter the theatre to prepare for the night's performance. Prince strode purposefully across Maiden Lane and stabbed Terriss three times. Terriss died where he fell, while Prince stood back in the roadway awaiting the consequences of his actions. The murder of a celebrity became the hottest story in the press and was covered extensively through to the trial at the Old Bailey on 13 January 1898. Prince initially pleaded guilty, offering a defence of provocation at an earlier hearing, but at his trial changed his plea to not guilty. The defendant called many witnesses including eminent doctors, and even his mother, to prove that he was not of sound mind. The jury found Prince guilty of murder but not responsible for his actions due to insanity, and he was sent to Broadmoor Criminal Asylum. Prince spent the rest of his days in Broadmoor; he died at the age of seventy-one in 1937.

* * *

The City of London Police suffered their heaviest loss of officers through a criminal act on the night of 16 December 1910. Max Weil, a shopkeeper in Houndsditch, heard strange noises from next-door, a jeweller's shop. He alerted police who turned up in force, entering a house in Exchange Buildings that backed on to the jewellers. The house contained several armed men who fired on the officers, killing three: Sergeants Bentley and Tucker and Constable Choat; two others were badly injured. Police enquiries and information from an informant led them to No. 100 Sidney Street where the wanted men were held up. The killers were a politically motivated gang of burglars led by anarchist Peter Piatkow, also known as 'Peter the Painter'. Winston Churchill, Home Secretary at the time, attended the scene and famously took charge of the siege, refusing to allow police and the fire brigade to approach the building when it caught fire. Two of the police killers died – Peter the Painter was never found.

17th – Their Last Christmas
Three police officers from the Metropolitan Police and three innocent bystanders were murdered by the PIRA in a devastating car bomb attack outside the Harrods store in Knightsbridge on this

day in 1983. PIRA had given a coded warning of a car bomb, but with only a few shopping days until Christmas the store and the area surrounding it was extremely busy; the warning, telephoned through to the Samaritans before being relayed to police, allowed inadequate time to evacuate before it exploded. Ninety people were also injured. PIRA apologised for the deaths of the civilians but not for the police officers, who probably had little or no personal opinion regarding the plight of Irish politics and were just carrying out their duty; according to the terrorists, they were legitimate targets. A memorial stands next to Harrods in Hans Crescent, where the three officers, Sergeant Noel Lane, Inspector Stephen Dodd and Constable Jane Arbuthnot, fell. The three civilians who had their lives so tragically cut short were journalist Philip Geddes, Jasmine Cochrane-Patrick and American Kenneth Salvesen, a twenty-eight-year-old business consultant from Chicago.

18th – 'Mr & Mrs Lloyd'

Most newly-wed couples spend the first few weeks of their married lives together celebrating and enjoying each other's company, forming a bond that will hopefully last a lifetime. Mr Lloyd spent this period convincing his new wife to draw up a new will, in which he would be the sole beneficiary, and to withdraw her savings in cash, before taking her to a doctor with worrying symptoms of dizzy drowsy spells that he had convinced her she was experiencing. Mr and Mrs Lloyd rented a first-floor room at No. 14 Bismarck Road, Holloway (renamed Waterlow Road). The day after the visit to the doctor, 18 December 1914, Mrs Lloyd decided to have a hot bath. Mr Lloyd would later claim he had gone out to buy some tomatoes. When he returned, he found his new wife dead in the bath. He called in the doctor he had previously taken his wife to see the day before: they both agreed that she must have experienced one of her dizzy spells and tragically drowned in the bath water. A death certificate was issued and Mr Lloyd had his wife buried without delay. The national media of the day made the most of such a tragic human story, which then resulted in two families in the south of England reporting to police two similar deaths of young ladies recently married and drowned in their baths. On each occasion, a very gullible physician had signed death certificates stating the cause of death to be drowning while suffering a fit. Detectives launched a multiple murder investigation, soon identifying 'Mr Lloyd' as George Joseph Smith, a charmer, bigamist and thief with a long record of dishonesty and imprisonment. Detectives unveiled a trail of bigamy and murder. His first victim was Beatrice Mundy in 1910: having stolen all she had, he drowned her in a bath at No. 80 High Street, Herne Bay, Kent. A second victim, Alice Burnham, followed in 1913, killed in a similar fashion. Finally (as far as detectives knew), Margaret Lofty, 'Mrs Lloyd', a young inexperienced girl, became his third victim, callously despatched in her bath at Bismarck Road.

Detectives knew they were dealing with a multiple murderer but had to prove Smith had killed the women. They turned to pathologist Bernard Spilsbury. Following the post-mortem on Margaret Lofty, Spilsbury came up with a theory that each girl had been pulled by their lower limbs until their heads were below water, and that if this was done forcefully enough with an element of surprise the water flooding into the nose and throat would cause loss of consciousness. Spilsbury's evidence was well presented to the court, reiterating his growing reputation as one of the best pathologists available in criminal investigation. Smith was found guilty and executed on 13 August 1915 at Maidstone Prison, Kent.

19th – A Weighty Weapon

Six days before Christmas, on 19 December 1958, the battered, naked body of thirty-one-year-old prostitute Veronica Murray was discovered in the front bed-sitting room of No. 58 Charteris Road in Kilburn; she had been beaten to death with a 6 lb dumbbell, which lay at her side. The only clue detectives found at the scene were a set of fingerprints alien to the house and presumed to be those of the killer. When police checked the prints against the fingerprint index at Scotland Yard, they found no trace – the killer had yet to come to their notice. The investigation stalled until a second violent attack took place on Mrs Mabel Hill in her flat at No. 5 Ismailia Road in Wandsworth on 10 October 1959, when a man she invited into her flat tried to rape and strangle her with one of her own stockings when she refused him sex. She lost consciousness, which probably saved her life as the killer left, presuming her dead, but Mabel survived and gave police a description of her attacker – the fingerprints found following the murder a year before were rediscovered at this crime scene.

Further assaults and burglaries, mainly in the Chelsea and Fulham areas, were linked to this individual by fingerprint evidence. During one such burglary a distinctive lighter was stolen with the brand name 'Texas Gulf Sulphur Co.' clearly marked on it. Detectives placed a picture of a similar lighter in the media, appealing for the identity of anybody who did or had possessed such a lighter. Within a week, detectives got the breakthrough they needed: a young guardsman stationed at Pirbright Barracks in Surrey had informed his commanding officer that a fellow guardsman called Michael Douglas Dowdall had one such lighter. Dowdall was eighteen years old and a member of the 1st Battalion Welsh Guards. It was relatively easy for detectives to check Dowdall's movements at the times of the offences he was suspected of committing. His military record showed that he was AWOL at the time of Veronica Murray's murder and either on weekend leave or AWOL when the other offences were committed. Dowdall's fingerprints were taken and matched to the outstanding marks at the crime scenes – the police had their man. At his trial, the jury found Dowdall guilty of manslaughter on the grounds of diminished responsibility and he was sentenced to be detained in a mental asylum. Having served nearly fifteen years, he was released on licence in July 1975, suffering from a serious illness from which he died a little over a year later, aged thirty-six.

20th – Got Away with Murder

Russell Christie, a thirty-four-year-old former computer programmer, was stabbed to death on Westbourne Park Road, Notting Hill on 20 December 1996. Police found Russell outside a cab office following reports of a fight; he had been stabbed with a Swiss Army knife. His killer, Simon Williams, knifed Christie during a dispute about drugs; he pleaded guilty to manslaughter at the Old Bailey in December 1997, and the prosecution accepted that he had not intended to kill Christie. He was sentenced to four years imprisonment.

21st – Bad Man-Management

A twenty-year-old storeroom hand named Ronald James Barclay worked at the Rest Hotel, Kenton, Middlesex. He stabbed forty-one-year-old manager Arthur Odell to death in the hotel's storeroom on 21 December 1951. Due to his insanity, the motive for the murder was never substantiated. The only witness to the killing was a young barmaid who saw Barclay and Odell talking and Barclay launching himself suddenly at the deceased, stabbing him in the chest. Police found the victim dead on their arrival, the knife protruding from his chest. Barclay gave himself up shortly after; he was declared insane and incarcerated in a mental asylum.

22nd – Honour to Dishonour

Theodore Papadopoulos was a proud Greek and served as a soldier in the Greek army until both his parents were killed by the Turks, turning his life on its head. He deserted the Greek Army and turned to crime. He was a wanted man in Greece for both his criminality and the fact that he was a deserter; in order to escape he joined the British Army as an interpreter and managed to get to London in 1918. He returned to his criminal ways – theft, bribery and fraud. On 22 December 1921, he decided to up the ante, choosing a soft target who would be low risk and lucrative, a moneylender, Stanley Theeman, who operated out of a first-floor office at No. 7 Maddox Street in the West End. He purchased a small automatic revolver and sat waiting patiently in the reception room to see Theeman. When called into his office, he simply handed Theeman a note that said, 'Silence, or you are a dead man. This is my last hope. If you do not give me a chance, you and I will die together. Remember delay is fatal. I need £300.' Things went badly wrong and, true to his word, Papadopoulos fired three shots that were heard by Theeman's secretary, Ivy Mcken, who rushed into the office to see Papadopoulos lying on the floor with a head wound and the smoking gun beside him. Theeman was seated behind his desk, groaning, having been shot twice, once in the leg and once through his chest. Both men died of their injuries in hospital.

23rd – A Plot That Would Make Agatha Proud

Late afternoon on 23 December 1924, elderly landlady Grace Goodall was found slumped at the foot of her stairs in Harrington Square near to Mornington Crescent Station. At first it was thought that the seventy-three-year-old had fallen, but while in hospital, just before she succumbed to her fatal injuries, she told medical staff she had been hit over the head before she fell. A murder investigation started, with detectives anxious to trace two men who had apparently answered an advertisement in the *YMCA Journal* for a furnished room at Grace Goodall's house. They had visited a few days before, leaving a deposit. At the time Goodall, who had eight rooms that she let, had several lodgers, and the police were faced with a whodunit that Agatha Christie would have been proud of. One long-term lodger, who lived at the house for twenty-five years, had been named in Grace's will. Another had had a falling out with Grace and left on bad terms, together with the mystery man who left a deposit and never returned – all were suspects. Unfortunately, the case did not conclude with a detective standing in the middle of the room explaining how the crime had been committed before revealing the identity of the murderer. Grace Goodall's killer was never brought to justice.

24th – Not Much Christmas Spirit Here

Sixty-four-year-old jeweller Ernest Percival Key was found murdered in his shop at No. 74 Victoria Road, Surbiton, on 24 December 1938; he had thirty stab wounds to his face and neck. The corpse was found by the victim's son, Jack Key, who had gone to the shop at 11.30 only to find it secure so used his own key to enter. When detectives arrived, they found a bowler hat, which, Jack Key informed them, did not belong to his father. Detectives were hopeful that the hat, sold by a Richmond outfitter, belonged to the killer and that it may well give up forensic clues to his identity. According to Jack Key, the only property missing was his father's blue overcoat that they believed the killer took to disguise the copious amount of blood on his clothing after such a violent attack.

From the injuries inflicted, detectives believed the attacker to be a large man who had utilised a razor as the murder weapon. The killer had suffered injury to his own hands during the attack and caught a taxi to Kingston Hospital where he was treated. He told casualty staff that he had sliced his hands on a woodcutting machine and gave the name of Charles Jackson. From the description given by hospital staff, detectives visited a married man with two children named William Thomas Butler of Laurel Road, Hampton Hill. They were able to confirm this to be the same man who attended the hospital and who provided the false name of Charles Jackson. Butler initially told police a different story to the one he gave at the hospital, claiming he had cut his hands when knocked down by a motorbike and given the false name to avoid paying any hospital charges. Butler was arrested and charged with the murder of Ernest Key. He claimed during his trial at the Old Bailey that he had acted in self-defence as he went to the shop to collect money owed to him by Key, who had refused and attacked him. The jury rejected his defence and convicted Butler of murder. He was executed at Wandsworth Prison on 29 March 1939.

25th – R.I.P Constable

Metropolitan PC Thomas Eldred Briggs Rowland was on patrol in the Walworth area of south-east London on Christmas Day 1919 when he witnessed an incident and attempted to detain an offender. During the arrest, Rowland was struck on the head, fracturing his skull, an injury that would prove fatal. His killer was never found.

26th – A Little Bit of Luck to Solve This One

At 5.15 a.m. on Boxing Day morning 1948, the night porter of a private block of flats called Fursecroft at No. 75 George Street, Marylebone heard desperate calls for help coming from the basement. He found resident and popular cartoonist Harry Saul Michaelson, whose nickname was 'One Minute Michaelson', bleeding profusely on the doorstep of his basement flat. He was taken to St Mary's Hospital, Paddington. Michaelson took a turn for the worst, doctors discovering fractures to his ribs and skull that needed immediate surgery – he never regained consciousness and died the following day. Detectives concluded that a burglar had broken into the flat, disturbed the sleeping Michaelson, who confronted the intruder and the killer struck the victim over the head with a tubular-steel -framed chair. A forensic examination discovered one fingerprint in the blood of the deceased that the police were confident belonged to the attacker. Of course, fingerprints are a great investigative tool for crime detection, as DNA is today, but only if the owner of the fingerprint is on the fingerprint database – the killer wasn't.

Murder investigation is about good, effective, methodical police work but is always accompanied by an element of good luck. That good luck arrived on 19 January 1949 when two PCs on a general patrol stopped a young Welshman of no fixed abode who refused to give any personal details; his fingerprints were taken and matched to the print found at the murder scene. The man's name was Harry Lewis, a belligerent individual who, if he had cooperated with the police in the first instance, may well have slipped through the net. Lewis was charged with the murder of Michaelson and made a full confession, stating that he entered the flat via an unlocked window and was going through the deceased's trousers when he was disturbed and struck him several times with the chair. Lewis told detectives that he normally wore gloves when breaking and entering – a mistake that would cost the killer his life. He was executed at Pentonville Prison on 21 April 1949.

27th – Street of Death

Hanbury Street, which dissects Brick Lane in London's East End, is the infamous location of one of 'Jack the Ripper's' victims. Annie Chapman was murdered at No. 29 Hanbury Street on 8 September 1888. Twenty-three years later, on 27 December 1911, the street witnessed two further murders at No. 62 Hanbury Street, a restaurant run by Russian Jews Annie and Solomon Millstein. The restaurant business was a front for a more lucrative gambling den in the basement. Early in the morning, the London Fire Brigade were called to put out a fire at the premises. When they entered to dampen down the debris, they found both of the Millstein's dead. Solomon had been stabbed with his own carving knife and Annie hit over the head with a poker before being stabbed and strangled. The motive seems to have been burglary as the cash box with the restaurant takings was missing. The murderer in his haste to leave the scene left bloody footprints and a distinctive scarf that was later identified as belonging to a local fish porter, Meyer Abramovitch. The porter was arrested wearing a suit belonging to Solomon together with his watch and chain. He admitted that the scarf was his and that he had killed the Millstein's because he had lost all his money in their basement. The cards were stacked against Abramovitch at his Old Bailey trial but he still pleaded not guilty, claiming he was insane; he was convicted and executed at Pentonville Prison on 8 March 1912.

28th – An Odious Woman

Flower-seller Walter Fensham led a sickly existence for most of his thirty years. He compensated for his ill health by drinking heavily and becoming addicted to the opium derivative laudanum, often used for ailments in Victorian and Edwardian Britain and prescribed plentifully by doctors. Even though Walter had a difficult life, he still loved and admired his father, James Fensham, who had remarried to an odious woman called Harriet who treated Walter with disdain. Walter would often visit his father at his home, No. 15 St James Road (now Mackenzie Road), Islington in order to make sure that he was being looked after and fed properly. On 28 December 1907, Walter made such a visit, and he and Harriet came to blows following a heated argument – probably about the intolerable way she treated his father. Florence, Walter's sister who still lived with his father and stepmother, found Harriet in the kitchen with a knife protruding from her neck; she died the following day. Walter fled the house after the stabbing and was later apprehended by police and stood trial for the murder of his stepmother Harriet. Walter claimed at his trial that he had been drinking and taking laudanum to ease the pain of headaches he frequently suffered following a previous fall from a horse. The jury took into account that he was wickedly provoked by his stepmother, who constantly berated him in his father's presence, but still convicted him of wilful murder but with a recommendation for mercy. Public opinion swelled with several petitions being raised, until Home Secretary William Gladstone gave Walter a conditional pardon in February 1908. He was still sent to prison but released, having recovered from many of his ailments, in 1920 and lived a long life.

29th – Stabbed Nine Times

A fight broke out in the lobby of the Boulevard nightclub in Ealing in the early hours of 29 December 1999, during which Babatunde Oba, a twenty-three-year-old trainee for hire firm HSS, was beaten and stabbed nine times, dying of his injuries a few hours later. John Richardson, a doorman at the club, was also stabbed but survived. Several people were charged with the murder and convicted, although their convictions were overturned in 2004.

30th – Two Confessions, No Conviction

The body of a young Polish Jew, aged about twenty-five, later identified as Dora Piernick, was discovered in her rooms at No. 115, Whitfield Street, at 5.30 p.m. on 30 December 1903; her throat had been cut. Dora, whose husband was serving a prison term, was last seen entering her address late on 29 December having met a friend in Tottenham Court Road just before midnight; she had not been seen alive again. Detectives established the motive as theft, as a number of rings and an amount of cash was missing. A witness, who lived in the same house, informed the coroner's court inquest that at approximately 6 a.m. on the morning of 30 December he heard a scream and the sound of a body falling to the floor, followed by the crash of glass similar to a lamp or glass ornament being smashed. He went upstairs and listened at the door but didn't knock or enquire about his neighbour's wellbeing. Six weeks after the murder, a man named John Ross confessed to the killing but later retracted the confession when he told a court that he was drunk when admitting the crime and could prove where he was on the night of the murder. In May 1905, another confession to the murder was forthcoming, this time from an opium smoker in Vancouver, Canada. John Jackson made a written confession to the murder of Dora Piernick but this was dismissed by detectives. The murder of Dora remains one of London's unsolved murders.

31st – I'm a Refugee – No You're a Spy

German spy and member of the Dutch Nazi Party Johannes Marinus Dronkers was picked up on a yacht (supplied by the German intelligence service) by a trawler in May 1942, claiming to be a refugee who had escaped from German occupied Holland.

He was so excited he had been rescued that he danced and sang on the trawler's deck. When he arrived in England he told the same story to the Security Services, but after interrogation admitted he was a German spy who had been sent to England in order to gather information, in particular on the amount of American and Canadian forces in the UK and their movements. He was to send the information back to addresses, already identified by British Security Services, using invisible ink. He was charged and tried at the Central Criminal Court in November 1942, convicted and sentenced to death. He appealed the sentence in December but his appeal was dismissed. Dronkers was executed at Wandsworth Prison on New Year's Eve 1942.

BIBLIOGRAPHY

Newspapers
Belfast News
Daily Herald
Daily Mail
Daily Telegraph
Derby Daily Telegraph
Dundee Courier
Hull Daily Mail
Illustrated Police News
Lloyds Weekly Newspaper
Manchester Courier
The Times
Windsor and Eaton Express
Western Morning News

Online
British Newspaper Archive: www.BritishNewspaperArchive.co.uk
Daily Mail Online
Old Bailey Online

Selected Books
Bondeson, Jan, *Murder Houses of London* (Stroud: Amberley Publishing, 2014)
Fido, Martin, *Murder Guide to London* (London: Grafton Books, 1987)
Hargram, Adam *Police Encyclopedia Vol V* (London: Blackfriars Publishing, 1920)

Hollington, Kris and Nina, *Criminal London: A Sightseer's Guide to the Capital of Crime* (London: Aurum Press Ltd, 2013)

Howse, Geoffrey, *The A-Z of London Murders* (Barnsley: Pen & Swords Ltd, 2007)

Kennison, Peter; Swinden, David; Moss, Alan, *Discovering More Behind the Blue Lamp* (Wickford: Coppermill Press, 2014)

Pepys, Samuel, *Pepys Diary Vol 1* (London: Folio Society, 1996).

Pillett, Rene, *Views of England During a Residence of Ten Years* (Boston: Parmenter and Norton, 1818)

Storey, Neil,R, *East End Murders from Jack the Ripper to Ronnie Kray* (Stroud: The History Press, 2008)

Webb, Simon, *Dynamite, Treason & Plot* (Stroud: The History Press, 2012)

Pictures/Illustrations/Sketches

The illustrations in this book originating from *Illustrated Police News, Lloyds Weekly Newspaper* and *Grantham Journal* are produced by kind permission of Newspaper Image © The British Library Board. All rights reserved. With thanks to the British Newspaper Archive (www.BritishNewspaperArchive.co.uk)

The images of Vine Street and Walham Green (Fulham) police stations were kindly supplied by Peter Kennison

INDEX OF OFFENDERS